CW00825739

The Leading Cities (
their Competitive Ac

The Perception of 'Citymakers'

Harry Grosveld

World Cities Research 2002

ISBN 90-9015 804-9

Distribution/Orders: Thela Thesis, Rozengracht 176 A 1016 NK Amsterdam
Tel.(+31) (0) 20 625 54 29, fax: (+31) (0) 20 6620 33 95
E-mail: office@thelathesis.nl

—

FOR INFORMATION:
World Cities Research
P.O. Box 5806
1410 GA Naarden
The Netherlands

worldcitiesresearch@planet.nl

—

COVER AND DESIGN:
Anja Felder

TRANSLATIONS:
Belinda Stratton

PRINTER:
Hentenaar boek B.V. Nieuwegein, The Netherlands

CONTENTS

Although lots of people weep
Because in cardboard they have to sleep
There is always something pretty
In every capital city
You can not help that people kill
In the capital of Brasil
And the situation has to be so
At the carnival of Rio
There are things that you will miss
When you're visiting Paris
And you think your city is the best
After visiting Bucarest.
Big cities are creations of men
And they all have things in common
Old gables in Amsterdam behind a tree
Compared with empty squares of Gaudi
St. Petersburg's Hermitage art
Compared with New York's Mondriaan start
Leonardo da Vinci in the Louvre
Compared with Amsterdam Vincent van Gogh's oevre
Some people know some cities well
The food, the drinks and their own smell
And no-one can visit every capital city
When you love city-life that is a pitty

Amsterdam, 'Pasta di Basta' , 29-9-1999

Jacob 't Dichtertje, epigrammatist

INTRODUCTION

Why write a book about 'leading cities', competitive advantages, perceptions and 'citymakers'? With hindsight it is easy to formulate an answer to this question. What began as little more than a collection of ideas – all rather vague, unstructured, unprioritized and often contradictory – developed in the course of about a year into a concrete plan. I shall try to describe this thought-process in a number of steps.

The idea was born at about the time (October 1995) that my period as Director of Economic Development of the city of Amsterdam came to an end. What has preoccupied me the most during the last twenty years, I asked myself? The answer came quickly: the competitive position of Amsterdam in relation to the region (the surrounding municipalities) and within the Netherlands (in relation to Rotterdam and The Hague), but especially in relation to the great cities of Europe and the rest of the world – its position in international competition. I had gained practical experience through working in this competitive environment, by talking to businesses and institutions that are connected to the (international) ups and downs of the city, and to foreign newcomers, and by occasional reading on the subject.

However, this knowledge was not systematized. This was partly due to the vague character of the concept 'competitive position'. Competition with whom, over what, with what? I had often been irritated by the weight given to lists of rankings, such as 'the best cities to locate your business.' There are so many different kinds of 'businesses' and, to pick a random example, a hotel will surely qualify a city as 'the best city' on the basis of different standards than an international distribution company. However the publications allowed no such doubt, it was presented as an indisputable fact – even if the year after (as, for example, with Fortune Magazine) a completely different list was published. It also had its advantages, from a PR point of view. You chose, from the wide variety available, the list that suited your interests best, and could simply overlook some or skip a less successful year.

Doubts therefore, even despair sometimes about the influence such publications have on the perceived image of a city. I had seen many comparative research studies and expensive reports, and also worked on some myself: on the quality of the city as a city of enterprise, as a city of culture or a city of conferences, or as capable of organizing the Olympic Games. Such reports are necessary in order to make a responsible decision, but I often had the impression that it was

1

■

not so much the facts as other kinds of arguments and feelings that determined the issue. However these were never publicly admitted. Retrospectively, a nice smooth argument was prepared: this is called cognitive dissonance, I have since learned. I asked myself continuously what role the image of the city plays in important investment decisions.

A completely different experience was interwoven with this. The last two decades of the 20th century had a dynamic that had never been seen before. Innovation, more free trade and 'shareholders value' forced companies to growth in a market with ever-increasing competition. This led to takeovers, mergers and joint ventures, at home but also increasingly across national borders. It is known as globalization, but for many companies it was 'consume or be consumed'. When you are involved in the economy of an international city, you are in the thick of things and you watch such events unfold. With pride when the local major bank works its way up the world rankings through foreign acquisitions. With disappointment when, following a merger, one of two headquarters has to close down and your city is not the lucky winner. For a city it is like a game of snakes and ladders (you win some, you lose some): but is the city just a spectator, or can it influence the result? Do the qualities of the cities involved play a role, in addition to the size and weight of the merger partners? The latter is an example of a situation in which cities so-called 'compete' with one another, but cities cannot do what businesses do in order to keep up with the competition: take over and merge across borders. So what can they do in order to be internationally competitive?

These are questions into which, after so many years, you might like to have greater and more systematic insight. So you go to your university library – you will, after all, need to test the thoughts in your own head against those that have already been published. The first impressions are overwhelming. What a lot has been written about cities! About their history, their present situation, and also fortunately about their future. About American cities, Asian, European and others. Poor and rich cities, global cities and world cities, megapolises and global villages. What a source of inspiration cities have been, for architects, city builders, planners, developers, historians, writers, composers, economists, geographers and last but not least sociologists. All these different approaches have led to all kinds of typologies, which you come across as you read the literature or just simply leaf through it. Early on I started to note these down, and I now have a diverse collection of about 140. They are reproduced on the inside cover of this book, as a gesture of respect to the many facets of the city.

A lot has also been written about competition between cities, especially in this era of globalization, but I could not detect any structure at first. I needed Porter's "The Competitive Advantages of Nations," which provided a breakthrough in the thought and search process: the many competitive factors and their relationships to one another, the dynamic of the model and the illustration with help of the 'diamond' which portrays the level of development and competitive profile of a country. What about a similar model for cities, a competitiveness model for cities? It was an idea that would not let me go. I had not seen one in the literature, and Porter himself had said explicitly that his model could be applied to regions and cities.

Enough reasons for a more focused and critical look at the literature on the subject – and a number of issues began to attract my attention. It appeared that cities were ranked almost entirely on economic elements (such as banks and head offices) with regard to their ability to compete. But a city is surely more than its economy alone? Yes of course, and this was also reported in the literature: a city is a construct of a number of extremely diverse factors. However this was then generally brushed aside with a single sentence under the heading 'social–cultural infrastructure.' Apparently there is not much more to say about it, nothing is known. If I want to carry on, I thought, I will have to do something about this knowledge gap.

It was also striking that the city 'rankings' were almost entirely based on quantitative data; so much of this, so much of that. Where was the human component, where were the feelings? Of course, you can read each year in Fortune which cities are 'the hottest places on earth' according to a number of senior executives. Life is indeed fast and everything changes, but do these 'top shots' really change their minds so quickly that each year different cities are suddenly 'hot'? Most remarkable, however, was that the publicists themselves decide what the relevant competitive factors for cities are. Without any kind of research they simply select them in accordance with their own opinions, or at least so it seems from discussions with such colleagues. Of course, each emphasizes slightly different aspects than the other. No wonder, then, that the ranking or typology of cities is different each time. The top three, the 'triad' New York – London – Tokyo, seem to enjoy complete consensus, but after that it becomes rather confused.

In this way the conviction grew that there was some room for a practitioner newcomer in the heavily populated academic world, room for someone who wanted to examine the international competitive position of cities - preferably by testing the theory in practice, as Porter did. He stated that, "The ability to upgrade an economy depends heavily on the position of a nation's firms in that portion of the economy exposed to international competition" (1990, p. 545). For that reason he focused his research on that part of the economy. In this way the idea was born of first examining the competitive advantages, competitive positions and related rankings through analysis of the literature, existing data and from experience and then to test the findings through research among the 'citymakers.' These are the businesses and institutions that (can) make a substantial contribution to the inter-

3

■

national competitive profile of a city. Their top executives deal implicitly and explicitly with international competition every day and should therefore know a great deal about the factors that are important in competition, and they will certainly know which cities go the furthest to meet their needs. Their insight, their perception must provide the data on the basis of which a competitiveness model for cities can be designed.

This is why this volume begins in Part I with an overview of what has and has not already been done in this area, based on the existing literature on the subject. The design of the research follows, and then quantitative and qualitative reports on the responses. Part II covers competitive factors and the design of a competitiveness model for cities 'à la Porter,' based both on theory and on the findings of the research. Part III is about the hierarchy of cities, in the integral and functional sense. The conclusions of Parts II and III are used in Part IV to flesh out the international competitive profile of a number of cities.

◆ ◆ ◆ ◆ ◆

PART I
THE RESEARCH

"The ability to upgrade an economy depends heavily on the position
of a nation's firms in that portion of the economy exposed to
international competition."
(M. Porter, "The Competitive Advantage of Nations", 1990, p. 545)

■

I.1   THE NEED FOR AND NECESSITY OF THE RESEARCH

John Friedmann and Goetz Wolff in 1982: "There is no specific literature on the world city concept ... there are no landmark studies .... Much of what is taking place in world cities is not documented or readily available in a form useful to the academic researcher."

John Friedmann in 1995: "Again I need to stress that we do not have clear-cut, agreed criteria that would allow us to validate world city claims unambiguously for any but the very top cities in the hierarchy."

Judging by the quotes given above, it seems there has been little progress in the last twenty years in the study of cities, their position in the world and the factors that determine this position. Although much has been written on competitive factors for cities, it tends to be hidden away in publications on the rankings and typologies of cities – a much more popular subject. It is, of course, impossible to make a ranking or typology without indicating which factors, elements, criteria, functions, indicators (whatever they are called in that particular study) are being used. Authors, not having done any original research themselves into the relevant factors, seem to rely on their analytical abilities or the publications of others in order to create a ranking or typology. They adopt all the factors from previous publications, select just some of them, and/or add new ones. All three methods are frequently encountered. The result is that there are enormous differences in what are seen as relevant factors, and consequently the rankings or typologies that are based on them also differ from publication to publication. Attempts are made to bring some kind of order into this diversity by dividing the publications into a number of groups, but this is little more than expediency in an attempt to gain greater insight. It certainly cannot claim to systematize competitive factors as some authors (including van den Berg J. & Bramezza I. 1991, Kresl P. 1995 and Begg I. 1999) have done. Their groupings are so different from one another that it is clear we are on thin ice, and the practical value has also yet to be proven.

1. First, there is the group of publications which attempt to provide a complete set of relevant factors: the integral approach. The most important member of this group is the 1989 Reclus/Datar report because it more or less represents the birth of literature on the ranking and typology of cities. It uses sixteen factors or criteria, and is the most comprehensive and concrete overview available. But why were these particular factors selected? Are they all equally relevant? Are there any others? No answer to these questions is given. Respect for this renowned publication does not increase when, in conclusion, the results of all the factors are added up like a grocery bill. On the basis of this – to put it mildly – arbitrary mathematical sum, a large number of European cities are divided into classes and types.

John Friedmann's 'World City Hypothesis' (1986 and 1995) can also be placed in this group. In his first publication he emphasizes, on the basis of a number of different starting-points or concepts, that the qualities of a city must be judged across a broad spectrum of factors, and certainly not only on economic ones. He indicates a number of these, such as the city's place in history, its multicultural character, integration into the world economy, cultural facilities, and its role as a capital city. The power lies in the combination, and he gives New York as an example. However, he does not go as far as an operational inventory. Despite the limitations – which he admits himself, thus hedging his bets ("a possible rank ordering of major cities, based on the presumed nature of their integration with the world economy" p. 319) – he nonetheless draws up a classification of cities. For this, he selects the following factors without giving any further reasoning behind his choice: financial centers, multinationals, international institutions, business services, industry, transport and communication, hotels, professional workforce, and number of inhabitants. There then follows a "world city formation," in which Paris, for example, scores low while cities such as Miami and Rotterdam score surprisingly high; and for which it is not possible to discover how the classification was made. As a result it is impossible to avoid the impression that it incorporates a substantial subjective element.

Into this group fall, in fact, all the other (previously cited) authors who have systematically organized such factors. They have had to make heavy use of their analytical abilities; original research on which their analyses are based could not be found. Iain Begg does introduce a number of determinants that, as he points out himself, remind one of Porter's national model. However, neither his attempt nor any of the others has provided a broadly recognized concept or model to illustrate the international competitive position of a city.

2. The other extreme is the classification of a city using one specific function, such as financial institutions, transport, congresses or hotels: the functional approach. All the studies, research, reports and indexes that classify cities according to one distinguishing factor, such as criminality, cost of living and quality of life, can also be placed within this group. There are many publications, academic and others, that use this approach and put cities in a good or less favorable light. In general it is easier and more reliable to classify and/or rank cities in this way than using the integral approach. The sources are usually easy to find, and they lend themselves to comparison from one year to the next. Whether or not these elements are also relevant to the international competitive position of the city is the question.

It becomes more difficult when authors use a variety of sources for the same aim. This may be extremely useful in an (academic) discussion, but the everyday (newspaper) reader can sometimes no longer see the wood for the trees. Newspapers are always so keen to publish the rankings of cities and countries! The more lists are published, the shorter the explanation; the necessary nuances in interpretation can sometimes be forgotten. Authors can be guilty of this even in the academic world: the titles of articles sometimes suggest an integral approach, while the content is little more than a systematization on the basis of a single function – leaving aside the question of whether or not it is an important one. A striking example in this context is the inclusion of 'European cities' in the title, while further reading shows that this qualification is linked to the presence of foreign consulates (Buursink J. 1991).

3. Saskia Sassen has pioneered the approach for a third group. In her book "The Global City" (1991) she argues that only three factors or functions ultimately determine which cities can count themselves at the top of a changed world order: the presence of headquarters of multinationals, of financial institutions, and the related management of corporate services. Her hypothesis is that, as globalization of the economy proceeds, the central functions will become concentrated in a decreasing number of centers. Since publication of her book, New York, London and Tokyo have become 'global cities' and the 'command centers' in the world economy.

Many authors have followed in her footsteps. Paul Knox writes in his collection, "it is clear that New York, London and Tokyo stand in a league of their own" (1995, p 8). However, no matter how authoritative this sounds, a city still has other aspects on which it can be judged, and the question is then whether Tokyo will continue to score so highly and whether Paris might perhaps be given a more comparable position. No matter how convincing the argumentation, it is once again striking that the selection of these three dominant factors is not based upon any original fieldwork/research.

4. Then there is still a mixed bunch of publications that do not fall under the previous three nor under the following two groups. These authors base their ranking or typology on a mixture of factors, but without striving to be comprehensive. The mixtures have some common factors – the economic functions of Sassen are usually included, for example – but each author includes different ones as well. To give some examples, with one it is international organizations (Palomäki M. 1991 and Knox P. 1995) or 'cultural centrality' (Knox P. 1995), while with another it is 'sites of global spectacles' (Short J. 1999) and by yet another 'multiculturality' (Lippman - Abu Lughad J. 1995) and 'urban governance' (van den Berg L. 1991). The consequence is, of course, that their lists of cities are all different. All the authors have interesting explanations for the particular emphasis they have chosen, but the question remains how relevant these selections are in the context of international competitive position. Some authors recognize this shortcoming themselves: "We have restricted our comments to a small range of data and a simple ranking of information. Much more work has to be done" (Short J. c.s. 1996).

5. A completely different approach is that of Cheshire (1990). Under the title of an 'urban problem index,' using data for immigration, unemployment, gross municipal product and what he calls the 'travel demand index,' he makes

an overview or ranking of 'successful and unsuccessful cities.' He deliberately excludes consideration of the frequently or less frequently used productivity functions that go with the other characteristics. This approach is an unusual one, and has not been much followed. The factors which he calls 'indicators' have been used by only a small number of other authors.

6. Finally there are some other publications that can be distinguished from the rest. These are the annual rankings published by Fortune Magazine ('the best cities for business') and by Cushman & Wakefield or Healy & Baker Real Estate Consulting ('Europe's Top Cities Monitor'). Both publications focus on a single function, the city as a center for enterprise (the establishment of businesses), but in order to determine this quality a (large) number of factors are assessed. An integral approach to a functional ranking, one could say. With Fortune, the factors can be deduced from the impressive questionnaire sent to the target group by Arthur Andersen Consultancy, who undertakes the study. The magazine publishes the results like a magician: each year it is a surprise which city has come out on top, especially as nothing in the explanatory notes indicates a particularly consistent assessment process. With Healy & Baker (Richard Harris undertakes the work) the factors themselves are also a subject of study each year, which is a strong point of this research. Using a formula, a 'weighted score' is calculated for each city. Which is a shame, as the quality of a center for enterprise is then once again expressed as a mathematical sum of unequal parts. This does not alter the fact that it is basically the only publication in which an integral ranking is determined through assessment of location factors that have been selected on the basis of previous research – in this case consulting 500 senior executives in Europe, who can be expected to know what they are talking about.

Despite this categorization, a feeling remains of great diversity, little systematization, perhaps even chaos. The academic world has not paid sufficient attention to classifying cities and determining competitive factors for them. Thoroughness has often been sacrificed for speed, the need to score quickly with a contribution to 'city formation.' Focused research, for example among people who are involved on a daily basis with competitive factors, cannot be found. In this context a lesson can be learned from the commercial publications, who seem to have taken Porter's recommendation much more to heart.

This is also recognized in academic circles. Peter J. Taylor wrote in 1997: "The world city hierarchy is the Achilles heel of research on world and/or global cities.... . The work is generally flawed either in data, theory or both... .Quite simply, currently available data do not allow for the specification of a world hierarchy... The argument is that if there are real tendencies towards a world city hierarchy, this can only be adequately assessed at a systems level, which means a global study over a series of years." (Cities, Vol 14, no. 16, pp 323 - 332). For completeness, it should be mentioned that he is thinking here of a study which will map the relations

■

between cities worldwide and on which he is working to this day.

Before Taylor, John Friedmann (1995) had already stated: "we do not have clear-cut criteria that would allow us to validate world city claims unambiguously for any but the very top cities in the hierarchy" (Friedmann, in Knox P. L. and Taylor P. (Eds.) 1995, p 23). In the same publication, (p. 9) Knox says, "(hierarchical classification of world cities is less and less satisfactory.... Cities hierarchical positions may be reversed according to the kind of functions considered... It may be more useful, therefore to think in terms of functional classification." Nonetheless he goes on to make a city ranking based on a combination of three functions (transnational business, international affairs and cultural centrality).

All of the above is summarized in Part II (Table II.1), where all of the competitive factors used or named by the various authors are placed next to one another. This table was included in Part II as its primary function is as part of the justification for the way in which the competitive factors used in this study have been selected.

* * *

Establishing that no research has been published on competitive factors for cities may be important in order to avoid repeating work that has already been done, but it does not resolve the question of the usefulness of the twin aims of the study: (1) constructing a model from which the international competitive position of a city can be determined and (2) making a list of, say, twenty of the most prominent cities in the world. How could such a city model be used and what is the value of a ranking list?

The answer to the second question can be found in daily experience. The fact that there are so many publications in which cities are ranked on the basis of all kinds of qualities is evidence enough of the demand for such lists. This demand comes initially, of course, from the authors and initiators themselves, and their ambition to add to their academic or commercial image. However, if there was no response then such initiatives would die an early death – and there is plenty of demand:

- First, the city authorities themselves: when they wish to succeed at an international level and are prepared to invest, they need to know where they stand in comparison to other cities. Indeed, it is not uncommon for them to commission these kinds of comparative studies themselves.
- Other government-level authorities are also interested in the international

position of the most important cities in their country, state or province. This can play an important role, for example, in determining policy on the quality and timetable for investment in national and regional infrastructure.

- Lobbying from associations of businesses, emphasizing the importance of certain action, can also influence not only the direction of the city authorities' policy but also the attitude of their own members. Their arguments are often supported with some kind of ranking list, in order to demonstrate that there is certainly room for improvement.
- Individual companies, institutions and people working in an international context (or with an ambition to do so) have a professional need for information on how cities are positioned as a factor in their plans for, for example, establishing a branch of their company, a concert tour, the sale of real estate or determining a schedule of conferences.

One should not underestimate, therefore, the influence of published lists of rankings: some of the information is bound to stick in people's minds. It is therefore important that such lists are based on careful research; some examples (of varying quality) were mentioned earlier.

Such research should not only address the question of which factors are relevant to the international competitive position of a city, but also how relevant these factors are. Otherwise it is impossible to judge the merits of rankings made on the basis of a single factor (or function). Of course it is interesting to know where the most expensive shopping streets are, but who has actually checked whether or not this is relevant?

It is also necessary to know which factors matter in order to design a model that can portray the international competitive position of a city. A model full of factors of unknown relevance would be, to put it mildly, of little practical use. Policy based upon it might risk money on one or more factors of less importance, while the quality of crucial functions could not withstand the test of criticism in an international context.

Conclusion

In this section an inventory has been made of the many academic and other publications on competitive factors and the classification of cities. In addition the usefulness of classifications has been discussed. The need for an operational model that can portray the competitive position of a city was noted and confirmed from a study of the literature. As a result, the following can be concluded:

1. In order to determine the international competitive position of a city on the basis of which policy can be developed, it is necessary to map the relevant competitive factors; including the weight each one carries. No evidence has been found that this has already been done. Therefore there is both room and necessity for research which could lead to the development of an operational competitiveness model for cities.

11

■

2. Classifying cities is a popular and useful task, and can be done in a number of ways – the most common being the integral and functional approaches. However, it is also a delicate task, as sloppy starting-points will lead to sloppy results. In addition, the fact that a city is more than the mathematical sum of a smaller or larger number of parts sometimes appears to be forgotten. These are reasons for putting together both an integral and functional ranking.

3. When examining the construction of lists of rankings, it is striking that the academic world predominantly uses 'hard facts' (so much of this, so much of that); the subjective element is addressed only in commercial publications, through opinion polls.

4. The commercial publications confirm Porter's assertion that insight into the competitive position of a city can best be determined through research among businesses and institutions who contribute to that competitive position and/or have a stake in it. The term 'citymakers' will be used for this group.

5. The literature on competitive factors for cities may have its shortcomings, but taken together it does deliver a diverse collection of potentially relevant competitive factors. These can be used, with gratitude, for further research.

A critical reader will be thinking: surely Porter has already determined these factors? Indeed he has, for a whole country, and he then goes on to say that his national competitiveness model could be applied to cities. So the research has already been done? If you are planning to construct a competitiveness model for cities à la Porter, you cannot avoid this question. In section II.1 Porter's national model and the publication in which he applied his model to inner cities will be thoroughly discussed. The latter publication from 1995 did not receive anywhere near as much praise as his standard work from 1990 – understandably, as will be explained in section II.1.

In order to construct a competitiveness model for cities – the first of the two aims – the factors that influence the competitive position have to be determined. This section covers what has already been achieved in this area. Now that it has been determined that further research is necessary, the following question is: what kind of research and among whom? This will be addressed in the following section. It will be followed by sections describing the structure and implementation of the research, and discussion of the validity of the results. Part I concludes with a report and evaluation of the experiences acquired during the research.

* * *

I. 2 THE RESEARCH INTO PERCEPTIONS

In the introduction to this book it was stated that, after twenty years of working in an international city, personal experience suggested that 'decision-makers' not only want to know all the facts but also give generous space to their own intuitive feelings and opinions on the object of their decision, which is a city in this case. Such a decision can determine whether or not a city is chosen as the location for establishing a business, for holding an annual world conference, for the organization of an international sporting event, for inclusion in an international tour, for the development and sale of real estate, for inclusion in an international comparative research study, for incorporation in an international network, as background for advertising campaigns, for the making of a movie, etc. This intuition, this subjective feeling, if shared by colleagues in one's field, can grow into such a shape that it takes on an aspect of objectivity, and starts to become a fact, a deciding factor. However, as stated above, this is purely personal experience and also limited, functionally and geographically, to the city of Amsterdam. Bringing some objectivity to this starting-point of the research is therefore required.

I. 2.1 THE IMPORTANCE OF PERCEPTIONS

Although perception might seem to be a subject belonging to the field of psychology, fortunately research (and plenty of it) has been done into the subjective element in decision-making in the field of geographical economics. However it took a long time for a widely accepted theory to be developed. In the classic theory (Weber, Von Thünen) and later the neo-classic (for example Christaller) the emphasis was still completely on rational, objective, purely economic motives such as market and costs; the entrepreneur as 'economic man' and 'optimizer.' Only in the second half of the 20th century does the 'behavioral' approach modify the (neo-)classic theory with the concept that entrepreneurs are also driven by other motives. It is no longer only normative considerations (what should influence the entrepreneur) but especially the factual ones (what actually does influence the entrepreneur) that take the central place in the theory. The entrepreneur is more of a 'satisficer' than an 'optimizer.' This theory is also sometimes summed up in the concept 'bounded rationality:' decisions are made rationally, but on the basis of limited information and with personal prejudices.

Immediately, concepts such as perception, cognition and image require consideration. In psychology, perception is described as the way in which (in the psychical sense) a phenomenon, person or object is seen or experienced. Cognition is the knowledge stored in our brains as a collection of facts and opinions. In practice, however, the term perception is often applied to what most psychologists would call cognition, and thus perception comes very close to image. If an image is described as the collective picture of a phenomenon, person or

13

object, then perception can be described as an individual image.

It may be appropriate to add a short personal comment here. The behavioral approach, which can be loosely translated as a combination of rationality and emotion, does indeed seem to be the most realistic in western cultures, but care must be taken in the interpretation. A factual or rational basis to a decision will always be needed. Even when the 'boss' her/himself does not require one, the people to whom s/he is accountable and her/his work colleagues are bound to ask for one. The greater the dominance of certain facts (such as labor or transport costs) and the size of the investment (for example a factory or terminal), the less room there will be for subjective elements. However, the greater the number of qualitative factors (intangibles) involved, for example in the establishment of a head office or the organization of an international event, the more room there will be for subjectively weighted arguments, and image and perception can play a more important role.

Yi-Fu Tuan (1977) postulates that perception is based on individual experience, and can range from a still-malleable initial impression to a fixed idea. That idea can be formed on the spot on the basis of a single personal experience or impression. Consider, to give a positive example, if it happened to be the place where you met the love of your life. However, it might also be a negative experience – it could equally easily be the place where you happened to be the victim of a robbery. In most cases, however, it is a combination of experiences, and can be formed without any direct experience. Impressions are built, confirmed and adjusted on the basis of what people pick up from the newspapers, magazines, TV, advertising, films, the internet, chatting at parties and in their local bar.

This reflects the overall picture of a city, the integral perception. However, there are also partial perceptions, built on specific, often work-related, experiences. Of course they influence the total picture, but do not necessarily correspond to it. An architect, the conductor of an orchestra and a tourism director (just to name a few examples) will all have their own particular picture of a city. These professional or functional perceptions will generally be based more on hard facts, but even professionals cannot escape their own subjectivity and experiences, and from basing their decisions on them. These are all reasons, therefore, to include in the questionnaire not only questions on the total image, the integral perception (question 1-A), but also on the functional perception (question 1-B).

The move from perception (individual image) to image (collective perception) is gradual. Not least because all kinds of forms of communication play upon perceptions that already exist or are latent. This continuous repetition can mean that a vague impression becomes fixed and sometimes indelible. In this way the image of city can be built up through direct and indirect publicity: the promotional campaign 'I love New York' is a pioneering example from the 1970s.

News can also create an image, but good news is not as newsworthy as bad news and image-forming through this route can quickly go wrong. The occasional report of a riot, demonstration or shooting is soon forgotten, but a continuous stream of such reports can be devastating. Little wonder that it is said that it is easy to lose a good reputation, but nigh on impossible to lose a bad one. Assuming that 'free publicity' contributes substantially to the way in which a city is perceived (although the questionnaire will need to confirm this), it is interesting to examine the relationship between the hierarchical position (the ranking) of a city and the frequency with which it has been in the news. The frequency and way in which the cities covered by the research have been in the news in recent years has therefore been explored, with regard to both the integral and functional picture. We will return to this point several times in parts II and III.

The step from image to (city) marketing is also quickly made – many books have been written on it, and much money spent. However, in the context of this thesis, it would be a step too far. On the other hand, if it is clear that important decisions are made on the basis of perception, and you are already approaching people who play an important role in these decision-making processes, it is hard to resist the temptation to ask them how the marketing of a city can best play upon these perceptions. A few questions, in the form of concepts, were therefore also included in the questionnaire on this point, which could confirm, sharpen or broaden existing insights. In the same context, a concept is included to give a definitive answer to the question: which parties have a stake in the image of the city? In this way, a number of interesting and operational findings can be reported on city marketing and the 'free publicity' issue.

The literature on this subject thus confirmed personal practical experience. Perception is an important, sometimes decisive, element in a decision-making process. 'Feelings,' built up from objective and subjective observations, are 'facts.' The feelings of 'citymakers' on competitive advantages and the ranking of cities, researched in this study, are therefore also much more than just indications. If any doubts remain, then the 'citymakers' are the ones best equipped to deal with them. The concept 'If cities have approximately equal qualities, then the perception of the decisionmaker(s) becomes decisive for investment or establishing a business' was therefore included in the questionnaire. A calculated risk – imagine if the response had been negative or 50:50, it would have destroyed one of the foundations of the questionnaire. However, with a convincing 'yes' (85%) it seems with hindsight to have been a rhetorical question. These data come ahead of the description and justification of the research, but illustrate so clearly how important perception can be in the decision-making process that it was felt nonetheless appropriate to include them here.

* * *

■

Table I.1 LIST OF 'CITYMAKERS'	
Clusters	**'Magnets'**
Performing Arts	• Symphony Orchestras • Ballet • Opera • Festivals and Facilities
Hospitality	• Congresses • Tourism • Hotels
Real Estate & Architecture	• Property Development • Architects
International Trade & Transport	• Aviation • Shipping • Trade Promotion
Corporate Services	• Accountants • Lawyers • Management Consultancy
Academia	• Universities
Museums	• Fine Arts Museums • Historical Museums • Other Museums
Media	• Press Agencies • Radio/TV
International Organizations	• Governmental • Professional • Non Profit
Multinationals	• Fortune 500 - companies • Other major companies
Finance	• Banking • Stock Market • Life Insurance

I. 2.2 THE TARGET GROUP OF THE RESEARCH

Porter (1990) asserted that the best way to gain a better insight into competitive advantages is to examine specific business sectors exposed to international competition, and he turned his words into action. He researched the dynamics and interconnections of a single specific and successful cluster in four different countries: the printing press industry in Germany, cardiological instrumentation in the United States, the ceramic tile industry in Italy and the robot industry in Japan. In addition, the service sector in general was also studied.

In order to chart the competitive factors for cities, it may also be advisable to consult the businesses and institutions that are most involved. In section I.1 it has already been established that the literature on the international competitive position of cities is indeed extensive and rich in content, but that the opinion has never been sought of the prominent players in the city: the 'citymakers,' who contribute to that international competitive profile and/or have a stake in it.

Citymakers

Who are these 'citymakers'? Which parties (businesses, organizations and institutions) work in an international competitive context and can contribute to the international profile of a city with their qualities? The literature, it must be repeated, does not provide a complete inventory; however, by gathering pieces from various different publications, it is possible to go quite a long way towards one. This, combined with a personal analysis made possible by extensive experience in city marketing, delivers a surprisingly large number of players (Table I.1). They are divided into eleven groups or clusters, according to type. As the term clusters is used in all the tables and graphics, let us now take an opportunity to become familiar with this concept.

Porter describes clusters as 'geographic concentrations of interconnected companies, specialized suppliers, service providers, firms in related industries and associated institutions in particular fields that compete but also cooperate' (1998, p. 197). This turns out to be a very broad definition of the concept cluster, particularly when he illustrates it with examples from countries and large regions; it could be called rather a network of businesses. If you consult a dictionary, you will repeatedly find the following key words: small, compact, same kind and grouped around a central point. An example is the definition in the Cambridge International Dictionary: 'a close group of usually similar elements, often surrounding something.' This is exactly the meaning that is adopted in this study. The size of the groups is limited, the activities are of similar kinds, and in most cases there are one or more 'magnets' around which the others group themselves. An airport, a home carrier and a seaport, banks and stock exchanges are clear examples of these. However, large museums and symphony orchestras are also 'magnets', as they create the cultural climate in which enterprises such as studios, impresarios, galleries

17

Table I.2	CITIES COVERED BY THE RESEARCH	
Division I	Division II	Not mentioned in questionnaire
EUROPE (31)		
Amsterdam	Barcelona	Athens*
Brussels	Berlin	Budapest*
Frankfurt	Madrid	Copenhagen
London	Moscow	Düsseldorf
Milan	Petersburg*	Geneva
Paris	Rome	Glasgow*
	Stockholm	Hamburg
	Vienna	Helsinki*
	Zürich	Lisbon
		Lyon
		Manchester*
		Munich
		Oslo
		Prague*
		Rotterdam
		Warsaw*
NORTH AMERICA (19)		
Atlanta	Boston	Cleveland*
Chicago	Dallas	Detroit
Los Angeles	Houston	Miami
New York	San Francisco	Minneapolis
Toronto	Seattle	Montreal
Washington	Vancouver	Philadelphia
		San Diego*
ASIA (16)		
Beijing	Jakarta	Kuala Lumpur
Bangkok	Manila	Melbourne
Hong Kong	Mumbai	
New Delhi*	Osaka	
Shanghai	Seoul	
Singapore	Taipei	
Sydney		
Tokyo		
LATIN AMERICA (9)		
Buenos Aires	Caracas	Bogotá*
Mexico City		Lima*
Rio de Janeiro		Montevideo*
Sao Paulo		Santiago
AFRICA (5)		
Johannesburg	Caïro	Cape Town
		Lagos*
		Nairobi
MIDDLE EAST (5)		
	Istanbul	Amman*
	Tel Aviv	Ankara*
		Jerusalem*

*not mentioned in "A roster of World Cities" by Beaverstock et al.

and training institutions can flourish. The 'citymakers' on which this study focuses can generally be considered as the magnets of the clusters.

These 'citymakers' contribute to the competitive profile of the city each in their own way and in varying degrees, determined not only by the importance of the cluster but also the international profile of the 'citymaker' itself. However, even if the profile of, for example, the symphony orchestra in a certain city is not particularly high, the orchestra can still be considered as a 'citymaker' because it has sufficient potential for further development, for example through its national status. In part II, section 3, the choice of clusters and their composition will be further examined. The way in which the addressees within the various clusters were selected will also be further examined in the discussion of results per cluster in section I.3, in which detailed information on numbers is included as well.

It should be noted that every effort has been made to achieve personal contact with the top executive, or someone from the highest executive level, within every institution. If 'the boss' could not personally participate, s/he was explicitly invited to involve someone else from within their top management team. This point will also be further examined in the discussion per cluster, and the results reported at the end of section I.3.

Eighty cities worldwide

The next selection involves the cities examined in the research. Which cities and where? The latter was easily determined: if you are trying to design a competitiveness model for cities in an era in which decisions are made on a global scale, then you cannot limit yourself to one or two continents. Opinions must be sought from around the world. Then there must be a selection of the cities in which the 'citymakers' will be approached. The following criteria were adopted for this:

- Cities which have sufficient 'citymakers', distributed over a number of clusters, to give (or potentially to give) an international profile to the city;
- Cities which qualify in the literature on the basis of one or more fields;
- Cities which qualified for consideration in various other studies;
- Being the capital city of a prominent country gave an extra qualification;
- A reasonable spread across the continents.

Having been measured against these criteria, around eighty cities were selected in which the 'citymakers' were approached. In table I.2 they are grouped alphabetically per continent. This number was too large and unwieldy to be used within the questionnaire, and was therefore reduced to fifty and subsequently divided into a first and second division, each with twenty-five cities. Further examination of this sub-division comes later, in the discussion of the first question on the questionnaire. The remaining cities were not included within the questionnaire but were still involved in the research. The relevant 'citymakers' were approached, and their answers are treated in the same way as those from their colleagues in the selected fifty.

■

While the research was ongoing, a publication appeared by Beaverstock et al (1999) with an overview of 79 cities that had already gained the status of world or international city in the literature. The cities (19) which are not found in that overview but were selected for this study are indicated in the table with an asterisk.

* * *

I. 2.3 THE RESEARCH METHOD

Written questionnaire
The 'citymakers' were approached in a traditional way, by post, with a questionnaire. Other methods were considered and discarded for various reasons. A survey by telephone was swiftly rejected on practical grounds: language problems, reaching the correct person, time differences, how to phrase the questions. The possibility of using e-mail was seriously considered, but again there would be substantial problems, both practical (few of the e-mail addresses were known) and technical (potentially incompatible systems). A face-to-face survey, perhaps the most desirable, would require a worldwide network of experienced people with excellent communication skills.

Research period
Designing, distributing and processing a written questionnaire requires a lot of work, especially when it involves eleven clusters with around eighty cities and on average about five or six 'citymakers' per city. A period of three years was therefore earmarked for the study. Existing research had shown that the topics of the questionnaire do not date particularly quickly: a city does not tend to drop from the top overnight, and the value given to a competitive factor does not change daily. The danger that the results of the research would quickly become outdated was therefore not considered to be very high. On the other hand, it is true that it can be difficult to interest people in conclusions that are based on research and data from years ago or (in a manner of speaking) from the previous century. In that sense there was some urgency.

The research was started in early 1998 with the Performing Arts. Every two to three months thereafter work on a new cluster was begun. At first it seemed as if the work on each cluster could also be completed within two or three months, but this ideal was soon abandoned. Sometimes it took more than a year, and for some clusters even longer, before there was sufficient response to allow plausible conclusions to be drawn. More on this later.

The questionnaire

The questions were the same for all clusters, but the presentation was altered during the study. The first three clusters received forms with substantially more explanatory notes on the questions. Reconsideration of the balance between presentation and information led to an extremely concise formulation for the first two questions, and also to very short annotations. All other additional information was collected into a leaflet that was sent together with the questionnaire.

However, the original form was itself the result of a test questionnaire which had been sent to around thirty people in the Amsterdam region, who were comparable to the target group for the research. A large number of valuable suggestions were made, amongst which 'make it shorter, more concise' was most common. So at the start, in the design of the first definitive form, much attention was paid to this. Nonetheless, experience showed that it had to be (and could be) even shorter and even more concise!

From the start the questionnaires were sent in eight languages: English, Spanish, French, German, Italian, Portuguese, Japanese and Chinese. Where appropriate (for example, for an English executive in Shanghai), a form was added with which a questionnaire in a different language could be requested. The questionnaire can be found in the appendices of this volume.

The main aims of the research, namely (1) the identification of the competitive factors for cities for the development of a competitiveness model for cities, and (2) the construction of not only an integral ranking list but also functional ranking lists of cities, are of course reflected in the questions. Not in the sequence of questions, however, as the first aim is included in the second question. As even 'citymakers' will not be thinking about competitive factors every hour of the day, it was considered to be the most difficult part of the questionnaire. It is not simple to answer and also not easy to formulate concisely. For reasons of presentation, therefore, it seemed advisable to start with a question of more immediate appeal.

QUESTION I is therefore aimed at obtaining a list from the 'citymakers' of the 20 to 25 most important cities in the world. The respondents are asked to base their judgement on overall impressions: the integral perception.

Why choose 20 to 25? Ask anyone to name the most important cities in the world, and you will frequently get the list: New York, London, Paris and Tokyo. This series is occasionally challenged; Sassen, for example, (and those following in her footsteps) and some other publicists do not include Paris in their comparative studies. However, the real doubts and differences only surface when a longer list is required, as is also demonstrated in the literature: apart from the Big Four, there are constant variations in the group that is taken into consideration. However, comparisons are usually limited to within a single continent, while in a world in which the borders between countries and continents are becoming blurred the need for comparisons at a global level is becoming increasingly urgent. Is the division between these first four and the rest indeed so sharp, and

21

can a reason be found for that? Can a broader category of cities be identified, that could also be considered 'global players'?

It is very tempting to use this term for the ranking list that is to be constructed of cities that play a leading role on the world stage. However, it is more often associated with businesses than with cities. A wide range of other terms can be found in the literature: some random examples are: Global City, Metropolis, World City, World Class City, Cosmopolitan City, International City. This research was aimed at identifying the 20 to 25 most prominent cities in the world; the word 'leading' is perhaps the most expressive. Therefore, with acknowledgements to a well-known hotel group, the term 'leading cities in the world' has been chosen.

Presentation of the question was very carefully considered. A scheme of all the cities that are involved in the research, as mentioned before, would have a damaging effect on the responses. An open question would certainly meet the needs of presentation, but would not help towards making it as easy as possible for the respondent, and could also encourage very limited answers. In addition, there has already been quite a lot of research on this point, the most well-known studies being those of Fortune Magazine and Healy & Baker Real Estate. Even though they have a more limited aim (examining the qualities of a city as a center for enterprise) and therefore also a more limited target group, they lend cities a certain status. This (fairly) objective finding would not be properly recognized in a totally open question. Fifty cities were therefore chosen, divided into two categories of twenty-five each: a provisional list of 'leading cities' (Division I) and a list of other important cities (Division II). The object was to obtain a definitive premier division by using the 'shift method'.

The 'SHIFT METHOD' reduces a number of the disadvantages and doubts mentioned above. As far as can be ascertained, it has not been used in this kind of research before, and it originated in budgeting techniques. Space in a budget can be created for new activities, if a number of existing, but less preferred, activities are abandoned. The method forces prioritization of new activities and so-called posteriorization of existing ones. In other words, if you want something new, you have to get rid of something equivalent from what you already have. Give with the left hand, take away with the right. For this research, cities in Division II had to be prioritized (which cities should be upgraded to Division I?) and the cities in Division I posteriorized (which cities had to be downgraded to Division II to make room for them?). Making choices is never easy, and the same applies to choosing cities, so firm instructions could do no harm. The respondents were therefore expressly requested to indicate at least five cities in both divisions – more if they wanted to, but preferably not fewer.

Putting together the first division may only be provisional, but must be done responsibly. The request to make (only) five changes implies that no more should be needed in order to come to a correct definitive list. A great deal of care was therefore spent on the pre-selection.

First, the literature was, of course, consulted. In addition, important weight was given to the above-mentioned studies by Fortune and Healy & Baker in both the choice of the fifty cities and splitting them into the two divisions. Another factor was the need to include at least one or two cities from each continent. At the same time a reasonably even geographical distribution was sought, both across the world and within the continents. Finally, the size of the country and the city, plus the function of capital city, was taken into consideration.

Each choice had its problems and raised doubts, and this led to a number of important cities failing to be placed in even the second division. To allow for this, space was deliberately offered in which other cities could be added, if wished. This led to only a small number of critical comments from respondents from these cities; one returned the questionnaire uncompleted as a form of protest. Others, however, happily added a city, frequently their own.

The target total of 20 to 25 cities should not be taken too seriously. It is only to indicate that the aim is to reach a clearly defined group of 'leading cities in the world.' The definitive total will ultimately be determined by the results. It is more important to recognize the clear lines of division between cities than the gradual differences in appreciation.

The second part of the first question (QUESTION 1-B) elicits a professional opinion on the quality of the cities in a certain specific area. This is obtained by asking the 'citymakers' which cities are at the top in their own professional field. To make it crystal clear, the professional field or cluster in question is indicated once more. A city can be appreciated as a whole, but also just in specific areas such as the arts, sciences or financial affairs. A city could score low as a whole, but be among the top cities in the world in a certain area – and vice versa is also possible, in principle. In short, the answer to this question provides a partial or functional ranking of cities, based on the opinion of professionals from that sector. Such a ranking meets the objection given to many other similar classifications: the 'best city,' that's nice, but best for what? The answer 'to locate your business!' is also nice, but what kind of business? With 1-B, question 1-A gains a dimension that, as far as could be ascertained, had not been introduced in earlier research.

The most important but at the same time most difficult question, getting a picture of the competitive factors for cities, is addressed in QUESTION II. The Shift Method is also applied here. For this purpose, the thirty-five selected factors are separated into a Division I (most important factors) and II (other important factors) and once again the respondents were asked to downgrade and upgrade respectively at least five. Section II.3 gives a detailed explanation of how the original selection was made. A substantial number of factors could be extracted from the existing literature. Personal (international) experience was heavily used in the separation into the two divisions. It was a consoling thought that application of the Shift Method would swiftly correct any obvious mistakes.

The overview of factors was also used to allow the 'citymakers' to put together an Agenda for the Future for their own city. In QUESTION 2-B they are asked which factors will require the most attention in their own city in the coming years. It is an attempt to collect an opinion on this point for each city. The data collected must, of course, have sufficient 'body' – if the number of answers is too small, then useful conclusions might only be possible per continent or per cluster, or perhaps only as a whole.

In QUESTION III a number of 'concepts' with regard to cities are presented. A characteristic of such concepts or propositions is that they do not require further explanation, as long as they are well formulated. It is also simple to 'agree' or 'disagree' with them. An efficient method, therefore, of eliciting judgements in a written questionnaire. The background of these concepts, however, and why they were presented, does deserve further explanation.

Concept 1 is intended to confirm that one of the two aims of this research, construction of a hierarchical overview of 'leading cities,' is useful in the opinion of 'citymakers;' does the title 'leading city in the world' give a competitive advantage? A risky initiative; imagine if they said no!

It is commonplace in the Netherlands for a doctoral thesis to be accompanied by a set of concepts or propositions, usually relevant to the subject of the thesis. Concepts 2, 3, 4, 6 and 7 could be appropriate for this purpose, if confirmed sufficiently in a positive sense.

Concept 5 also has this background, but in addition it is aimed at contributing to a potential future study on the administrative structure of large conurbations.

The eighth concept, in addition to the first, is aimed at confirming an assumption on the basis of which this research was begun: studies, comparisons and analyses are important, but the perception that exists of the qualities of a city (or country) can be decisive.

Concepts 9 to 11 relate to the international profile, image and marketing of a city. It is certainly not a primary aim to dedicate a separate section to these elements. It is more that, as explained earlier in paragraph 1.1 on perception, the opportunity was too good to be missed. The replies will determine whether or not substantial conclusions can be drawn. While this research was still ongoing, work was also begun on making an inventory of which cities had generated the most 'free publicity,' anticipating the results for concept 11.3. That was not without risk; if the concept had not been endorsed then that would have been a lot of work for nothing.

FINALLY a few data were collected on the respondent him/herself: age, professional background (varying per cluster), and job title.

The question whether s/he also lives in the city in which s/he works was asked with concept 5 in mind. It is important to know whether or not the opinions of city residents differ greatly from those of commuters.

Research should be undertaken as objectively and neutrally as possible. It may be focused on the perceptions of the 'citymakers,' but it is not the intention that this should be influenced by the origin of the sender. Hence the question if any constraint was felt in responding because the research was conducted from the Netherlands and/or the doctoral thesis is for the University of Amsterdam.

The questionnaire market is very competitive. Businesses and other bodies are assailed with all kinds of questions; for legal reasons, official statistics, academic research and of course especially commercial reasons. As a result a few have made it company policy to refuse to participate in any such surveys. You therefore need to use your own competitive advantages in order to be noticed in this crowd. An interesting subject and a good presentation are, of course, of paramount importance, and offering to send the results of the research has become almost taken for granted. This is why a roundtrip to a number of European cities was offered to the respondents in a prize draw. It is impossible to tell whether or not this incentive positively influenced the level of response, but the fact that 63% indicated that they wished to be entered into the prize draw shows that it appealed to a large proportion of the respondents.

* * *

I. 2.4 FRAMES OF REFERENCE

It does not suffice to research the perceptions that 'citymakers' have with regard to relevant competitive factors and the ranking of cities. Research into perceptions that covers eleven clusters and eighty cities spread across the entire world calls for frames of reference, additional data that can confirm, reinforce or put into perspective the results. These data were obtained from (1) the literature, (2) lists of rankings and (3) overviews of free publicity.

This (additional) part of the research relates, however, only to the ranking of cities. As explained above, little systematic information on competitive factors for cities can be found in the literature and other publications, let alone ranking lists that display their relevance to competitive positions. Most information on competitive factors is hidden in contributions on the ranking of cities; sometimes it seems as if it is embarrassing to pay any attention to it or to try to justify it. However, by gathering a little information here and a little information there, it proved possible to construct an overview that was useful as a frame of reference both in the design of the research and in the analysis of the results. As it was more appropriate for the latter, this table is included in part II.

Table I.3	**SOURCES OF REFERENCE**			
Clusters/ Categories	Sources of Reference			
	Literature	Free Publicity	Available Rankings	Ranks newly prepared
Performing Arts		International Arts Manager		International Competitions
Hospitality		Business Traveller		
• Hotels			Institutional Investor	
• Congresses			ICCA and IUA	
Real Estate & Architecture				
• Development		World Architecture	Richard Ellis (office rents) Healy & Baker (retail rents)	
• Architecture				Largest Architectural Firms
Trade & Transport				
• Aviation			Airports Council International	
Academia	Mattiessen et al.			Cited Publications
Corporate Services	Beaverstock et al.			
Museums				Art Galleries etc.
Media		Time magazine		
Int. Organizations			UIA Yearbook	
Multinationals & Finance				
• Multinationals	Godfrey en Zhou	Fortune Magazine		
• Finance		The Bankers Journal		
All clusters	Beaverstock et al.	Time Magazine		

Meanwhile, drawing up all kinds of ranking lists for cities has become a popular occupation for both the academic world and the profit sector. Depending on their position in the list, one city may be over the moon, while the others simply shrug their shoulders. The quality of the lists cannot always withstand criticism, especially with regard to integral classifications of cities, as explained earlier, but there are not so many of these. There is no shortage of functional classifications, however, which cover a most diverse range, but they are almost all based on hard data, not on perceptions. Each ranking list, whether integral or functional, qualitatively good or not, will influence perceptions, especially now that they are increasingly being publicized. More than enough reasons, therefore, to examine such lists critically. On the occasions that this does happen, it is understandably almost always done by the cities that were placed in less favorable positions in the list. Criticisms from that quarter are quickly dealt with. Whatever the case, there are functional ranking lists available for a number of clusters which can serve as a frame of reference for the research. If important differences are observed, then this could contribute to the debate on the best basis for such research: data or perception.

Publicity, or rather being the subject of publicity, is an important factor in forming a city's international profile – at least, that is the impression from personal experience, and confirmation will be sought in the responses to concept 3.11 in the questionnaire. Anticipating the results, over a number of years a study has been made of how often a city has attracted attention in one or more authoritative periodicals, for a few clusters and integrally. It could be through a special article, a mention in a headline or accompanying map, a photo, a calendar of events, etc. If the 'citymakers' agree with the concept, then so-called 'publicity rankings' could be constructed on the basis of these inventories and subsequently used as a frame of reference.

Various routes have therefore been followed in order to obtain lists of rankings: those in the literature, published by research bureaus or magazines and – such as the publicity rankings – self-made. Table I.3 indicates how successful this has been per cluster. The already existing lists of rankings have been included without assessing their worth, insofar as their quality did not play a decisive role in their selection. Precisely by placing the results of the perception research next to rankings obtained by other means, and establishing the similarities and especially the differences, a contribution can be made to a critical evaluation of the diverse methods of ranking. It is a first insight. Relevant specific information (such as the sources) will be given in the discussion of the different clusters.

* * *

27

Table I.4 NUMBERS OF ADDRESSES AND RESPONSES

CLUSTERS & TIMETABLE	Overall			Europe			North America			Asia			Latin America			Africa			Middle East		
	Adr.	Resp.	%	Adr.	Resp.	%	Adr.	Resp.	%	Adr.	Resp.	%	Adr.	Resp.	%	Adr.	Resp.	%	Adr.	Resp.	%
Performing Arts 01.1998 - 04.1998	320	159	50	134	63	47	97	58	60	50	20	40	26	12	46	3	2	67	10	4	40
Hospitality 05.1998 - 05.1999	871	199	23	296	78	26	283	44	16	150	37	25	66	16	24	45	11	24	31	13	42
Real Estate & Architecture 09.1998 - 08.2000	835	131	16	314	62	20	240	26	11	205	31	15	53	9	17	13	3	23	10	0	0
Int. Trade & Transport 10.1998 - 08.2000	408	127	31	149	62	42	84	21	25	97	28	29	38	8	21	20	5	25	20	3	15
Academia 02.1999 - 04.2000	355	151	43	108	59	55	101	24	24	81	40	49	35	16	46	12	6	50	18	6	33
Corporate Services 09.1999 - 08.2000	913	121	13	347	49	14	218	23	11	195	29	15	95	7	7	32	5	16	26	8	31
Museums 02.2000 - 06.2000	432	148	34	221	88	40	76	19	25	71	20	28	35	11	31	19	5	26	10	5	50
Media 03.2000 - 02.2001	764	92	12	306	38	12	118	12	10	185	24	13	101	11	11	35	7	20	19	0	0
Int. Organizations 06.2000 - 03.2001	405	102	25	208	58	28	62	13	21	67	13	19	36	8	22	32	10	31	0	0	0
Multinationals & Finance 09.2000 - 03.2001	1219	137	11	495	74	15	310	16	5	269	30	11	86	10	12	32	3	9	27	4	15
ALL CLUSTERS 01.1998 - 03.2001	6522	1367	21	2578	631	24	1589	256	16	1370	272	20	571	108	19	243	57	23	171	43	25

28

I. 3 EVALUATION OF THE RESEARCH INTO PERCEPTIONS

In section I.2 a report is given on the composition of the target groups ('the citymakers') and on the cities involved in the research. From this can be deduced that relevant addresses had to be selected in eighty cities for each of the eleven clusters. It was expected to be an extensive and difficult task, and was there-fore approached cluster by cluster. In order to provide help with this when necessary, but also to make it possible to approach the addressees more directly with reminders (if required) at a later date, contact persons were sought in the cities involved. This was successful in about forty cities, most of them working for the city autho-rities or at the Chamber of Commerce. However, it was necessary to promise faithfully that they would be called upon only in a dire emergency. They were kept up-to-date with the aims, content and progress of the research via bulletins; at first every three months, later every six months. The collection of addresses went much more smoothly than expected – further information on this will be given in the discussion of the results – and the assistance of a contact person was required in only one or two instances. The initial response rate also meant that their assistance was not strictly necessary, leaving aside the fact that chasing 'citymakers' to return a questionnaire is, of course, not a particularly attractive task.

Addresses and response rates

Table I.4 shows, per cluster and per continent, the number of addresses to which a questionnaire was sent, and the number of questionnaires returned. The dates on which the studies of the different clusters were started and closed are given alongside. The Performing Arts (part of the culture cluster) were tackled first, for no particular reason; at most, the fact that the research was to cover non-economic factors as well may have played a role. It turned out to be an excellent choice. The response rate was more than 50%, beyond all expectations. It was a wonderful incentive to continue, and a real confidence boost. Next was the cluster Hospitality (tourism, congresses, hotels), a group that is connected intimately to the city. Couldn't go wrong, you might think, but disenchantment came quickly. The required response rate could only be reached with a great deal of extra effort, and thanks to the fact that it is a broad target group. Subsequent experiences were not dissimilar. As inspiring as it had begun with the Performing Arts, so it ended in difficulties with the clusters Multinationals and the Financial world. There were more than enough addresses for the last target group, but the willing-ness to reply was close to non-existent.

This meant that the help of the contact persons had to be requested for the first time. Their own reactions were not exactly encouraging. First, around half had changed job, and attempts to find a replacement usually failed as soon as they heard what they were expected to do. This was also the case with the other half who, in principle, had agreed to help; when the request for help became concrete, they were suddenly too busy or could not be reached. Eventually there was only

29

a very small group of faithfuls left, who worked personally towards securing a good result using their local networks. It helped, but was not enough to complete these two last clusters successfully. If it had been absolutely necessary it might have been possible, but the effort required would have been out of all proportion to the results. After nine clusters the results were already more or less clear, and around seventy responses had already shown that neither the Multinationals nor the Financial world were going to be much different. That meant that only two reasons remained for continuing: to deserve a medal for pig-headed persistence, and to get an answer to question 2-B (the top cities for the cluster). Regarding the latter, it is fortunate that the available literature is focused on precisely these two clusters, and that there are sufficient data to construct a hierarchy using an alternative route to that of perception. In addition, many banks and life insurance companies are also multinationals. Enough reasons, therefore, to say goodbye to a chance at a medal, and to combine the two clusters.

Looking back, it can be seen that the peak response was in the second and third week following the mailing. After that, responses just trickled in. Precisely in that phase, while there was still hope (not to be confused with expectation) of a satisfactory conclusion, the envelopes that could not be delivered also started to return, each one the cause of some gnashing of teeth.

Two to three months after the first mailing, a reminder was sent. A personal handwritten note was added to the reminder letter (a very time-consuming task) and, of course, a new questionnaire was enclosed. Keeping in mind the need for a balanced geographical spread, the continents that were most weakly represented after the first round were handled first. Usually the other continents had to be added later as well, in order to achieve the desired minimum total (100) of replies. If this second round did not deliver the desired result, then extra addresses were sought and/or a third mailing was sent, but with a letter or note of recommendation from someone within a relevant international organization. Selecting extra addresses was only possible when the target group was broad enough, for example the corporate services and hotels. Other target groups were limited by their very nature, such as congress centers, concert halls or airlines. The starting-point was always that the company or institution must be a 'city-maker,' i.e. a contributor to the international status of a city. Regional orchestras or charter companies, for example, were not approached. Where efforts in a few cases remained unsuccessful, then the work on that cluster was temporarily halted, to be picked up again after about a year. This happened, for example, with the cluster Hospitality, especially with the hotels. In many cases they had come under new management in the meantime, so it was new to them anyway; the others had more than likely forgotten the earlier mailings. In this way each reminder mailing delivered some results. Together with the first wave of responses, the numbers recorded in Table I.4 were achieved.

The following observations can be made on this overview.

1. A form was sent to around 6500 'citymakers;' ultimately, around 1400 responses were received, which is 21%. Before the research was started it was pointed out that a response rate of 20% to a written questionnaire is extremely good; at least if the study is limited to your own country. In the end this percentage did emerge, but for a worldwide study. The only reason that this percentage is reported here is because everyone will ask for it or work it out for themselves, but it should not be linked to how representative, or not, the responses are. The plausibility of the results is what is important. In order to measure this, a **Plausibility check** has been developed. In the following section this is explained further, and the results of the check reported.

2. The response rate from within Europe was above average, from Asia and the 'other continents' about average, while from North America it was well below average. This lagging-behind by North America was observed in all the clusters, with one exception: the Performing Arts. The response rate here was actually well above the already exceptional average! Afterwards it was clear that this was the proverbial swallow that, at least for this continent, did not make the summer. This dazzling peak at the start was sadly matched by a depressing low at the end. By combining the clusters Multinationals and Finance it was eventually possible to form three groups for the Plausibility check.

3. The response rate per cluster varies widely. However, a certain pattern can be identified if they are divided into profit and non-profit clusters. The latter includes the clusters Performing Arts, Academia, Museums and International Organizations. They all score well above average. Of the profit clusters, only International Trade & Transport and Hospitality are above average. However, this is in no small way due to the non-profit institutions represented in these clusters.

Plausibility check
With some forty categories, grouped into ten clusters, spread across six continents and eighty cities, with one category narrowly defined (such as stock exchanges) and another loosely measured (such as hotels and consultancy) and when, in addition, it was not certain for all the clusters in advance if and how the necessary addresses would be obtained ... it did not seem sensible to try and achieve a statistically accountable sample or result. Instead, an approach was chosen which would lead to plausible conclusions for as many clusters as possible, preferably for all of them. Most dictionaries define plausible as 'seeming to be true or reasonable.'

In order to determine how plausible, how reasonable or worthy of belief, the responses received were, a check was developed and applied to all clusters. The test gives the degree of plausibility, the plausibility value (PL index) expressed in a percentage. The higher the percentage, the greater the level of agreement in the responses. The PL index can be calculated for:

■

- the total of all answers,
- the answers to the different questions,
- the answers per cluster,
- the answers per continent,
- and even for each separate competitive factor, city or concept.

The check is built up of the following elements

1. For each cluster, a group was formed of the first 50 completed questionnaires to be received. A good balance between the continents was sought by maintaining as far as possible an 'ideal city mix.' This mix was based on the number of cities per continent involved in the research, with the cities of London, New York, Paris and Tokyo – because of the much greater number of addressees –

Ideal City-Mix		
Continents	Number of Cities	Ideal % of responses
Europe	31	38
North America	19	24
Asia	16	20
Other Continents	19	18
Asia+	35	38
World	85	100

counting for two. The 'ideal' group has therefore the composition shown above.

However, such a mix can only be achieved when there is a sufficient mass, and with certain clusters in certain continents it was insufficient from the start. This was the case, for example, for the Performing Arts in Asia, Africa and the Middle East. However, even if there are sufficient addresses, the response can be so disappointing or arrive so irregularly over time, that it is not possible to keep to the 'ideal' composition. For this reason the Plausibility check could not always cover all four continents. For comparability and transparency, the results for Asia and the other continents are therefore collected under the term Asia+. Please note, this only applies to the Plausibility check: in the later sections, the results for Asia and for the other continents are discussed separately.

A first group of replies reflecting the ideal mix could be put together for each cluster, but it was not always possible to form a second group; for some clusters the number of replies left over was sufficient to be included in the check as a remainder group.

2. The percentage of votes received for a competitive factor, a city or a concept is an observation. Each well-balanced group delivered at least four observations: one for each of the three continents (Europe, North America and Asia+) and one for the average for the group. A second group delivered in most cases another four observations, and in a few clusters there was even a remainder group which was large enough for yet another observation, making eight or nine in total. In one case (Hospitality) observations could be made for Asia as well as for the other continents (Latin America, Africa and the Middle East), which provided

32

yet another two observations for that cluster. On the other hand, the poor level of response from North America meant that it sometimes did not appear in the second group, or that it was not possible to form a well-balanced second group, and there are then one or two fewer observations. The maximum number of observations per cluster is therefore eleven and the minimum is six. The maximum was reached only in the cluster Hospitality; most cases gave eight or nine, with only the clusters Media and International Organizations providing fewer than this. Below is an overview of the number of observations per cluster:

Number of observations (by continent and cluster)

	Group Average	Europe	North America	Asia+	Remainders	Total
Performing Arts	2	2	2	2		8
Hospitality	2	2	2	4	1	11
Real Estate	2	2	2	2	1	9
Trade & Transport	2	2	2	2		8
Academia	2	2	2	2	1	9
Corporate Services	2	2	2	2	1	9
Museums	2	2	2	2	1	9
Media	1	2	1	2	1	7
Int. Organizations	1	2	1	1	1	6
Multinationals/Finance	1	2	1	1	3	8
All	17	20	17	20	10	84

3. Each observation was recorded in a graphical figure. The observations were recorded per city (for questions 1-A and 1-B), per competitive factor (for question 2-A) and per concept (for question 3). For the question about Leading Cities (1-A) and Top Cities (1-B), the minimum threshold used was that 10% of the votes had been awarded to a city. On average (it varied a little from cluster to cluster) this gave respectively 40 and 15 cities for which observations were noted. In addition there were 34 competitive factors and 16 concepts. Together this made approximately 105 elements for which observations were recorded. Multiplied by 84, for the total of clusters, this would work out at about 9000 observations, and in fact it was 8955.

4. In the figures, all these observations are shown, per cluster, against the average score received by a city, competitive factor or concept from the cluster as a whole. Lines are drawn around each average, demarcating the area covered by 10% above and 10% below the average. In this way it can be determined how many or what percentage of the observations lie outside these margins. The percentage within the margins is the PL index (PLI).

33

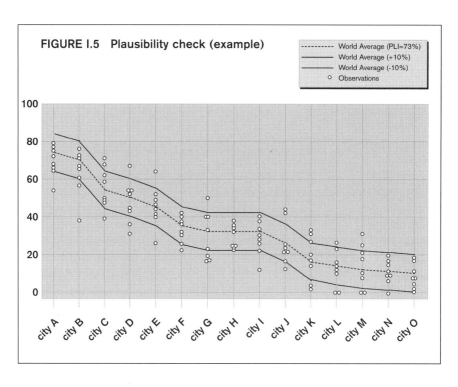

FIGURE I.5   Plausibility check (example)

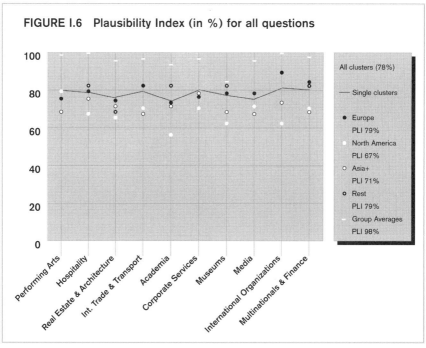

FIGURE I.6   Plausibility Index (in %) for all questions

5. In total, forty figures were constructed from which the PL index could be determined; four questions for each of the ten clusters. They give such a detailed picture, that it would go too far to publish them all, and therefore a single example is shown (Figure I.5). It is taken from one of the clusters and shows the answers to the question (1-B) about the Top Cities for that specific field.

A.	Number of observations for the cluster	8
B.	Number of cities selected	15
C.	Total number of observations (A x B)	120
D.	Number of observations outside the 10% zone (not specified per continent owing to space limitations)	32
E.	Number of observations inside the 10% zone	88
F.	PL value for the cluster's answer to the question on Top Cities (E as a percentage of C)	73%

The PL index therefore gives the percentage of observations that lies within the zone of 10% above or below the average result. The closer the observations are to each other or the more they are gathered close to the average, the higher the plausibility of the response. In order to give an indication of the degree of reliability that can be associated with a certain score, the following scale has been made:

- PL index = 90–100%: there is no doubt that the results represent the opinion of the relevant group(s);
- PL index = 70 - 90%: 'sans risque d'erreur';
- PL index = 50 - 70%: reason for caution and therefore a reason to examine the results more closely;
- PL index < 50%: insufficient to draw conclusions.

The results of the check described above for the study as a whole (in other words, the four questions taken together) are given in Figure I.6. In parts II and III similar overviews will be given of the PL indexes for, respectively, the question on competitive factors for cities (2-A) and the question about Leading Cities (1-A) and Top Cities (1-B). Anticipating this, it can be revealed now that the PL indexes for these questions deviate little from the PL index for the whole study. From Figure I.6, the following results can be determined:

1. The PL index for the whole study – in other words, for the four questions, all clusters and all continents together. This total PL index, shown by the straight black line, is about 80%. This percentage is built up from a total of 8955 observations, 22% of which therefore lie outside the 10% zone. This does not necessarily make it an unreliable part of the research, as shall be explained later.

2. The PL indexes for each of the ten clusters for all continents. These cluster PL indexes are shown by the points on the other black line. This line
   has been drawn only to illustrate more clearly the differences with the
   average. The PL indexes for the individual clusters lie between 74%
   (Academia) and 81% (International Organizations) and thus differ little.

3. The PL indexes for the three continents per cluster. The PL indexes for the
   continents vary somewhat more. The picture for Europe is in reasonable
   accordance with the total picture. For North America and Asia+ it is about
   10% less. If separate conclusions are to be drawn for these continents,
   then the exact composition of the PL index will have to be examined per
   case. The continental PL indexes (the continental average for all clusters)
   are not recorded in the Figure itself but in the key, in order to preserve the
   clarity of the Figure.

4. The other observations on which the total PL index is based, especially the
   remainder groups and the group averages.
   The remainder groups score better than average. This is rather noteworthy,
   as they are of limited size (between 30 and 50) and have very diverse (continental) compositions. This strengthens confidence in the plausibility of
   the results.
   The group average lies outside the zone in only 41 cases (about 2%), which
   means that the observations with a low PL index barely influence the total
   of the group and thus that the deviations that lie outside the 10% zone are
   not very large in general.

5. The more one goes into details, the more precarious it becomes. This is
   demonstrated by the cluster PL indexes for the continents. These show, for
   example, PL indexes for the response from North America that are 20 percentage points below the average for three clusters (Academia,
   International Organizations and Museums). Caution is required in such
   cases.

However, the most detailed cases are the unpublished figures. From these
the PL index per city, competitive factor or concept can be deduced, as desired.
In order to provide a complete picture of this, as mentioned before, it would be
necessary to reproduce all 40 figures and describe their relationships to each
other. It will be considered sufficient here, in addition to the example given
above, to make some remarks on the results that throw a little more light on the
observations that fall outside the 10% zone.

- It is not surprising but still important to note that the PL index is particularly high for high scores (75–100%) and for low ones (0–25%). The greatest
  deviations lie in the middle. This could be interpreted as making it risky to
  draw conclusions for that section. However, the deviations could simply
  be confirming that the opinions on or perceptions of a certain factor or

city are rather diverse. A more detailed judgement can be made on the basis of the concrete situation.

- An average smoothes out the differences, and it is the differences that are of interest for this research. A city or a competitive factor may be viewed much more positively (or the reverse) from a certain continent or from a certain cluster than the average (continental or professional component respectively). This will be expressed by two observations falling outside the margins, but it does not in fact adversely affect the plausibility.

- The absolute numbers for certain individual clusters are sometimes rather small. A minimum of 10 answers per continent was required. In these cases, just two deviating votes will place the observation outside the 10% zone.

Further examination of target groups, responses and plausibility

Earlier in this section it was explained that the ten clusters involved in the research were composed of businesses and institutions that can be considered as 'magnets' around which other activities group themselves and on which they are to some degree dependent. The overview shown earlier (Table I.4) is limited to the clusters as a whole. Most of them are, however, composed of more 'magnets.' Justification of the quantitative results of the research would not be complete without providing more insight into the selected categories from which the clusters' address lists were composed and also into the responses from the different categories. Table I.7 (next page) provides this information.

In this overview the sources are given from which the companies, organizations and institutions to be approached were chosen. This extensive and crucial process was the silent precursor to sending the questionnaires. Apart from the name of a company, the sources also had to provide an address and – in order to allow the questionnaires to be addressed personally – the names of one or more top management figures. This process proved to be simpler than originally expected, especially thanks to help from good contacts acquired during one's previous professional career. There are also many international organizations, including ones for the groups researched. Most of these publish an annual report or membership directory, and it usually proved possible to obtain a copy by one means or another.

It was more difficult when the international organizations had a federal character, i.e. when their members were national organizations. In this case the directories could not help; national organizations have not been classified as 'citymakers.' In addition, a few professional groups are not organized internationally at all; this applied especially to the clusters Corporate Services, the

Table I.7   Sources, Mailings and Responses

Clusters/categories	Main Sources of Addresses	Mailings		Response in % of	
		abs	%	mailings	all responses
Performing Arts					
• Symphonic Music		111	35	51	36
• Opera		58	18	55	20
• Ballet		59	18	59	22
• Others		92	29	38	22
• Totals	Paye and Mod Yearbook	320	100		100
Hospitality					
• Congresses & Tourism	Directories of ICCA and FECTO, Hotel Yearbook	199	23	49	49
• Hotels	Hotel Yearbook	672	77	15	51
• Totals		871	100		100
Real Estate & Architecture					
• Architects	World Architecture	373	45	24	69
• Development & Brokerage	Directories of Healy & Baker, Jones Lang Wootton Cushman & Wakefield and Richard Ellis Directories of Real Estate Federation and International Association of Corporate Real Estate Executives	462	55	9	31
• Totals		835	100		100
Trade & Transport					
• Aviation	Airport Yearbook	145	36	36	41
• Shipping	Directory of International Association of Ports & Harbours	74	18	22	13
• Trade	Directories of European Chambers of Commerce and World Trade Centers Association The Europa World Year Book	189	46	31	46
• Totals		408	100		100
Academia					
• Universities	International Handbook of Universities	355	100	43	100
Corporate Services					
• Accountants	Directories of KPMG, Ernst & Young, Deloitte/Touche/ Tohmatsu and PriceWaterhouseCoopers	377	41	15	46
• Lawyers	Directories of Clifford Chance, Legal Network International, Lex Mundi, Baker & McKenzie	139	15	20	23
• Management Consultancy	Directories of Bain & Company, The Boston Consulting Group,McKinsey, McCann Erickson, Young & Rubicam, Booz-Allen & Hamilton, Korn/Ferry International, Oracle	397	44	9	31
• Totals		913	100		100
Museums					
• Fine Arts Museums		246	57	33	55
• Historical Museums		103	24	46	32
• Other Museums		83	19	23	13
• Totals	The Museum Yearbook	432	100		100
Media					
• Newspapers		309	40	17	55
• News Agencies		186	25	9	18
• Others		269	35	9	27
• Totals	The Europa World Yearbook	764	100		100
International Organizations					
• Governmental		192	48	23	44
• Professional		147	36	29	41
• Non Profit		66	16	23	15
• Totals	Yearbook of the International Organizations	405	100		100
Multinationals & Finance					
• Multinationals	Fortune-500 List, Global Researcher Worldscope Data Base, Annual Reports	639	52	13	62
• Finance				9	38
• Banks	The Banker-1000 List and Global Researcher Worldscope Data Base	237	20		
• Stock Market	Directory of International Federation of Stock Exchanges, Directories of Barclays Capital, Bear Stearns, Chase Manhattan, Goldman Sachs, ING Barings, Lehman Brothers, Merrill Lynch, J.P. Morgan, Morgan Stanley Dean Witter, Nikko Securities	269	22		
• Life Insurance	Global Researcher Worldscope Data Base	74	6		
• Totals		1219	100		100

Multinationals and Finance. Overviews of international networks or offices and commercial databases were required to provide answers in a few cases. As a last resort there was always the 'Europa World Year Book' with a large collection of data for the whole world, per country, and sometimes even subdivided for the most important cities, but not always up to date.

Below, the composition of the clusters and the sources used to select the addresses will be examined briefly for each cluster. When a conspicuous number of deviations from the total picture were observed for a cluster, or other note-worthy observations were made, these will be highlighted in the explanation. In addition, attention will be paid, when relevant, to other interesting results of the Plausibility check.

For the **PERFORMING ARTS** use was made of a commercial publication in which the names, addresses and executives are listed for symphony orchestras, opera and ballet companies, cultural facilities and international festivals across the entire world. Data on size and turnover are also included. Using this, together with personal knowledge, it was fairly easy to make the selection. This was limited primarily to the large national companies. Most cities in Europe and North America have such companies for symphony music and for opera and ballet. By adding to this at least one cultural facility plus an international festival, it was possible to select four to six addresses (sometimes more) for each city in Europe and North America. The number was lower for Latin America and Asia, while the selection choices for Africa and the Middle East, using the same criteria, were very limited.

The remarkably high response, especially from North America, was evenly spread across both the continents and the diverse categories, with a slight peak for opera and ballet and a small dip for the group 'other.' The latter was comprised mostly of the management of international festivals and cultural facilities. The high response makes it possible to draw conclusions per category (part III).

The Plausibility check for this cluster shows a conspicuous deviation for North America. As stated earlier, in general this continent scored around 10% less than the total average. However, in this case, the respondents from North America are way out in front.

Various sources had to be consulted for the cluster **HOSPITALITY**. The congress side has a worldwide organization, but institutions for promoting tourism are only organized up to continental level. There are also national and municipal institutions. The promotion of tourism and conferences is often combined. This created a fairly complicated selection process, in which fortunately use could be made of the Worldwide Hotel Directory. In this way a total of 199 addresses were collected of institutions that are involved in the promotion of tourism and congresses and in accommodating congresses. Any further subdivision was prevented by practical constraints. The promotional bureaus in particular are not easy to distinguish, and conference centers (and hotels) often have their own marketing bureau. However, by studying their names, it would be correct to say that at least a third of this group is concentrated, to a lesser or greater degree, on the promotion of tourism.

In addition, the Hotel Directory mentioned above was the source for the hotel world. Containing the names and addresses of more than 10 000 hotels across the world, it seemed to be a bottomless well. This was shown clearly when insufficient responses were received from the first selection; it was very easy to make an additional selection of equal quality. With regard to quality, a choice had to be made on the basis of size (number of beds) and price. As the questionnaire was intended for 'citymakers' – hotels that (can) give an extra international status to a city – it was generally the larger and more expensive hotels that were approached. In addition, a limited number of hotels were selected from the middle and budget class, using the criterion of inclusion in an international chain, as this gives a certain guarantee of quality and international orientation. In general, a spread of respectively 60, 20 and 20% was sought.

The response from the two categories was very different. The congress centers and promotional bureaus together had a response rate of nearly 50%. However, it took long hard work to achieve this – a bit of a shock after the wonderful response from the Performing Arts. On the other hand, the hotels, despite the additions to the list of addresses, did not get further than 15%. Thanks only to the large size of this target group, this percentage represents, in absolute terms, a fairly high number. The response rate from hotels in the top and middle classes was a little higher than that from the budget class.

The PL index for the response from North America shows large differences for this cluster. On the positive side (79%) for the question about 'leading cities'; but in the other direction (57%) for the question about competitive factors. For Europe, the high score (91%) for the sixteen concepts is striking.

Originally it was intended to split the cluster **REAL ESTATE & ARCHITEC-TURE** into three categories: architects, agents, developers and investors. From the responses it became clear that the agents and developers groups overlap, so that they form a single category. No start was made in selecting investors; not only because there are no obvious sources, but also because of the strong relationship with the financial world. Both in the selection of the addresses and in the processing of the results, the emphasis was placed on the world of architects. Architects operating at an international level have an excellent viewpoint, from their own work and through the literature, on the important developments in real estate in both the planning and implementation phases. The monthly periodical World Architecture was used as a source for this category. Each year it publishes an overview of the 500 largest architect bureaus in the world, complete with addresses and contact persons. For the other category (agents/developers) use was made of the directories of offices with international networks and of a few international organizations.

Much time was needed in order to get a sufficient number of responses. It was particularly difficult with the agents/investors and it certainly did not reach the level that would allow separate conclusions to be drawn for this category (if desired). The response rate from the world of architects was much better. Together they provided a total that, certainly in absolute terms, can be compared favorably with the other clusters.

The PL index of 75% does not differ from the total picture. For the separate subjects, however, it lies visibly below the average in two cases: 54% for Asia regarding the question about Top Cities and 56% for North America for the concepts. The 69% for Europe for the competitive factors is also noteworthy. There are no obvious positive deviations.

A target group must have sufficient 'body' in order to have a chance of success. Neither of the separate categories **INTERNATIONAL TRADE or TRANS-PORT** has that 'body', and this was the main reason for combining them into one cluster. In addition, they are activities that are regularly reported in combination in statistics. There is also a clear relation between the activities; trade simply has to be transported.

For the category trade, institutions were selected that facilitate trade, such as Chambers of Commerce and World Trade Centers, as well as large international trading companies. Of the latter, there are not many left in the western world. In the Far East they are found largely in Korea. The category trade taken together forms about half the total cluster.

The category transport is divided into air and sea transport. International air and sea transport companies were selected, as well as the managers of international airports and seaports. Together they provide the other half of the cluster. The air transport portion is, however, twice the size of that for sea transport.

Almost two years were spent working on this cluster. This was largely because work was started with the trade category and only later it was decided to combine it with transport. The work therefore lay dormant for a while. In addition, substantial extra efforts were required in order to bring in sufficient responses for both categories. The response from sea transport is below that of trade and air transport and that of the average for the whole cluster. The number is too small for separate conclusions.

With regard to the PL indexes, there are no particular deviations to report for this cluster.

41

The cluster **ACADEMIA** is limited to universities. Much research and development (R&D) is concentrated in the universities or linked to them and to the multinationals. In addition the remaining institutions are by no means all located in the big cities. Most business schools also seem to be linked to a university in one way or another. As the questionnaires were addressed to the universities' top management, it was assumed that the respondents would also include research activities and business schools in their total judgement.

For the selection, use could be made of the International Handbook of Universities in which the addresses and executives of all universities and similar institutions are collected. Additional names of executives were found in the membership directories of a couple of international organizations.

The latter was only necessary for North America. The response rate from Europe (55%), Asia (49%) and the other continents (43%) had been terrific and – coming about halfway through the study – an enormous incentive to persevere with the research. With help from additional material a sufficient response was eventually received from North America, but the response rate for the Performing Arts was never rivaled.

The PL index of 74% for this cluster may be the lowest, but it is only four percentage points less than the average. This is caused by the relatively low values for Europe (70%) and North America (56%).

The **CORPORATE SERVICES** form a multifaceted cluster. It includes accountants, legal practices, organizational advice bureaus, IT consultants, executive searchers, advertising bureaus and perhaps a few other specialized, high quality service activities. An attempt is made to compress this diversity into three categories. The accountants and legal practices are reasonably easy to distinguish as separate categories, however diverse their activities may be and however many interconnections there may be with other service providers. All the other service providers are gathered in a third category under the heading management consultancy.

Only companies that formed part of an international network were approached. For the accountants this was then the 'big four;' they had one or more branches in almost all the cities studied. Legal practices started setting up international office networks only recently. In fact there are only two with extensive networks: Baker & McKenzie en Clifford Chance. In addition there are international alliances and light cooperative links. The service providers placed in the third category are also without exception part of a worldwide office network, even if one is somewhat more comprehensive than the other.

A large number of executives could be selected using the address books, but not all of them were approached in the first mailing. In this way it was possible, when the response rate left something to be desired, to approach an extra number through which this cluster could be brought to a reasonable conclusion. A low response rate of 13% combined with a limited group of addressees was never going to provide the number of answers required for the Plausibility check, and this modest response was observed for all continents. Was the subject not interesting enough, were they too busy with the economic boom, are people not used to giving their opinions for free or do they attach little importance to the international competitive position of their city? These are just speculative questions. The reaction to concept 10 can provide an answer (negatory) to only the last one. Conspicuous in this cluster was the fact that the addressees often completed the questionnaire themselves; in the other clusters it was not uncommon for it to be passed on to a colleague or deputy.

The PL index for this cluster as a whole deviates positively from the average. There are no conspicuously low scores.

There are many **MUSEUMS** in the world, all shapes and sizes, in large and small cities. Fortunately a museum book is produced each year in which the museums are neatly listed per country and city and the type of museum is also indicated. In this way it was fairly simple to select the museums that could be defined as 'citymakers.' These included in any case the museums that foreign visitors regard as a 'must see,' which belong to the categories 'fine arts' and 'historical' and made up about 80% of the total selection. The other 20% was comprised of museums that may not be a 'must,' but are of such a character that they attract a specific but still reasonably broad group of visitors. This category includes maritime and technological museums in particular.

The desired response rate was achieved within a reasonably short time period. With a score of 34% this cluster was one of the most successful. This does not take away the fact that the museums in North America had to be pushed hard to produce a result. The responses are reasonably well spread across the three categories, even if the remainder category is a little thin on the ground. The 'must sees' are well represented, however.

In general the PL indexes for this cluster show a fairly stable picture. However, for the question about the Top Cities it lies ten percentage points below the average. For the question about the concepts a (uniquely) low score of 31% can be recorded for Asia. On the basis of such scores, it is not possible to draw conclusions.

The **MEDIA** formed a richly varied cluster. Addresses were selected from the Europa World Yearbook of the most important daily newspapers, periodicals, press agencies, news correspondents, television and radio stations and publishing companies. In most cases it was possible to address the questionnaire to the editor in chief. The news correspondents often had the nationality of the press agency, so that for example an American was approached who worked in Moscow for Associated Press, a Briton working for Reuters and stationed in Sydney, or a

Japanese working for Kyodo Tsushin in Vienna. Taken all together, there was plenty of choice. This was fortunate, as this sector may be quick with unsolicited opinions, but it was much more difficult to obtain solicited ones from them. At least on this subject. Did they doubt whether they qualified as 'citymakers' and did the subject therefore not appeal to them? In section II.2 further motivation will be given to involving this cluster in the questionnaire, while the answer to concept no. 10 (Figure II.12') gives an indication of their stake in the city.

The quantitative aim, two groups of fifty questionnaires, was not achieved. North America lagged behind once again, and therefore the balance of cities was also not ideal. In the end the response rate from the daily newspapers was a reasonable average, but the news agencies and correspondents, the editors of periodicals and publishing companies, only managed 9%. A higher response rate could probably have been achieved by approaching German, French, Spanish and Italian correspondents, but this would have led to an even stronger European representation in the results.

Whether this cluster, despite these shortcomings, has been successfully concluded depends on the PL index of the responses. This shows a very stable picture. A fractionally lower score than the total average, and no conspicuous deviations for the separate questions and/or continents. Conclusions for the cluster as a whole can therefore be drawn with confidence. However, more caution will be required for statements about the separate continents.

The **INTERNATIONAL ORGANIZATIONS** form an exceptional cluster. At first sight, there is an enormously rich pool when you look at the impressive Yearbook of International Organizations. However, when you start to make selections and pick out the 'citymakers,' the number shrinks rapidly and what remains is also concentrated in a limited number of cities. The selection criteria used were that the organization is preferably worldwide in structure or at least covers a whole continent, and is preferably not a federation of national organizations. This not only rapidly shrinks the book, but for a large number of cities you need a magnifying glass to find one or more suitable addressees. This does not apply in Europe to London, Paris, Geneva or Vienna; nor in North America to New York or Washington; nor in Asia to Bangkok or Manila; nor in Africa to Cairo or Nairobi. However, beyond these it required long and hard searching. For the Middle East it was not possible to find a single organization that qualified. The overrepresentation of Europe in the address list meant that from the start it was unlikely that a good balance of cities could be achieved.

The organizations were divided into three categories. The GOs or govern-mental organizations, such as head and regional offices of the United Nations, form about half the selection. The NGOs or non-governmental organizations were split into two categories: organizations of professional groups (such as journalists or doctors) and non-profit organizations including, for example, charities and international sport organizations. The latter group was at 16% clearly the smallest.

In all cases the top executive of the organization was approached. It must be remembered that these addressees, like the news correspondents, often came from a different country than the one in which they were stationed. In the allocation of the responses to the different continents no account is taken of this.

The response rate from this cluster, compared to the total average, can be called reasonably good. A number of messages were sent from governmental organizations in particular, stating that their independent position did not allow them to answer the questions posed. Eventually the response, divided over the three categories, almost matched (percentage-wise) the number of questionnaires sent. The response from Europe, as with the mailing, forms about half of the total.

These are reasons to look carefully at the PL index. At 81% it is the highest for all of the clusters. The response from Europe, with a value of 89%, makes an important contribution to this. This means that the values for North America and Asia etc. are lower, but this is the same for all clusters. However, there is one striking deviation to report: the PL index for the response from North America to the question about the Top Cities is no higher than 43%. Generally a good picture for the total and for Europe, but without examining the details more closely, a certain caution is required for the other continents.

At the start of this section some information was given on experiences in obtaining the necessary responses, and reasons why in the end the two clusters **MULTINATIONALS and FINANCE** were combined into one. From the beginning there was a premonition that it could be difficult, and this is why many extra addresses were selected. For this, access was obtained to the Global Researcher Worldscope Database, and the data collected for around 300 companies that feature on the Fortune 500 list. To these were added other prominent, usually industrial, businesses, with a turnover of more than US$ 1 billion. For the financial category, stock exchanges and the offices of financial agents with a worldwide network were also added.

The initial response from the Multinationals was of such a nature that a reminder was sent. This ultimately resulted in around 80 questionnaires being returned. For the financial category it was clear from the first round: these would not reply even if a reminder was sent. The intervention of contact persons in a limited number of cities did provide some results.

Taken together it can even be called a good result, especially if the PL index is examined. This matches closely the total for all the clusters. Even the (merely) fifty questionnaires from the financial category fit the total picture so neatly that it is tempting to make a separate cluster from them after all, but this would not be sensible. It is possible, however, in part III, to make some remarks on subsections of this category.

■

A closer look at the participants

The background of the respondents is also covered by a few questions in the questionnaire. These data are summarized in Table I.8. It covers the age, gender and position of the respondent within the company or institution. It was also asked whether the fact that the research was initiated from the Netherlands and the doctorate would be awarded by the University of Amsterdam might have any influence on the response. With a view to possible further analysis of concept 5, it was asked in addition if the respondent both lived and worked in the same city. Finally, the respondent could indicate whether or not s/he wished to receive a summary of the results for her/his cluster and whether s/he wished to be included in the prize draw for a European trip. Further explanation is given below.

Table I.8 Personal Data	
	in % of respondents
Respondent's Position	
Senior Management	78
Others	22
Respondent's Age	
< 40	24
40 - 60	65
> 60	11
Respondent's Sex	
Male	80
Female	20
Respondent's Residence	
In city	72
In another municipality	28
No constraints in responding	97
Wants an abstract	73
Participates in prize draw	63

The target group of the research comprised the executives of businesses and institutions that contribute to the international competitive position of the city ('citymakers'). Depending on the source, the highest executive or someone of management level was approached. It was assumed that not every boss would fill in the questionnaire her/himself but that, for example, s/he would ask her/his deputy or assistant. In the accompanying letter this possibility was emphasized. It is often not possible to be sure who eventually filled out the questionnaire and what function they had. Therefore it was important to know at what level the respondent worked inside the company. As almost 80% on average described that level as senior management, it can be concluded that the aim of the research on this point was achieved. Figure I.9 shows that the differences per cluster are not conspicuous; they are found mostly at about 10% around the average.

It is then probably not surprising that around the same proportion of the respondents are men. However, women are much better represented in the senior management of the clusters Museums and Performing Arts, with almost 40%.

The division across the age groups is equally unsurprising. Far and away the largest proportion of the respondents is middle-aged. Only in the clusters Hospitality, Performing Arts and Transport are there more young people, while in Academia there is a higher proportion of older people.

Finally, it is important to note that almost no-one felt restricted or influenced by the fact that the questionnaire was initiated from the Netherlands and that the doctoral thesis was being written for the University of Amsterdam. Possible criticism with regard to the results has therefore been dealt with in advance.

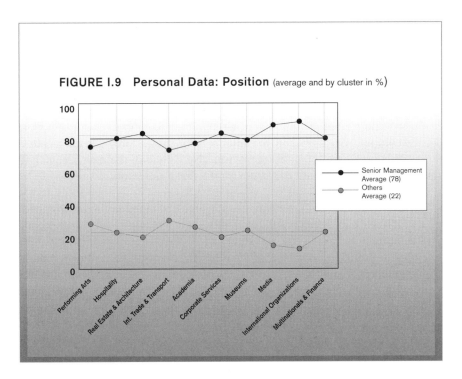

FIGURE I.9   **Personal Data: Position** (average and by cluster in %)

Other findings

Nonetheless, the questionnaire was not equally successful in all areas. Without going so far as to speak of shortcomings, there are a few items that are worthy of note.

1. During the research it was noted that the questionnaire functioned less well on a number of points. Where this reflected the presentation, it was fairly easy to improve. As mentioned earlier, from the fourth cluster onwards the formulation of the questions was drastically shortened. Altering the (ready printed) answers, because they were open to broader explanation, would, however, have had an immediate impact on the content of the question and therefore the comparability. These kinds of changes were therefore avoided. The best example of this sort is the fourth concept of question 3: 'It's culture that makes cities different.' Culture is meant here in the broad sense of a social phenomenon, different peoples, different customs, different expressions, but could also be understood in a narrow sense, as a collection of artistic expressions. It is not possible to know which sense the respondents understood. When examining the answers to this concept this must not be forgotten.

Similarly with the formulation of the competitive factor 'network.' Here it was meant as a multiplicity of functional relations and interconnections, but could also be interpreted in terms of physical infrastructure. If it was confusing, then the confusion was lifted by placing the factor in the group 'Knowledge' during the revision.

In question 2-A it was a less fortunate choice to include both the accommodation (the conference center) and the international congresses themselves as factors. This was not done for comparable factors, such as airports and performing arts. The fact that a judgement was given in the first column on the importance of the accommodation, could influence the judgement about congresses in the second column. For this reason, the latter is not included further in the results.

The factor 'seat of government' was also shifted in the new design, and this is a reason not to count this factor for the first four sectors.

2. When part of a questionnaire is regularly skipped in the answers, it is clear that it is less than successful. This was the case with question 2-B: the agenda for the future of one's own city. Less than half answered this question, which was intended to provide an overview of the most important tasks, in the opinion of the 'citymakers,' facing their own city in the coming years. With around five hundred answers divided over ten clusters such an overview is not possible. Perhaps an article could be written on this. As question 1-B was also missed occasionally, the cause was at first sought in the presentation. The position of both questions was shifted a number of times: first above the scheme, then underneath it and then above it again with a note below that the B question should not be missed out. Only the latter change appeared to bring about a visible improvement for question 1-B and to a lesser extent also for question 2-B. Aside from the presentation, there could be other factors involved: perhaps people did not feel qualified to answer the question or maybe they just did not want to.

3. Then there was the 'problem' of the 'home referee': A respondent could vote for her/his own city. In some cases this did happen. With the question 'Any city that is missing?' the respondents' own city was not infrequently put forward, if it was not already in the list. However, it also happened in the upgrading to the first division and in the indication of Top Cities. In all these cases this vote was given an annotation during processing. These votes were only added when, at the end of a cluster's count, it was clear that the city had scored above ten percent under its own power, in other words without the 'home votes.'

4. It should also be reported that occasionally one returned form could be used for two clusters. For example, the form for an international organization of accountants or of publishers, can also be used for, respectively, the clusters Corporate Services and Media as well as for International Organizations. This possibility was used only for the sectors Finance, Multinationals and Media. It involved not more than twenty forms in total.

5. Finally, the formulation of the questions could play a role. Apparently

the concepts in question three were so clear that all participants felt able to respond to them, and processing the answers gave no problems. This cannot be said about the first two questions in all cases. It was obvious that the respondents occasionally struggled with the question or rather with the 'Shift method': the downgrading of at least five factors or cities to the second division and the upgrading of an equal number to the first. This led to corrections and extra clarifications being added. Sometimes crosses were used when circles had been asked for, and there were respondents who settled for less than five or who moved unequal numbers. The quality was not the same for all continents and clusters. Fortunately, after some experience had been gained in processing the question-naires, and a certain consistency in the way the answers were made had been dis-covered, it became possible in most cases to understand what the respondent had meant. The number of rejected answers could therefore be limited. It was interesting to note that respondents had mastered the shift method much better by the time they answered the second question, while this question was certainly not any easier.

These imperfections, understandably, made the processing of the results a little more complicated. On the other hand, they are also clearly the result of a struggle, and therefore a sign of how seriously the work was undertaken. This confirms a general impression: from very many forms it was clear that careful consideration had taken place.

Closing remarks

An overview has been given above, per cluster and per continent, of the addresses approached and the questionnaires returned. Finally the background of the respondents, including the level at which they function, has been analysed.

To be absolutely clear, this research is tentative; an exploration into the per-ceptions of 'citymakers'. A statistically accountable result was not aimed at because of the complexity of the target group. Instead, an approach was chosen which would lead to plausible conclusions. In order to measure the plausibility of the responses a special check was developed; not as a statistical test, but as a tool to verify sufficient consistency in the responses registered. On this basis it can be stated that the results of the survey give a reliable picture - both for the total and for the separate clusters - of what the 'citymakers' perceive as important with regard to competitive factors and the ranking of cities, the two aims of the research.

This conclusion is most convincing for the cities and factors with a high or low score. The middle scores have a lower plausibility value. This does not necessarily mean that these results are less reliable. A continental component can be involved, for example. It is also possible that there are simply diverse opinions on the position of a city or the importance of a factor. In this case the low PL index accurately reflects the real situation.

■

If, in the description of this process, the impression has been given that the research has been a struggle, especially in the final phase, then this reflects the truth. It was extremely difficult to obtain an accountable response for the commercial clusters; for the non-profit clusters it was merely a little less difficult. However, this impression must not overshadow another fact: almost 1400 people from eighty cities made the effort to complete the questionnaire and to return it, sometimes even by courier. This demonstrates great interest in the subject, in the international competitive position of big cities and also, it can be safely concluded, great commitment to one's own city. This is underlined by the fact that around three-quarters requested a summary of the results of the research.

The results of this research will not date particularly quickly; if perceptions change, they will generally change gradually. This could be interpreted as an argument for repeating this research (only) after a number of years have passed. The approach used, however, may not be suitable for re-application. 'Over-questionnaired' and 'busy, busy, busy' are worldwide phenomena. Perhaps from the beginning there should have been more active contact with the (original) forty contact persons, so that they would have remained more involved in the research; who can say? However, this question emphasizes that if such a worldwide study is repeated in the future, its strength will lie especially in the local networks of the institution undertaking the research.

◆ ◆ ◆ ◆ ◆

PART II
THE COMPETITIVE ADVANTAGES

"Plainly, cities compete.
They do so internationally, nationally and at the regional level, so that is,
pace Krugman, appropriate to explore the determinants of urban competitiveness."
(Ian Begg, Urban Studies, 1999, p. 807)

II. 1 INTRODUCTION

Do cities compete with one another? The answer is yes and no, according to the literature. Krugman (1996) is the most forthright in his denial, and states that cities are simply places from which companies compete with one another. Porter (1990) thinks along similar lines, and, judging from personal experience, one tends to agree with them. It is often little more than a feeling that cities compete with one another, a feeling that tends to be strongly encouraged by the media and by the cities themselves. In fact it is almost always companies and institutions that actually compete. Whether it concerns conferences, tourists, air and sea freight, universities, stock markets, orchestras etc., the city generally functions at most as a partner, financier and/or promoter. However, the picture is a little more complicated if we distinguish three geographical levels of competition: regional, national and international.

Of course, a city competes within its own conurbation with the surrounding municipalities for the building of homes and the establishment of enterprises. If the city doesn't, then the neighboring municipalities do. But that is not competition between more or less equal cities. What is called competition is often little more than rivalry or envy.

Of course, cities compete with other cities within their own countries for the largest possible share of public and private funding for, for example, support of infrastructure, employment and cultural facilities. Depending on the targeting of the funding, the city may have to adopt an optimistic or somber attitude. Cities also compete for the establishment of enterprises. If Boeing announced it wanted to move its headquarters from Seattle, then many American cities (and states!) would race to be the one to land this big fish. However, if the management of Renault threatened to move within France, it would not be taken seriously. Within France there is really no alternative to Paris.

National quickly becomes international, especially in Europe where the borders are becoming blurred. Brussels or London is therefore more likely to be Paris' competitor for Renault's headquarters than Lyon or Bordeaux. That looks like competition between cities – but only looks like, because a decision to move and, if yes, where to, is determined in the first instance on national competitive factors, including emotional ones. What about the Olympic Games, that is surely an example of competition between cities? Here again, it only looks that way. In fact it is the National Olympic Committees that compete with one another, the city is the stake. When selecting the candidates for the headquarters of international institutions, such as an international development bank or a tribunal, it is once again the country that is the first consideration.

In this context there are few situations in which cities are directly in competition with other cities abroad. It is, as Porter said (1990), the companies that are at the forefront of competition and not the (national) governments. Whether it involves attracting a world congress, a new intercontinental flight schedule, an international academic course, a music festival, the bid from a prominent local company for shares of a foreign brewery – and many more examples could be given – it is the conference organizer, the airport, the university, the concert hall and the local brewer that compete. Depending on the nature of the business, the city will identify itself with the project, support it financially, act as a partner, or simply be an interested spectator.

In fact the government must have done its work much earlier. It has to help create the climate in which companies and institutions will have a good chance of succeeding in competing at an international level. From Porter (1990) we know what is required at a national level for this. What more is needed at the level of the city in order to be able to compete internationally? Or, in other words: what are the most important factors that make a city internationally competitive, prominent, leading? In part II an attempt is made to find answers to this question.

* * *

■

II. 2 THE NATIONAL DIAMOND

"The national theory is just as relevant to smaller areas such as the inner city" (M. Porter, 1995, p. 57)

"This is a work which will become the standard for all further discussions of global competition and the sources of the new wealth of nations," is the claim on the cover of Michael Porter's book "The Competitive Advantage of Nations" (1990). Those kinds of claims are rarely justified, but this is an exception. His book has been the inspiration for the first aim of this thesis: to develop a model à la Porter that can illustrate the international competitive power of a city.

Porter distinguishes four decisive determinants that determine the competitive position of an industrial cluster in a country. These are (1) the factor conditions, such as raw materials, labor, capital, expertise, infrastructure; (2) the demand conditions, especially from the home market, (3) the network of related and supporting industries and (4) the entrepreneurial culture in a country. He describes how one factor influences another and concludes that the four factors cannot be considered in isolation from one another. Together they form the national business climate within which an industrial cluster develops and can compete internationally. He illustrates this interdependence in his famous 'diamond' (Figure II.1).

Figure II.1

THE DETERMINANTS OF NATIONAL ADVANTAGE
IN INTERNATIONAL COMPETITION

THE NATIONAL DIAMOND

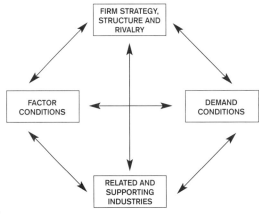

Porter then adds two elements to this diamond. The first is 'chance,' a more or less coincidental event such as a variation in exchange rates, war, a technological breakthrough, etc. The government is also given a place in the system, and can influence the factors in a number of ways. However, it is not seen as a real element of the system itself, because it cannot create a competitive advantage. "It is not the government but business life at the front line of international competition."

Using an analysis of industrial clusters in a number of countries, he describes the characteristics of the four phases of development of a country. In the first phase the competitive advantage is found in one or more of the factor conditions (factor-driven). Entrepreneurship and demand from the market stimulate a broad scale of investment in a country (investment-driven). In the third phase the economy is driven further by the development of (high value) new products (innovation-driven). All four of the factors in the diamond are then fully developed across a broad section of the national economy. There then follows a phase of consolidation (wealth-driven), in which a lack of challenge and motivation forms the greatest threat to the wealth that has been acquired.

The key to growth but also to survival in global competition lies in recognizing your competitive advantage and continuously enhancing it. A competitive advantage can arise spontaneously, but further development does not happen automatically. It develops in the face of pressures, challenges, reversals, seldom on the basis of an easy life. That is the central theme of the book, in fact of Porter's entire oeuvre. The following quotes are also characteristic, and of interest in the context of this study.

- "The search is for the decisive characteristics of a nation that allow its firms to create and sustain competitive advantage in particular fields, that is, the competitive advantage of nations" (p. 18);
- "In reality, every determinant can affect every other determinant, though some interactions are stronger and more important than others" (p. 132);
- "The theory can be readily extended to explain why some cities or regions are more successful than others" (p. 158).
- "The ability to upgrade an economy depends heavily on the position of a nation's firms in that portion of the economy exposed to international competition" (p. 545).

The latter sounds like a challenge at a time when books and magazines are full of articles on cities, competition, globalization and the various interactions and potential consequences. But is it as simple as Porter says?

A successful model for the inner city?
Porter took on the challenge himself a few years later by publishing a contribution on "The Competitive Advantage of the Inner City" (1995). His attempt to make a case for a radically different approach to the revitalization of inner cities using his model and his four determinants is, however, much less convincing than his original work. The following arguments may help explain why.

1. The functioning of a national economy, especially of a large country such as the United States, can be explained using globally formulated factors. Policy that is designed around these factors also has a global character. Take, for

■

example, the factor infrastructure. This is counted as one of the factor conditions. In a book of around 800 pages he devotes exactly seven sentences to this, and interprets the concept so broadly that it covers the availability of housing, cultural institutions and quality of life (p. 75). As the working area becomes smaller then the factors will have to be described more concretely in order to make it possible to formulate operational policies.

2. All businesses, whether they are established in a city, in the inner city, or in the countryside, are affected to a lesser or greater degree by national competitive factors. Examples include the tax regime, legislation, and the cost of living. In addition there are typical local factors. If the national model is to be applied to a (smaller) region, then it is necessary to analyse the specific factors that (together with the national factors) create the climate which businesses in that region or in close proximity need in order to compete internationally.

3. The demand from the market – quantitative and especially qualitative – is one of the determinants in Porter's national model. This is self-evident for a large country that is pretty much self-supporting. It can also be applied, for example, to a local shopping mall that is dependent on customers from the immediate neighborhood. However, imagine if the demand from the inner city was decisive for the competitive power of the businesses located there; that could become a very small-scale affair indeed. In other words, the determinants from the national model cannot simply be transferred to a regional, city or inner city model.

4. Porter did not distinguish any differences in priority in his standard work, nor have others who have written about or reported on competitive factors. The impression is that all factors are important. This may well be true, but they are not all equally important. When Porter does select four dominant factors in his later analysis of the inner city, his arguments for his choice ("ongoing research," 1995 p. 57) are left unexplained.

5. Finally, the various industrial clusters will not all have the same interest in the different competitive factors. For one cluster the labor market may be decisive, for another the infrastructure or one particular aspect of it, and for yet another the business network. The transport cluster, for example, can be expected to view the importance of a seaport somewhat differently than, say, the financial cluster.

Cluster formation
There has also been an important development in Porter's work. In later publications he emphasizes increasingly the positive influence of economic clusters on the competitive position of a country, region or city. He goes on to acknowledge a more important role for the national government and interest groups.

In Porter's view, clusters are geographical concentrations of (manufacturing) companies, suppliers, services and related enterprises. Companies can belong to more than one cluster within this broad definition. They are perfect examples of the interdependence of all the factors in the model. They affect competition through increased productivity, innovation and establishing new businesses. They are a competitive advantage in themselves. Personal contacts and the relationships and interactions between people and institutions are essential: the network. Porter not only states that clusters make his model more operational, but also implies that they are a part of it.

Clusters vary in composition, rate of development, size and location. With regard to the latter, there are clusters that are contained within national boundaries and regional boundaries, but also within city boundaries and even city neighborhoods. The proximity of businesses and thus of people can strongly promote the exchange of information. In this way the city is perhaps the ideal place for cluster formation: "the most enduring competitive advantages in a global economy will often be local" (1998, p. 266). As explained in Part I, section 2.2, this local or city level was an important reason for choosing a narrower interpretation of the concept 'cluster' for this study.

An adjusted role for Government
The humility that descends on a civil servant on reading Porter's standard work will disappear when he or she sets eyes on "Clusters and Competition." Never before had the government, and also interest groups, been given the role of driving force, particularly with regard to cluster formation and development. Porter enlarges this role so much, makes it so decisive for success or disappointment, that the government (at last) has the place that Europeans felt it deserved much earlier: a full determinant within the model. Porter, however, still does not translate his words into actions: neither cluster formation nor the important role of the government is included as a determinant in the model. The 'diamond' does not become a pentagon, let alone a hexagon.

Porter's model has regularly been the inspiration for national, regional and local or city-level studies that portray the competitive power of the area as a whole or of a certain cluster. However, his model uses a very large number of factors, and these are not always easily measurable. Many a study has therefore limited itself to a pre-selected number of factors. The selection is often made more on the basis of instinct than on the basis of research into the degree of relevance to the subject.

This cannot be said of the World Competitiveness Yearbook (WCY), which certainly strives to be comprehensive. No less than 249 criteria are measured annually via statistics and interviews, in order to calculate and portray the competitive power of a country using a specially developed model. A large number of Porter's factors can be recognized in this model. Some are, however, notable by their absence, such as the composition of demand and cluster formation, which are surely not amongst the most unimportant. This can be explained by the different aims of the two models. In section II.4.1 we shall discuss this in more detail.

World Economic Forum publishes the Global Competitiveness Report (GCR) together with the Center for International Development at Harvard University. The Report focuses on two distinct but complementary approaches to the analysis of economic competitiveness: (1) the prospects for economic growth (prior to 2000 known as the Competitiveness Index) and (2) evaluation of the underlying conditions defining the current level of productivity. The second approach, started in 2000, is led by Porter himself and focuses not surprisingly on company sophistication and on the quality of the national business environment. Central to both indexes is the yearly Executive Opinion Survey.

Both the WCY and the GCR aim to classify or rank the competitiveness of a large number of countries. A more detailed description of the reports, covering their qualities and differences, is outside the scope of this book. For the time being, however, the use of the WCY report is to be preferred, primarily for reasons of continuity.

Conclusions

If we want to make an operational competitiveness model for the city à la Porter, then a number of conclusions can be drawn from the above:

1. National and local factors together determine the competitive power of a city. They must, however, be clearly distinguished from one another. National competitive power is a given for the city model. As such, it is an independent determinant within that model.

2. The city is an ideal breeding-ground for clusters. These have a decisive role in both the competitive power of the city and the country. As such they are also an independent determinant in the competitiveness model for the city.

3. The role of government is being increasingly acknowledged as significant, in particular with regard to cluster formation. In a city the policy of the local authorities will be much more specific. These are reasons to give the (local) government a full place in the model for the city.

4. Research among the relevant clusters must demonstrate which factors determine the competitive position of a city. At the same time it should be distinguished to what degree they contribute to the competitive position: in other words, exactly how important are they? The results will be the building blocks for a model for the city as a whole.

A rough outline has therefore been given for a model for cities that has been inspired by Porter's model for countries, and contains many of its elements, but is not a copy of it. In the following sections an inventory will be made of the separate competitive factors, their interactions will then be described, and finally they will be allocated a place in the model for cities. This model can then be visualized.

* * *

II. 3 MAPPING THE CITIES' COMPETITIVE ADVANTAGES

"Every attempt to classify cities or place them in some sort of order stands or falls with the choice of criteria"
(J. G. Lambooy and H. W. ter Hart: "Les capitales, villes pilotes?" 1975)

In Part I.1 it was established that a large number of competitive factors for cities can be found in the literature, but that they are largely personal selections. Focused research, designed to map all the relevant factors and incorporating their degree of relevance, was not encountered. It was concluded that there was sufficient justification for research on this issue, within which grateful use could be made of existing selections.

Competitive factors in the World Literature

Turning words into deeds, an inventory has been made of the competitive factors indicated by a large number of authors. They were sometimes explicitly listed, but occasionally a magnifying glass was needed in order to find them. There is also a great diversity in the terminology used: functions, criteria, characteristics, elements, indicators, standards, qualities, variables, conditions; and, of course, factors. Whichever term was used, it always concerned the standards by which the (competitive) power of a city economy is revealed.

The inventory is quite different to the grouping in section 1.1, where an attempt was made to group the diverse publications according to their character or approach. Here, the emphasis is on which factors are frequently used and which are not, or at least to a lesser degree. In addition, it aims to justify the choice that was made when putting together the list of factors that was used in the research. How far does this match what is often encountered in the literature, where does it deviate from it and why?

A fair amount of information is revealed in Table II.2 (page 60 and 62), but it cannot be guaranteed as being completely comprehensive. However, as there is much cross-referencing between publications, it is extremely unlikely that any authors have been missed out who have published something quite different. The competitive factors are given in the left-hand column. The wording of the descriptions will not match exactly that used in some publications, but the meanings should be the same. In the rest of the table an asterisk indicates which factors are used by which authors.

Further selection

When they are gathered together like this, it appears that a substantial number of factors can be collected from the literature and previous studies. It is at the very least a solid basis for research into their relevancy. However, a selection will have to be made from this large number of factors. With this in mind, the number of times a factor appears in the table was considered, and this also played a role in allocating a factor to the first of second division. However, some personal

59

Table II.2 Factors/indicators of urban competitiveness mentioned in literature (1)

Factors/indicators	Begg I. (1999)	Berg van den L. (1996)	Bramezza I. (1996)	Cheshire P. (1989)	Conti S. et al (1990)	Driehuis W. (1992)	Fortune Magazine (annual)	Friedmann J. (1986 + 1995)	Hall P. (1966)	Healy & Baker (annual)	Jensen-Butler et al (1995 + 1997)	Knox P. (1995)	Kresl P. (1995 + 1999)	Lever W. (1999)	Lippman - Abu-Lughod J. (1995)	Lo F. & Marcotullio P. (1999)	Palomäki M. (1991)	Reclus/Datar (1989)	Rimmer P. (1996)	Sassen S. (1994)	Schachar A. (1990 + 1996)	Short J. R. (1996)	Sánchez J. E. (1997)	Selected for World Cities Research
Population																								
• Very large population								•			•	•	•	•		•	•				•			•
• Highly skilled labour		•		•				•			•	•		•		•	•				•			•
• Open to an international world												•												•
• Multicultural community								•	•							•								•
Economy and Management																								
• Home for Multinationals	•			•				•	•			•				•	•	•	•	•	•	•		•
• Major Stock Exchange				•				•	•							•	•	•	•	•	•	•	•	•
• Home for international banks				•				•	•							•	•	•	•	•	•	•	•	•
• Seat of international organizations								•				•					•		•					•
• Major production facilities								•								•	•							•
• Home for major media firms								•											•		•			•
Government and Politics																								
• Positive international performance											•													•
• Political leadership		•						•	•															•
• Favourable local tax climate								•		•			•											•
• Good public safety								•				•												•
• Commitment to invest																								•
• Seat national government																								•
Physical infrastructure					•	•		•			•			•	•						•			
• Intercontinental airport		•	•													•		•	•			•		•
• International seaport		•														•		•	•					•
• High-speed train service		•																						•
Knowledge															•									
• Leading university(ies)	•			•	•									•				•				•		•
• Renowned R&D institutes			•											•				•				•		•
• Prominent business schools																								•
• Large, rich network	•															•					•			•
Other Facilities															•									
• Congress and exhibition facilities																			•			•		•
• International-class hotels																								•
• Prestigious shopping facilities																			•					•
• International professional services			•		•			•	•				•	•					•	•		•		•

(1) For more information on these publications please refer to the bibliograpphy. Continued on page 62 ▶

analysis or rather personal experience was also used. Firstly, to include some factors that were probably meant by the authors but not explicitly mentioned. Secondly, to include some factors that were rarely mentioned in the literature.

In the end, 35 local factors were selected and included in the questionnaire. These are indicated in the right-hand column of Table II.2. A large number, admittedly, and of course they are not all equally important. However, this happens to be one of the aims of the research: to establish the degree of relevancy of the factors.

In the following sections the selections will be discussed in more detail per group. Where certain factors that are featured in the table were not included in the selection, one or more of the following reasons usually lay behind this:
• It was a more national than city-level factor, or the factor is strongly influenced by national developments. Unemployment levels in a city, for example, certainly have a city component, but are still largely a result of the state of the national economy.
• We have learnt from Porter that 'basic and generalized factors' can be distinguished from 'advanced and specialized factors.' Basic facilities such as roads, subways, and even telecommunication facilities, are no longer a specific competitive advantage. They are a competitive disadvantage when they do not meet present-day needs. 'Specialized factors' were the focus for the survey.
• In order to get operational results from the questionnaire, it was necessary to work with operational concepts; descriptions with which the respondent could immediately identify because they arise in his/her daily work or s/he can easily imagine what they mean. They have to be simple, or rather their meaning has to be unambiguous. So-called 'container concepts' are not unambiguous; 'quality of life' is an example. Some will interpret this very narrowly, others will use it to cover almost everything.

In order to make the large number of factors more accessible to the respondents, it seemed a good idea to divide them into recognizable groups. It was natural to consider first of all the division that Porter used to portray national competitive factors: demand, related and supporting industries, factor conditions, and entrepreneurial culture. In the previous section it was already indicated that this division cannot be used unadjusted in a competitiveness model for cities. In addition, it is too academic, too unrecognizable, for a practically oriented target group like the 'citymakers.' In the literature, two other divisions can be found: (1) into economic and strategic factors (Kresl P, 1995) and (2) into structural and functional factors (v.d. Berg L & Bramezza I, 1996). However, neither of these would generate the immediate recognition among the 'citymakers' that is required.

A completely different course was chosen, dividing the factors into eight categories, with no other aim than designing the most effective possible questionnaire. These categories, and their respective factors, are briefly described below.

■

Table II.2   Factors/indicators of urban competitiveness mentioned in literature (1)

Continuation

Factors/indicators	Begg I. (1999)	Berg van den L. (1996)	Bramezza I. (1996)	Cheshire P. (1989)	Conti S. et al (1990)	Driehuis W. (1992)	Fortune Magazine (annual)	Friedmann J. (1986 + 1995)	Hall P. (1966)	Healy & Baker (annual)	Jensen-Butler et al (1995 + 1997)	Knox P. (1995)	Kresl P. (1995 + 1999)	Lever W. (1999)	Lippman - Abu-Lughod J. (1995)	Lo F. & Marcotullio P. (1999)	Palomäki M. (1991)	Reclus/Datar (1989)	Rimmer P. (1996)	Sassen S. (1994)	Schachar A. (1990 + 1996)	Short J. R. (1996)	Sánchez J. E. (1997)	Selected for World Cities Research
Cultural and Social Life								•								•								
• Famous museums								•	•			•						•			•	•		•
• High standard performing arts								•	•			•						•			•			•
• Attractive nightlife																								•
• Mega events																			•		•			•
• Major congresses and fairs						•		•										•						•
• High standard sportlife																								•
General																								
• It happens there!																								•
• Impressive skyline																					•			•
Various																								
• Acces to markets	•											•												
• Quality of life	•	•			•							•		•										
• Performance national economy	•											•												
• Business locations		•			•	•						•							•		•			
• Proximity clients		•																						
• Housing		•		•	•							•												
• GDP per capita			•									•	•	•										
• Net immigration rate			•	•										•										
• Unemployment rate			•	•										•										
• Travel demand index			•									•												
• Highways			•																					
• Telecommunication												•	•				•					•	•	
• Freedom from pollution								•				•	•											
• National urban primacy														•										
• Favourable location													•											
• (Transnational) investment															•									
• International trade									•							•	•							•
• Public-private partnership	•														•									
• Real increase in land value												•												
• Others		•				•		•		•		•	•				•					•		

(1) For more information on these publications please refer to the bibliograpphy.

Population

The size of the population is included as a factor in this category. Important cities are often associated with large numbers of residents: is this a clear advantage, is it neutral or perhaps even a disadvantage? The presence of a highly skilled labor force is generally acknowledged as a competitive factor and also plays an essential role in Porter's national level model.

To what degree does greater openness and a multicultural population provide a competitive advantage or perhaps disadvantage? The literature is less clear on these two factors, and they are indeed difficult to measure. Countries have very different natures, with the two extremes being introversion and extroversion. These differences can also be observed within a country, for example between urban and rural areas. Many aspects play a role in this. Religion is one, as is curiosity about foreign things and cultures, but also tolerance, and certainly the ability (and willingness) to speak foreign languages. The answer to this question could teach us a great deal.

Center of economy and management

According to a number of respected authors on world cities, the first three factors should be sufficient for this category. That may be a little exaggerated, but Sassen in particular does emphasize heavily the importance of financial institutions and the headquarters of multinationals, in order to make clear that it is this kind of enterprise that makes a city a command center of the world. In any case, at this stage they certainly belong at the top of this category.

Many cities in the world developed on the basis of industrial manufacturing. It has also been the downfall of some. These days, at least in the western world, cities are no longer primarily associated with (major) industrial complexes. In general more are leaving the cities than moving to them. However, there are still quite a few in which industry represents a large part of the city product. Does this give a competitive advantage?

Also, what about international organizations? In a world that is 'shrinking,' the need for international cooperation is rapidly increasing. This applies as much to the (national) government as it does to private professional organizations and interest groups. The palette of international organizations is not only large, but also extremely diverse in terms of size, character and aim. Countries and cities will go to great lengths to become the seat for such organizations. Is it then worth the effort? For a large one like the United Nations the answer seems clear, but is a bunch of small ones equivalent to a large one? The 'citymakers' will have to tell us, as the literature is not clear on this point. This applies also to influential media companies, such as authoritative newspapers, magazines, radio and TV stations and press agencies. How important are they to the competitive profile of a city?

Governance

The national government does not create a competitive advantage itself,

63

but it can influence the competitive profile. This was the justification for Porter to place governance on the sidelines in his model, together with "chance." Looking at Table II.1, the literature would seem to agree with him. Earlier it was stated that, from a European standpoint, this position does not do justice to governance, especially if one considers its role in cluster formation. Will the 'city-makers' think the same, and will there be differences per continent?

Personal experience was again used within this group for the selection of factors, combined with input from the test questionnaire (see section I.2.3), but less use was made of the literature as it does not give much coverage to this subject.

The factor 'positive international performance' would not have been out of place in the final category ('General'). The fact that this performance is often considered to be embodied, particularly in the media, by the city government, and in turn by its leader (usually the mayor), was decisive in placing it here.

The factor 'political leadership' is also linked to the mayor in many countries. It is a concept for which not everyone will give an identical definition, but which is generally associated with clarity, consistency, continuity and authority. In this case, the leadership is also expected to ensure that the natural tension between the city and its surrounding regions, which exists almost everywhere, is guided in a constructive direction. The city authorities, however, can also be clear and consistent in their rejection of issues that benefit the international competitive position of a city. This is why the factor 'Commitment to invest in quality' was included. Quality is a 'container concept;' it is possible to imagine all kinds of meanings. For the target group selected, however – the 'citymakers' – this does not seem very likely. They will tend to associate this quality with the factors in the list. Further confirmation of this can be sought using the subjects that they select for the 'Agenda for the Future' for their city (question 2-B).

If you talk about investment you have to talk about taxes, and it seemed useful to emphasize once more that in this case it means exclusively the local taxes. There are large differences across the world in this area. It would therefore be interesting to see if, for example, the opinions from American cities differ from those from European ones. This does, however, make extra demands on the composition of the response.

'Public safety' could be called the Achilles heel of the public authorities. It appears to be a basic condition and would therefore not qualify for inclusion in this list. Public safety is, however, a worldwide problem, faced by almost every city authority. It can, therefore, become a competitive advantage for the city that, exceptionally, has it under control.

Many important cities are also capital cities. However, there are also important cities that have to manage without the seat of government and everything that goes with it. Is this factor valued? Nothing can be found on this in the literature.

Infrastructure
This is again a collective term. In the narrow, traditional, sense it covers the

roads, airports and seaports, and the railways. All kinds of additions, especially in the social–cultural sphere, dilute the concept and make it impossible to draw operational conclusions. The traditional meaning has therefore been selected in this case, and within it only the facilities that (could) give an international dimension to the city: an airport, a seaport and also, albeit with some hesitation as it is a factor that is not relevant everywhere, a high-speed train service. Other facilities, such as highways, subways, car parks, industrial estates, office buildings and even cable networks, were not included because they are among the normal facilities (the basis) of any city. Which is not to say that they are not important. A city can, however, only distinguish itself in a negative sense with these basic conditions, by failing to offer adequate facilities.

Knowledge

This is a part of the infrastructure that has become a separate category. The limited number of publications on the relation between the city and its institutions of knowledge played an important role in this division, as it is the only way we can learn more. It is true that universities have become part of the standard 'equipment' of a city, but there are still such differences in size, differentiation, level and profile, that they can function as a competitive factor. The question is whether the 'city-makers' also see it this way.

Institutions for Research & Development are often part of a university, others are linked to multinationals and some are the product of international cooperation. It would have been going too far to make this distinction in the questionnaire.

There are world-famous business schools and cities are proud to host one or more. Does this pride cut any ice, is the presence of such an institution indeed a significant factor? A separate issue is that the concept 'business school' can also be said to have been subject to inflation in the meantime. Perhaps the international character of the school should have been emphasized, in addition to its prominence.

The rise of the 'worldwide web' has confused the academics. Some are predicting the death of the city, as proximity will not be a criterion any more, while others see only more new opportunities in this development, and emphasize that the many impersonal business contacts via the web will mean that personal encounters and the exchange of thoughts and experiences will become increasingly important – and then preferably between all sorts and kinds of people. No place could be better for this than a city, whether it is the main auditorium of the university, a circle of professional associates, a renowned elite club or a bar somewhere in the city center. That is the sort of network meant here. It does not necessarily have to be linked to an institution of knowledge and this factor would not, therefore, have been out of place in the 'General' category. In practice, however, it is often these institutions that are the first to take the initiative to set up formal and informal platforms for the exchange of knowledge and for doing business.

Cultural and other facilities

It is characteristic of a city that there is much to see and do: the social–cultural infrastructure. The importance of this is acknowledged in the literature, but that is mostly where the discussion stops.

Of course, there have been studies on the success and failures of the Olympic Games, and it has also been calculated that international conferences make a significant contribution. Everyone can see that certain museums are strong magnets for tourists. Manchester goes wild when one of its soccer teams wins the World Cup, the shopping streets are the pride of many a city at Christmas, Vienna and its Philharmoniker are on the TV worldwide on New Year's Day, the carnival of Rio is a phenomenon, experiencing the nightlife of certain cities is a 'must' and any mayor takes notice if one or more hotels in his/her city are counted among the top so-many in the world. However, what does this contribute, compared to the other factors, to the international competitive position of the city? In order to obtain the most operational possible answer, these facilities were divided into two categories (cultural and other) with, respectively, six and four different factors each.

Finally, the internationally operating accountants, lawyers and other management consultants had to be given a place. After some hesitation – they would not have been out of place within Center of Economy and Management – they were placed with the 'other facilities.'

General

Many of the above-mentioned factors would be placed under 'quality of life' in the existing literature and especially in reports of studies. It is a 'container concept,' as described earlier, containing numerous elements, especially the normal everyday items and facilities, often defined in a similar way but the definitions are rarely exactly the same. In addition, national and city qualities are merrily intertwined. If it was featured in the list, then this factor would undoubtedly score highly, but not much could be done with it after the processing of the results. Sufficient justification for not including it.

Why, then, is 'It happens there!' included? That is equally unsuitable for operational conclusions and is very similar to a number of the other factors. The answer is that it clearly reflects the city and the position of the city in the world. Through their response the 'citymakers' can make clear how important they believe it is for a city to be a trendsetter, lively, active, exuberant, exhilarating.

Finally, the skyline of the city is included as a factor in this category. This may not be obvious to a European, but when you visit an American city and want to send a postcard home, you will have a choice between the skyline at sunset … or the skyline at dawn. Asia has also been infected with the 'higher the better' syndrome, and even in Europe there are now cities that are more readily recognized for their skyscrapers than for their church towers. Is this only important to developers, architects and city leaders or does a wider circle value it as well? At the very least it will be interesting to find out.

The above selection is reflected in question 2-A of the questionnaire. The aim, let us repeat, is to determine which factors are really important and which, in comparison, are less important. The respondent will tend to regard all the factors as important, and will therefore have to be forced a little to make a choice. This is why the shift method was used for this question, as described in section I.2.3. Two divisions were therefore constructed. The factors in the first division are those that stood out after examining the existing literature and on the basis of personal experience. It is not intended to be a perfect list, and the split between the two divisions is here and there quite arbitrary. The shift method, however, forces a choice; so the respondent must get the feeling that there is something to choose. Again, this method has the advantage that the respondent can correct imperfections him/herself through upgrading and downgrading. In addition, s/he has an opportunity to add any missing factors in the space provided. With regard to this, it was explained earlier why certain factors, particularly basic facilities for a city, were deliberately omitted. The respondent, however, can have other ideas and might consider public transport in a city to be very important, and can then communicate this. S/he might also be of the opinion that, in the age of the New Economy, a city gains an important competitive advantage through the presence of important ITC companies and of a cluster of ICT companies. They were not included as a factor because this sector is constantly changing and therefore insufficiently crystallized. In addition, a not insignificant proportion of these activities can be found in the Media cluster. These are good reasons, but the respondent may not necessarily see things the same way. In that case the extra space will certainly be used.

Despite 'globalization' there are still striking cultural differences across the world, and also between cities. Does this mean that, for example, the 'citymakers' in Latin America will value the factors differently to their colleagues in Asia? The results of the study will demonstrate this. They will also show whether the 'citymakers' from, for example, the financial world give the factors a different valuation compared to 'citymakers' from the academic world. This question (2-A in the questionnaire) can then also provide the following:
- A priority list of competitive factors for cities, according to the opinions of all the 'citymakers' in six continents and 80 important cities in the world (total picture);
- A priority list per continent (continental picture);
- A priority list per separate cluster (functional picture).

These results are included in section II.4. First we address the question of how the (34) selected factors can be integrated into the model for cities à la Porter.

* * *

II.4 THE CITY DIAMOND

II. 4.1 GROUPING THE CITY FACTORS

In the previous section an inventory was made of the competitive factors for cities using the existing literature and practical experience, and they were divided into groups. It was established that an identical grouping to that used in Porter's national model, even if that were possible, would not benefit the presentation. As there were no other examples to follow, a division into eight categories was created. There was only one aim: the most transparent possible presentation of a question that is not easy to answer.

In this section the aim is to group the listed factors in such a way that they fit into a city model. It has already been established that Porter's national model, despite his encouragement of the idea, cannot simply be copied and used for a city. The city model will have to be à la national model. The greatest possible correspondence or similarity will, however, be sought. The starting point is that all the relevant city factors must find a place in the model and be grouped in determinants. Exactly which determinant is not so important; after all, a model describes the interdependence of factors, competitive factors in this case, both within and outside the determinant.

Porter's 'diamond' had four determinants. His thoughts on competitiveness have, over time, focused on the formation of business clusters; so much so that cluster formation has become a competitive factor in itself. This gives room to contemplate adding a fifth determinant, or even a sixth, if governance – left on the sidelines in the original model – is allotted a very dominant place in cluster formation. In the following, it will be seen how far the competitive factors from the inventory made in the previous section can be transplanted into a city model through allocation to one of these determinants.

1. Porter's determinant Factor Conditions is a diverse collection of elements, including potential employment, knowledge centers, available investment capital and infrastructure. The latter is itself comprised of a rich variety of qualities, including health care and cultural institutions, which influence living and working conditions. Of course, the fundamental structure of a model must be kept simple. However, if we place the competitive factors covered by the research (34) alongside the description given above, then at least 13 of them belong to Porter's determinant 'Factor Conditions':

- Highly educated labor force;
- Airport, seaport and high-speed train service;
- Universities, R&D institutions and business schools;

- Congress centers, hotels and shops;
- Museums, performing arts and nightlife.

At a national level this would already be confusing, but when this division is followed for a city model it becomes unbalanced and non-operational. A good enough reason to see if these factors can be allocated to another determinant. The clusters chosen as target groups for the research are the first to catch one's eye. All the factors except one can be grouped in the clusters Transport, the Academic world, Hospitality and Culture. Both the hard infrastructure (such as the concert hall) and the users (such as the symphony orchestra) would be allocated to the clusters. The factor labor force remains as the only Factor Condition. If we can find another logical place for this factor, then there remains no reason to include the determinant Factor Condition in the model for cities.

2. A second determinant in Porter's national model, 'Structure and Rivalry' encompasses a number of qualitative factors. These are the context in which enterprises are initiated, organized and led, and the character of the competition within the country. They are factors that have to do with the culture and ambition of both the business world and the government. For the outside world they manifest themselves primarily at national level and are not therefore typical factors for cities, but that does not mean that within a country there are not significant differences. Consider, for example, the now-outdated saying that "Rotterdam is where the money is made, and Amsterdam is where it is spent."

The factors that Porter names are focused on action: entrepreneurship and competition. At a city level this will translate into the international profiling of companies and institutions and, as a result, of the city as a whole, which is a reason to include 'INTERNATIONAL PROFILE' as a determinant for cities. Among the competitive factors for cities that have been listed, this could embrace: a positive international performance, mega events, top-level sport, skyline and 'it happens there!'.

In this connection the following deserves attention. In the third question of the written questionnaire, one of the 11 concepts featured is focused on the city center and another one is focused on the hotels. The tenor of these is that both are decisive for the international profile of a city. If the concept on the city center is endorsed then this would have to be added to the above-mentioned list of factors. In this way a place has also been found for the factors shopping and nightlife, as these are found predominantly in the heart of the city.

For the hotels it is different. They come under the cluster Hospitality. It would be confusing to express their significance for the international profile of a city in yet another determinant. Admittedly this reinforces the idea that the distribution of factors among the determinants is somewhat arbitrary. However, let it be stated once again, the place they are given in the model is less important than the fact that they are included at all. On the other hand, this example makes it clear how intensive the interrelations between the factors and the determinants can be.

■

But what about the element competition that Porter emphasizes so strongly in this determinant? The fact that his model is for a country as a whole does not diminish the fact that, as he points out, competition is more effective the closer you are. A good example in this context is the hotel sector. This is strongly concentrated in a city, and you can feel your competitor's breath on the back of your neck. This is also true for business services such as accountants, lawyers and so on. For the headquarters of a bank and certainly for a multinational it is, however, quite different and, for some facilities, there can only be one or two of their kind. Examples in this context are airports and seaports, opera halls and museums. The difference between competition at a national and city level cannot therefore be sharply defined. The most important motive to exclude this element from the model for cities lies in the cluster formation that was discussed earlier. Both cooperation and competition are inherent in cluster formation. If clusters are included as an independent determinant, then the competition element is also implicitly represented in the model for cities.

3. Porter's third determinant is 'Demand from the home market.' He considers in particular its composition, size, growth and international allure to be a solid stimulus for the quality of enterprises in a country. It has been established earlier that including a similar determinant in a model for cities or, as he did, in a model for the inner city, is a risky business. The development of a city's industriousness quickly becomes associated with the size and especially the quality of the demand within the city. That can be done in a justifiable fashion for the domestic service industry that, as Krugman says, always accounts for by far the most employment in a city. It must not then be restricted to the butcher and baker, but also embrace the entire shop and restaurant world, and also orchestras, ballet and opera companies, who – however much they may profile themselves internationally – will still be largely dependent on the home market. Many a university also attracts a large proportion of its student population from the city and its immediate surroundings.

The 'drivers' in the service industry will associate the home market especially with national demand and beyond. An example from my professional past. I once asked the director of a prominent (service sector) company who was determined to move his offices to the southern edge of Amsterdam, why he was so keen to go there, to a spot where we could offer him no help whatsoever. "It's perfect" he replied; "I look out over the country where most of my clients are located, and lean with my back against the city where you will find my most demanding ones." Which is intended to demonstrate that national and local demand are too interlinked to be included as independent determinants in a model for cities. The national component includes the city, and vice versa. On top of that only one of the listed competitive factors (rich choice of highly skilled labor) falls under this determinant. Therefore another suitable determinant will have to be found for it.

4. With his fourth determinant 'Related and Supporting Industries' Porter describes how companies in a country benefit maximally when their national suppliers are themselves competitive at an international level. It is also very probable that a national cluster is successful when the country itself has a competitive advantage in related activities. Although they were not described as such then (in 1990), this refers in fact to clusters. Later he describes them as "a geographically proximate group of interconnected companies and associated institutions in a particular field, linked by commonalities and complementarities" (1998, p. 199) and further "Clusters constitute one facet of the diamond (related and supporting industries) but they are best seen as manifestation of the interactions among all four facets"(p. 213). With some limitations (which will be examined later) the original title of this determinant can be replaced by CLUSTERS. In this way 'his' total of six determinants can be restored to five.

According to Porter, cities are the ideal breeding grounds for clusters. Silicon Valley shows that other routes are also possible. It also proves that an international trendsetting cluster does not necessarily transform a modest town into a prominent city. The question now is: which clusters are relevant to the international competitive position of a city; which industrial sectors and activities give a city a more international profile, make it more prominent than other cities, give it a competitive advantage? Four clusters have already been put forward as possibilities: airports and seaports, hotels, universities, museums and the performing arts, all in the determinant Factor Conditions. The following comments can be made on these.

The first thing that a new nation-state does, after "choosing" a president and selecting a capital city, is to set up a national airline with at least one (if necessary borrowed) aircraft. We are all very conscious of the international allure of air travel, but it also has an enormous impact on a city. All kinds of transport, storage and distribution activities gather around an international airport, if we limit ourselves to this example. The same applies to an international seaport. However, transport is also closely linked to trade; without trade there is no freight. Traders and distributors were two of a kind, and were sometimes one and the same person or company. This relationship has diminished over the years, but there are still enough interconnections to allow us to regard TRADE AND TRANSPORT as a single cluster and to involve it in the research.

Hotels offer accommodation to people who are staying in a city temporarily, whether it is for a business meeting, a congress, a holiday or something else. They are the personification of the hospitality of the city, quantitatively and qualitatively. However, as has been stated earlier, they are mainly dependent on the visits generated by companies and tourist and congress organizations. Air travel, equally dominant in the previous cluster, must also not be forgotten in this context. However, even if everything is clearly interconnected, over-large and complex clusters do not enhance the trans-parency and must be avoided. The degree of

71

interdependence seems to be a good measure for determining the composition of the clusters. In this case it means that not only hotels but also tourist and congress organizations will be allocated to the cluster HOSPITALITY.

Universities are clusters themselves, if you consider the great diversity of faculties. Around them can also be found large numbers of businesses and institutions. Together they form the ACADEMIC WORLD, a cluster that Porter allocates to the infrastructure, because of the knowledge it generates and its impact on the innovative capacity of industry. This impact is felt within the city as well as within the country and even across borders, but proximity does play a very positive role here.

An unexplored region is the interaction between a city and the cultural or artistic activities that take place there. The importance of these for a city is, of course, recognized in the literature, but usually they are covered by a footnote or an aside or are found as an element within the Quality of Life. However, if posters can be seen hanging in Tokyo announcing a performance of the Wiener Philharmoniker, to name but one possible example from many, then this has a positive impact on Vienna as a city. It is no different with famous museums. You read or hear about a particular exhibition somewhere, and add that city to your travel scheme. If we collect all of this within the cluster CULTURE, then a cluster is created for which everyone recognizes the importance, but does not know how to structure it or to define it precisely.

However, apart from these four, there are more clusters that can be distinguished that give a city a competitive advantage. Obvious ones are, of course, the two clusters that have been strongly emphasized by Sassen: the headquarters of MULTINATIONALS and the FINANCIAL WORLD. The concentration of these in a limited number of cities makes these cities, according to her, 'global command centers.' The financial world especially combines a broad net of businesses and activities that can have a worldwide impact. The best evidence for this comes from the daily reports of stock exchange activities.

Many multinationals still have their headquarters in the cities where they once began production. Those industrial companies were then the source of economic progress; the cities were the centers for industry, and derived their power and position from it, nationally and internationally. This situation changed dramatically in the second half of the twentieth century. Industrialization has spread across the whole world and cities have turned to becoming national and international centers for tertiary and quartiary service industries. This does not mean that industrial manufacturing has been reduced to a negligible activity. Many prominent cities are still very important industrial centers. The question in this context is how far this gives a city an extra international competitive advantage. A reason to include PRODUCTION FACILITIES as a cluster.

INTERNATIONAL ORGANIZATIONS are a quite different case. There are many thousands of them: a few truly large ones but very many small ones, some world-famous but many less well-known, rich ones but also many with a limited budget. They can be roughly divided into organizations and institutions that have been founded by governments (for example the United Nations, Unctad, NATO, IMF, the World Bank), organizations that represent the interests of professional groups (for example IATA, FIFA) and charities and organizations for the general good (for example the Red Cross, Amnesty International, Greenpeace). The fact that countries, and especially cities, like to be the center for this kind of organization is clear from the competition that starts well before their foundation. Because of the employment opportunities, of course, but even more because of the international allure that a prominent organization can give a country or city.

Important cities are usually magnets for businesses (and the people connected to them) that are involved in offering news, knowledge and entertainment. Consider newspapers, TV and radio stations, magazine publishers and so on. The world of the MEDIA is a rich and varied one. However, this is not sufficient to justify including this cluster in the world of the 'citymakers.' What is written in the Brussels paper 'Le Soir' is seldom seen outside Belgium, 'RAI Uno' attracts few viewers in Sweden, and in Canada it is nigh on impossible to find 'O Estado de Sao Paulo' at the local newsagents. However important they may be for the city, the media do not contribute directly (with a few exceptions) to its international profile. Indirectly, however, they contribute much more, especially the newspapers. They are the window on the world for their professional or general readership. They select the news from the world that is received via press agencies and correspondents. Who, in turn, pick it up from their local news circuit. In this way, as messengers from the city to the rest of the world, they are perhaps 'citymakers' *par excellence.*

The world of REAL ESTATE is again quite different. According to Porter, buildings are themselves nothing special: just basic conditions. They can only contribute to competitive power when they distinguish themselves in a positive manner. This could be through quantity and/or quality. A city in which a great deal is being built for the commercial sector can profile itself as a successful growth point (investment driven). Interesting buildings, in their turn, attract international attention, and not only in professional circles. The skyline of a remarkable building ('landmark') can even, in special cases, be immediately associated with a city. Builders, developers and especially architects can be placed in this cluster. They are also, literally, 'citymakers.' Their contribution to the international competitive position of a city is probably less spectacular than their contribution to the way it looks, but is certainly important enough to allow this cluster to be distinguished and to involve it in the research.

■

Accountants, lawyers, organizational advisors, headhunters and advertising agencies establish themselves in a city if there is a market for them. At a city level (and also national level) they are more 'followers' than 'leaders.' However, this picture is changing. A cluster of PROFESSIONAL SERVICES, especially when they are specialized and highly qualified, can give a city a profile that attracts other companies and institutions. It is also a cluster that responds to globalization with mergers and takeovers in order to form as quickly as possible a worldwide network of branches. This network in turn leads to commissions that far exceed its original dimension. In brief, a fast-moving cluster with an international profile.

It is not only ministries and the associated institutions that gather around the SEAT OF GOVERNMENT of a country, but also all kinds of other institutions, many of them focused on lobbying for certain interests. The national character is predominant, but foreign embassies certainly provide an inter-national dimension. It is a cluster that at a national level certainly contributes importantly to the profile of a city. The significance for the international competitive position of a city is difficult to estimate.

Using the (11) clusters given above, it would seem that most of the companies and institutions have been covered that, each in their own way, contribute to the competitive profile of a city. They form the nucleus, the magnet for the clusters. This is the background to the limitation that was mentioned in the opening paragraph. The clusters as a whole contain many more businesses, and many of them are also part of one or more other clusters. The Corporate Services are a good example of this; as a specialized function they can be part of, for example, the cluster Finance, but together with other specialized services they also form their own cluster. Then there are clusters that overlap, such as the Transport and Hospitality clusters. In fact, all the clusters form a single network within which the elements can be distinguished but not separated. Within that network the 'city-makers' can be recognised as the representatives of their cluster.

5. Of the factors not yet allocated, five have the common characteristic that they involve human qualities; people's skills, character and mentality. The skills are, of course, closely connected to the level of education of the labor force. This is a competitive factor that is perhaps increasingly independent of location, and is no longer even constrained by national boundaries, but it is still the local clusters that provide the raison d'être for specialist training courses and ensure that this is in fact a factor for cities, clearly distinguishable from the national.

The way in which people respond to different (foreign) influences is another quality. If they are open to other cultures and languages and approach them in an unreserved and helpful way, this is an important characteristic in a world in which physical distance is hardly an obstacle any more. History, race, religion and especially language play an important role in this.

74

For centuries cities have been the melting-pots for the various races and cultures found within a country, and this has had a positive influence on the openness of city residents. Being such a melting-pot can bring social problems to the community, but it can also be enriching. It ensures characteristic differences that give a city its own special flavour.

This (multicultural) factor is again linked to the size of the population. The larger it is, the more 'space' there is for cultural differences. The size of the population, and its composition, also affects the support basis for services and events with an international dimension in the cultural, educative and recreational spheres.

With these four 'human' factors the third determinant for the city model, THE HUMAN FACTOR, seems to be well filled. It is up to the 'citymakers' to indicate its significance to the international competitive position of the city.

6. There remains the determinant 'governance.' In the previous section it is stated that its place on the sidelines in the national model meant that the role of governance had been neglected, and that it should be given a full place (i.e. determinant) in the model for cities.

Porter argued that the governance structures may be able to influence all the determinants positively or negatively, but they do not have the power to create a competitive advantage themselves. This seems to be fundamental. However, it can perhaps be stated with equal justification that a government that has the intention and ambition of stimulating the international competitive power of the business sector does provide a competitive advantage and is therefore a determinant itself. Porter gives plenty of room for this explanation in his later work in which he increasingly emphasizes the importance of the role of governance. In particular, he abandoned all reserve when he applied his theory to clusters and developed a new theory for them. Perhaps it was the stereotypical American suspicion of the influence of government that prevented him from including governance, at least visually, as a full determinant in his model. From a European perspective it is not so problematic. From this starting point, four factors can be placed within this determinant.

Taxes are always a significant factor. However, a city model will only involve local taxes, and there are huge differences between countries and cities on this point. The national tax regime belongs together with the national competitive position to the determinant that will be discussed next.

The next specific local factor is Leadership, of which the mayor is often the personification, and which translates into charisma, authority and the ability to turn words into actions.

Public safety has more nuances. In very general terms, there is a higher level of criminality in the cities than in the country as a whole. However, there is a very close relation between the two. The city is, in this sense, a product of the country. On the other hand, the city can in fact distinguish itself by minimizing that difference. Public order is therefore both a national and local factor when considering the competitive position.

Finally, there is the (visible) effort by local government to invest in a city, particularly in cases in which the city can then distinguish itself qualitatively from other cities. This could involve any of the clusters mentioned above, plus the hard infrastructure that is required. For the latter in particular the local government is primarily responsible, it is the initiator. This is a prime example of a local factor, even if the national government is often indispensable as a co-financier.

A city is not an island, isolated within a country. The clusters that are found in the city are also, in all kinds of ways, affected by the competitive factors that apply to the country as a whole. The New York of today is, for example, unthinkable in Mexico, or Tokyo in Thailand. A city cannot build a competitive advantage on its own. Exceptions are the so-called city states, such as Singapore and (until recently) Hong Kong. In designing a model for cities, it is about highlighting the factors that give a city a clear competitive advantage compared to other cities at home and abroad. The national competitive position of the country is in this sense an essential part of the model for cities.

The World Competitiveness Yearbook (WCY) appears annually. This measures and compares the competitive power of 47 countries. Many factors from Porter's model can be recognized among the input factors used. However, there is one conspicuous difference: cluster formation in a country is not included explicitly as an input factor. A possible explanation is as follows: The competitive power, the business climate of a country on the one hand, and the competitive power of companies on the other, are two separate but interdependent concepts. WCY focuses on the climate for the business world as a whole; Porter's model shows why a country scores internationally in a certain branch of business or cluster: "firms compete in industries, not nations" (1990, p. 619). Considering the input factors that are used and the great similarities between the two models, the difference seems to be of more theoretical than practical significance. The question remains whether competitive power, or parts of it, can ultimately be expressed with a single number or index, in the manner of the WCY. However, as the model has been applied unchanged for years, it does give a reliable indication of development in competitive power of a country. As such it can be included as data in the model for cities. In this way the national government also gets a place in the model; around 15% of the input factors involve the role of government.

In the foregoing it has been attempted to group the 35 selected competitive factors for cities into determinants. The obvious first step was to use the determinants from Porter's national model, but this was only partially successful. It confirmed once again that his national model cannot simply be applied to a city. Two determinants ('factor conditions' and 'demand') have been dropped completely and two others ('structure & rivalry' and 'related and supporting industries') have been transformed into, respectively, International Profile and Clusters.

Governance is no longer on the sidelines but included in the team, and, last but not least, national competitive power has been included as a separate determinant. In this way the adjusted model for cities has acquired five determinants in which all the (provisionally) selected competitive factors, as shown above, can be placed. All this is portrayed in the 'city diamond' in Figure II.3.

Whether Porter intended such a model when he stated "The theory can be readily extended to explain why some cities or regions are more successful than

Figure II.3   **THE CITY DIAMOND**

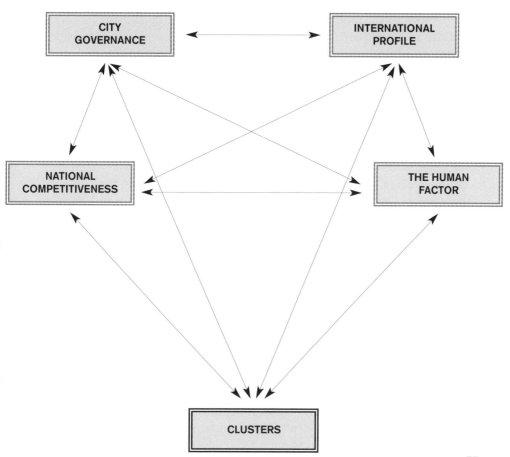

others" (1990, p. 158) is doubtful, considering the rigid way in which he himself applied his own model to the inner city. It does, however, meet the original aim of this study as described in the introduction: a model à la Porter. His model was the inspiration.

As in Porter's model, the arrows symbolize the relations between the diverse determinants and the factors within them. In the following section these will be examined further.

* * *

II. 4.2 INTERACTIONS

Now that an inventory has been made of the factors that give cities a competitive advantage, and they have been sorted into groups, the variables in their interactions should be examined. "In reality, every determinant can affect every other determinant, though some interactions are stronger and more important than others", according to Porter (1990, p. 132). He describes this interaction in detail and convincingly; but says little about its intensity. An order of priority cannot therefore be determined, and the operational value of the model is limited by this.

Following in Porter's footsteps, this section will describe the interactions between the determinants for cities and their associated factors. This will be done on the basis of insights that can be found in the literature and from personal experience. The intention is to test the model for cities on, in particular, its completeness and consistency. The final judgement can, however, best be left in the hands of the practitioners: the professionals, the 'citymakers.' Each of them belongs to a certain cluster. By indicating in the questionnaire what, in their professional opinion, are the most important factors for cities, they create an authoritative picture per cluster of both the interactions and their intensity.

CLUSTERS ◄———————► THE HUMAN FACTOR

Any success, in any cluster, is based on people, on their commitment and qualities. This is the essence of the relationship between these two determinants. More can be said, however, if only in general.

The **level of education** of the labor force is important for all clusters. Some clusters benefit, however, from a high level of education and specialization. This encourages innovation and inventive entrepreneurship. The Financial cluster, the Multinationals, the Academic and Cultural worlds and the Professional Services are the most typical examples. Other clusters, on the other hand, attach more importance to a poorly educated labor force in order to maintain their competitive power. The clusters Hospitality, Industry and also Transport are the most obvious ones. Clusters have certain needs and on the basis of these they create all kinds of training pathways, alone or in cooperative set-ups and with co-sponsorship. Universities and higher education institutions respond to the needs of clusters with specialized chairs and (sub)faculties. This is another example of how clusters reinforce one another.

Banks and multinationals are the perfect example of companies that can only do business internationally if they respect other cultures and know how to work with them. If you encounter a variety of cultures at home, then you must surely benefit from this experience when you go out into the wide world. It is these two clusters that are involved in takeovers, mergers and joint ventures, for which an **open approach** to business and people is a first requirement.

In addition, multinationals and large banks own factories and offices spread across the whole world. The degree to which the culture of the mother company penetrates other countries and cities depends on the structure of the organization and the end product. A Coca Cola factory has no degree of freedom, nor does a producer of McDonald's hamburgers. A Ford factory in England, on the other hand, will be run 'at a distance' from Detroit, while the headquarters in Japan will feel very close to a Toyota factory in Belgium. International banks also keep a firm grip on their foreign branches, as local failures can affect their world-wide reputation.

Whether such foreign branches are able to take root and flourish depends on the way in which the labor force responds to the different business culture. The interdependence goes both ways; a foreign owner who shows no respect for the business culture of another country, whatever he or she may think of it, will learn a hard lesson.

Openness to other opinions and influences and relating to the outside world is inherent in academia. A university with a leadership, staff or student body that cuts itself off from this will stay in the shadows and not be able to take its place in the international spotlight. Publishing and the exchange of information are the tried and tested methods. Knowledge of and ability in the English language play a key role here.

Of all the clusters, international trade and transport seems to be the one that is most dependent for success on the way it handles the diverse cultures of consumers and businesses. Respecting one another's differences and remaining yourself is a golden rule in trade. Those involved in transport can only make connections both literally and figuratively when their focus is outwards and they can bring together apparently conflicting interests. No other cluster is so intensely confronted with the results of internationalization and globalization, and has been for centuries.

The practitioners of international consultancy (Professional or Corporate Services) may not agree totally with the last statement. They must also conti-nuously make strategic choices. To participate in international networks or to concentrate on the traditional home market? The latter is easier than the former. The chances of success as part of an international network depend to a large extent on the way in which clients who are used to something else are approached, and the extent to which it is possible to get across one's own knowledge and creativity to foreign colleagues.

The cultural cluster cannot retreat into its shell either, if it wants to extend its ambitions to the world. Broadly oriented museums have always opened their doors, literally, to other cultures. Museums of modern art cannot afford to restrict themselves to home-grown creations either, particularly if they are to fulfil their educative task. Opera and ballet companies, and in particular symphony orchestras, have to be open to a huge international variety of artistic direction and compositions if they want to be counted as a player in their competitive field. A lack of openness can quickly become a blot on a beautiful international reputation, as the Wiener Philharmoniker has found.

Another cluster has to literally open its doors to influences from outside: this is implicit in hospitality, and hotels are the perfect example. They have to be able to place themselves in the mind of the foreigner in order to make him or her feel at home in their new surroundings. No less is expected from those who organize conferences and incentive trips and who operate in an extremely competition-sensitive international market. The risk is that a uniform product is created which does not differ from city to city, while the unique characteristics of the country and city should be used as a competitive advantage. Quite a challenge for all those working in the Hospitality cluster. However, if the challenge is met successfully, then globalization will take its toll in a positive sense: good examples are swiftly followed!

The danger of worldwide uniformity comes even closer to realization in the cluster Real Estate. Perhaps architects, investors and developers are too open to ideas from outside. The uniformity of cities, especially of office towerblocks, is disturbing. Openness that simply leads to copying what has already been done elsewhere does not have much added value, and does not provide a competitive advantage. Here again the challenge is to find a balance between openness and originality.

Finally, how will foreign employees feel in a city that, particularly in its daily life, has little or no consideration for the foreigner? Like a fish out of water. That news spreads so fast that a yet-to-be-established organization, or at least one that is free to choose its location, will not place such a city on its shortlist.

Summarizing the above briefly, 'openness to the world' is a characteristic of people at various levels, and pretty much any cluster that is subject to international competition can make good use of it.

The **multicultural** society has so many facets, that it is difficult to limit a description to its interaction with clusters. These interactions mostly involve the labor market, and its underside in particular. The clusters that benefit most from a wide choice at this end of the market are those that focus primarily on the unskilled.

In this context the clusters industry, hospitality and to a lesser degree transport were mentioned earlier. Unskilled people from other cultures are also often found in the service sector, which does not operate in an internationally competitive field. Airlines and telecom companies have the advantage that newcomers tend to keep a long-standing relationship with their country of origin; the competitive advantage of specialized demand from the home market, Porter would say. Of course it does not really make much of a significant contribution.

Cities attract people, both from afar and from close to. Sometimes so many that the process can no longer be controlled and desperate situations arise. Huge conurbations have been established. The condition of the national economy determines this trend; in countries with a high degree of economic development opposite trends have been observed for some decades. If you focus on the uncontrollability of the process, and with some cities this is inescapable, then hardly any advantage can be detected in having a **large population**.

However, many people collected together also form a huge resource pool. When multinationals set up production companies in low wage countries, they often seek out the large cities. In the more developed countries, this pool, through both its size and certainly its diversity, is of benefit to many a cluster. A rich and diverse contribution to the labor market is the most obvious, and the importance of this has been discussed earlier. The cultural and academic clusters also rely substantially on their immediate surroundings. The competitive advantage that Porter attaches to the home market, and then especially to the sophisticated part of the demand, may be a less dominant factor for cities, but for a number of clusters is certainly not to be neglected.

In his later theory Porter laid even more emphasis on the competitive advantage that clusters deliver. This advantage is created by, amongst other things, proximity, which greatly facilitates business and personal contacts. **Networks**, that's what it's all about. An important role is given to governance and to professional interest groups in the creation of these. It is difficult to say if networks are the result of clusters or vice versa. We will limit ourselves to noting that networks are required in order to realize potential clusters. Networks can be created in all kinds of ways. They are often institutionalized, in the form of committees, working groups, task forces and so on, but are also often informal. For the latter, proximity, people with the relevant expertise, and an open atmosphere are required. A city is the perfect environment. It is therefore no coincidence that a potential cluster such as New Economy is growing fastest in the cities.

Not all clusters are equally dependent on networking. The intensity depends on common interests that can be recognized, on the mutual benefits that are expected, and not least on the culture of the individual cluster. The clusters Professional Services and Media do nothing else but network, in a manner of speaking, while the Multinationals are more a coincidental collection. International Organizations come together for yet other reasons (advantages of scale, tax climate, accommodation) and national organizations cluster for explicable reasons around the seat of the national government.

In general, there are many interactions between the determinants Clusters and the Human Factor. The intensity of these is quite varied. The interactions appear to be most intense on the point of an educated labor force and openness to other influences. The questionnaire should be able to give a more precise answer to this, both in general and per cluster.

CLUSTERS ◄————————► INTERNATIONAL PROFILE

For this interaction the question is in fact what is the significance to the clusters of the international profile of the city in which they are established? That profile is formed by a number of elements, but the general impression is of importance.

The cluster Hospitality appears to be the one with the most interest in a good international profile for the city. In fact, the cluster depends on it. All the parties involved, the tourist and congress industry and the hotels, benefit from a lively city with a high quality center that is constantly in the news, with facilities, events and achievements at international level. In this case the transport cluster, and the home carrier of the international airport in particular, can also be included.

The interaction with other clusters appears to be less. Of course, an international bank does have an interest in the skyline of a city – banks do not build impressive skyscrapers for no reason – and multinationals can profile themselves worldwide via famous sport teams and mega events. Did either Coca Cola or NBC bring the Olympic Games to Atlanta, or did they do it together? However, they do not need the city *per se.*

On the other hand, clusters contribute substantially to the international profile of the city. This is also true for the financial world (especially the stock exchanges) and the multinationals, but probably even more so for (for example) famous universities, orchestras and museums, for authoritative newspapers, a popular airport or a port for cruise-ships, for a high-profile international organization or for film companies.

The interactions exist, therefore, but it seems clear that the international profile is more dependent on the clusters than vice versa. Whether that also means that clusters which have less of a stake in their city's international profile also attach less significance to it must be sought in the results of the survey.

CLUSTERS ◄————————► CITY GOVERNANCE

There are no two countries in which the responsibilities of the various governmental levels (city, region, country) are arranged in the same way. To attempt to give a global description of the interactions between clusters and city governance would therefore be pretentious. It will not be possible to do much more than outline some rather general areas of responsibility and the interactions flowing from them.

A striking example of this great diversity can be found in the ways in which city governance is funded. The interaction with the clusters is greater and more sensitive the more a city is dependent on income from local taxes. It then also becomes a competitive factor in relation to neighboring municipalities and other cities in the country. However, this does not apply equally to all clusters; large businesses and the world of real estate would appear to be the most sensitive to this factor.

When clusters are dependent on investment from local authorities, with or without contributions from regional and national governments, then the factors leadership and commitment to investment are very closely related in their eyes. Investment by local authorities, especially in projects and activities that provide no cash return, requires political choices and therefore courage and the ability to turn words into actions. The clusters hospitality and culture (the latter because of the preservation of cultural heritage, for instance) are almost always dependent on the local authorities' commitment to investment. However, seaports, airports and universities in many countries could not exist without it either. Finally, the world of real estate cannot make any progress if the authorities do not invest sufficiently in the necessary infrastructure.

Public safety is regarded instinctively as a very important factor. However, viewed purely functionally, only a few clusters have a direct interest in it. Once again there is the cluster Hospitality: there is no doubt that a poor public safety image has a negative impact on the flow of conference and tourist visitors to a city. If a city is under pressure as a destination, then the home carrier will feel the effect of this as well. In addition, an unsafe city loses its attractiveness for international organizations and embassies. However, it is quite possible that other clusters will also give this factor a high value. This will be primarily because an unsafe image is bad for the international profile of the city.

Finally, only a few words need to be said here on the role that Porter subscribes to city governance as a stimulus for existing and potential clusters. It is not an easy task to convince those who are used to minding their own business to acknowledge their common interests with others. It is even more difficult to keep them on track and to ensure that words are turned into actions. This is the kind of leadership that the business world looks for and greatly appreciates.

In conclusion, the interactions between clusters and governance are varied in intensity, in many cases they are lacking or scarcely detectable, and they are strongly dependent on the way in which the governance and especially the tax regime of a country is organized. The interactions seem, at first sight, to be rather one-sided: the clusters are dependent on the authorities. However, if a city authority is aiming to profile the city internationally, then it cannot achieve this without the clusters. To paraphrase Porter: clusters, not city governments, are on the frontline of international profiling.

■

THE HUMAN FACTOR ◄————► INTERNATIONAL PROFILE
At first sight there seems to be little interrelationship between the characteristics of a city's population and its international profile. Take the level of education for example; if the level of education and specialization of the population is
significantly enhanced it does not necessarily mean that the international profile
of the city is similarly improved. There is also no direct relationship between a
large population and, for example, noteworthy performances in international
sport. Tokyo is an interesting example of this. On the other hand, a rich mixture
of population groups does make a very vibrant city; take New York, for example.
Openness to foreign, different influences implies tolerance. When minority
groups feel free to express themselves, it can sometimes deliver world fame: Rosen
Sonntag in Berlin and the Red Light District in Amsterdam are striking examples
of this. In top-level sport the integration of the races is not only commonplace,
but also improves performance. These are just some examples; examples of
interrelationships that, where they exist, cannot always be easily defined.

THE HUMAN FACTOR ◄————► CITY GOVERNANCE
In a well-functioning democracy, the nature and composition of the population have a direct influence on city governance. They are expressed in its political
composition and manifestos. However, when the issue is, for instance, to tackle
the problems of disadvantaged population groups, the balance in the relationship
shifts towards the city government. It is up to the local authorities to address the
negative aspects of a large and multicultural population, and turn them into
benefits for the people and the city as a whole. A city authority that can make
strengths from weaknesses will steal the show internationally, and therefore be
an advantage. This requires leadership.
When the function of city governance as a stimulus for networks was raised
for discussion, it was not only on the basis of economic interests. Through their
networks, local authorities can recruit interested partners for the realization of
certain social ends; reducing, for example, the number of young people who
drop-out of education. An illustration in this context that has stuck in my mind is
'London Compact,' an organization in which businesses adopt underprivileged
schools .

INTERNATIONAL PROFILE ◄————► CITY GOVERNANCE
Clusters seem to have the most interest in the international profile of the city;
city governance, however, usually feels primarily responsible for it and is also
regarded as such by the clusters. That is the characteristic of this interrelationship.
Once again it will depend on the leadership whether or not the city governance
can meet this responsibility. More important than financial investment will be its
ability to bring together and link interested parties. The structure needs them

both: the 'citymakers' are the bricks and the city governance the mortar.

The public safety image is primarily under the control of city governance. The interested clusters (and citizens!) address it continuously on this. Misunderstandings, which arise easily on this issue, can be avoided through good communication.

City governance is also regarded as primarily responsible for the image of the inner city. A city center needs much maintenance and continual renewal. Commitment to investment in the center should be self-evident. The more this happens in cooperation with the business world, the more added value these investments generate. This is why you will always see the partners and the mayor together on the information boards for the large urban renewal projects in American inner cities (the mayor, however, is always the most prominent).

A city 'where it happens' is always in the news. 'It' will include more or less spontaneous events, such as demonstrations, but also all kinds of city initiatives. The initiative-takers need to know that they can rely on an ambitious city governance that is ready to help with serious plans. However, it demands a high level of ambition and inventiveness not only from the leadership but also from the residents and the business sector. There are endless examples, from cultural festivals to the Olympic Games. Even after two years it is still fresh in our minds how cities strove to distinguish themselves in the celebration of the new millennium. However, globalization was seen to strike again: all pretty much the same! Small wonder that only a few, the most original, got the publicity.

There is no doubt that an international profile, strong civic sense and an ambitious city governance go hand in hand. Sometimes this combination only springs to life as a last desperate measure. However, as the Dutch say, it is better to repair the roof while the weather is still fine.

THE NATIONAL COMPETITIVE PROFILE ◄——► OTHER DETERMINANTS

Yet another anecdote from my personal past. It was the early 1980s and the Amsterdam economy was not going well. Asked how we could get it back on track, a professor and former minister who had been taken on as an advisor gave this reply: "the recovery of the Amsterdam economy will start with the recovery of the Dutch economy." A statement not to be forgotten. It indicates exactly how dependent a city is on the economic ups and downs of the country.

This interrelationship is clearest with the clusters. Clusters operating worldwide can compensate partially for a poor economic climate at home with their activities abroad, it is true. However, many remain dependent to a great degree on their original market, and this is more the country than the city. The automobile industry and the banks are good examples of this. On the other hand, a flourishing economy at home can give businesses the courage to try their luck in the wider world. For the non-profit clusters (Culture and Academia) that are wholly or partly dependent on government subsidies the relationship is not much different; the Treasury of a country with a less-than-flourishing economy will not usually be particularly generous with its handouts. Only the clusters International Organizations and National Government seem to be less sensitive to variations in the national economic climate.

On the other hand, the national economy is itself dependent on the clusters. Companies that are less dependent on the home market and achieve good results elsewhere can provide a positive stimulus to the home economy. Possible examples are worldwide manufacturing multinationals, international transport companies, businesses in the hospitality cluster, internationally operating media companies and, increasingly, financial institutions. Their success and prestige reflect not only on the city but also on the country. France and Italy are fashion nations because of the clusters in Paris and Milan, the United States is a movie nation because of the cluster in Los Angeles, the Netherlands is a transport nation because of the clusters in Rotterdam and Amsterdam and a flower nation because of Aalsmeer. Clusters give, according to Porter, a competitive advantage to a country.

There is also a clear relationship between the determinant THE HUMAN FACTOR and the national competitive profile. Cities may have a spearhead position in many areas, but they do not function in isolation. London may have a broad multicultural population, but it remains a (magnified) reflection of the composition of the population of other large and small English cities. Istanbul is located on the European continent, but remains a Turkish city. A city reveals more of a country than a country does of a city. It is no different with the labor force, especially the highly skilled. They spread themselves just as easily across the country or concentrate in the city, depending on the demand. Even national boundaries are scarcely a barrier any more for specialists. Language and ties to one's own culture seem to be the only remaining obstacles. A country that is open and internationally oriented seems to give its cities a competitive advantage.

There is less connection between the competitive profile of the country and that of the city. Cities such as Mexico City, Rio de Janeiro, Buenos Aires, New Delhi or Cairo may score reasonably well in ranking lists of cities, while the competitive profile of the country is quite low. The Scandinavian countries show that the opposite can also be true. In general, a city will be able to profile itself internationally more easily with a strong nation behind it. The reverse is seldom the case. The position of a city is not so dominating that it can drag a whole country with it. London, Paris and Tokyo are perhaps exceptions to this rule; the combination of economic power is so great there that a 'local case of the 'flu' can infect the whole country.

The relationship between the determinants CITY GOVERNANCE and national competitive profile is focused largely on the factors public safety and public investment. Both are part of the national and city competitive profile. These are clearly tasks for the government, at both national and city level.

In general, the requirements for public safety are greater in a city. However, once again, the city is usually a product of the country, and no huge differences can generally be distinguished: no super dangerous cities in a safe country, and vice versa even less. Special projects on this issue in a city (such as in New York) are either temporary or have a structural effect elsewhere as well.

A city cannot function without connections to the rest of the country and neighboring countries. On this point a city is therefore completely dependent on public investment by the national government. In most countries this also applies to cultural heritage (such as museums) and academia (universities).

The availability of national funds and the way and timing in which they are used therefore determine the development potential of a city to an important degree. Tradition plays an important role in this. The rivalry between Moscow and St. Petersburg is legendary, the connection France–Paris exemplary and the reserve in the United States occasionally astonishing. Alongside tradition, however, political leadership, especially in city governance, plays an important role.

* * *

In the fourth section of part II an inventory was made of the determinants and their competitive factors for cities, making use of the existing literature. In this fourth section the interactions between both the determinants and the competitive factors were described in broad terms. On this basis a competitiveness model for cities could be developed that was inspired by Porter's national model, but adjusted to the specific situation of the city.

On the basis of the inventory in section II.3, 34 competitive factors for cities could be included in the model, grouped in the four city determinants. This number of factors is, however, unselective and also too large for a competitiveness analysis that is of any practical use. From this collection, the factors will have to be selected that are of real relevance to the international competitive position of the city; there could also be new ones added. This was the task of the 'citymakers.' They were asked in question 2-A of the questionnaire, on the basis of their professional knowledge and experience, to make this selection. With around 1300 answers, they have delivered the foundations for a competitiveness analysis that every city with international ambition should undertake from time to time. In the following section a report is given of the results from this research.

II. 5 THE RESULTS OF THE RESEARCH

All competitive factors are important; it is just that some are more important than others

Not a quote this time, but an opportunity to make a personal statement. For the time has come to report on the results of the research on the 34 competitive factors, and in particular on their relative significance for the international competitive position of a city. This means reporting scores, and with scores there is always the danger that those scoring the least (in this case the competitive factors) will be dismissed as less important or even as completely unimportant. This must be avoided, and therefore the above statement will be repeated frequently.

It will be recalled that in part I there was a thorough discussion of the usefulness and necessity of research into the factors that determine the international competitive position of a city. It was established that the existing literature on the subject often makes use of such factors in order to place cities in a ranking order or typology, but that the selection of these factors relies on personal analyses. Focused research on the relevance of these factors has never been undertaken. Without such knowledge, it is difficult for a city government, for example, to analyse the city's competitive position covering all important aspects, and then on the basis of this to develop policy. This lack is indicated in the literature, but is packaged in the form of an invitation to undertake further research (sic!) on this point. This challenge has been accepted. In accordance with Porter's own advice, the research has been conducted amongst those who, in a manner of speaking, deal with these factors on a day-to-day basis in their professional lives: the executives of companies and institutions that contribute to the international competitive position of a city, the 'citymakers.'

Following a study of the literature, 35 factors were included in the questionnaire, of which one was later dropped during the processing of results. The questionnaire is included in the appendices of this volume, for those who wish to refer to it. The factors belong to four of the five determinants of the 'city diamond.' In the questionnaire, they were collected into groups that were more recognizable for the target groups and then divided between a first and second division. The respondent was asked to indicate which factors make a city, prominent, trend-setting, 'leading,' by downgrading at least five factors from the first division to the second, and upgrading an equal number from the second division to the first to replace them.

In this section the results of this part of the research will be reported. Following some general observations, an overall picture will be given of the results for all clusters taken together, plus a division per continent. Then the individual competitive factors will be discussed separately. In the accompanying figures, a (straight) line indicates the average score and another line connects the scores for the ten separate clusters. In this way it is easy to see how far the score of a certain cluster deviates from the average. In order to avoid making the figures overcomplicated, the scores for the continents have not been included in the figures for the separate continents. Where there are important deviations, these are reported in the accompanying notes.

Links with the existing literature on competitive factors for cities will be highlighted throughout the discussion of the results; Table II.2 will be the reference point for this. Wherever possible, reference will also be made to examples in the literature where the factors have been handled in a different way, for example on their significance to the economic development of a city.

Finally, each discussion of a group of factors will be closed with a conclusion on the relevance of the diverse competitive factors. At the end of the section it will then be possible to use these as a basis to construct an overview of the factors that should be a standard part of any analysis of the international competitive position of a city.

II.5.1 GENERAL OBSERVATIONS

Before examining the results in detail, a few points of a more general nature.

1. In general, the returned questionnaires had been correctly completed. For the question on competitive factors this means that, in most cases, five factors were indicated in both divisions, as had been requested. Occasionally there were more or an unequal total, but these have simply been included. There were also respondents who clearly had difficulty with the so-called 'shift method' and not only indicated the five factors in the second column that they found most important and wished to upgrade, but also indicated the most important ones in the first column. In these cases, the first column was not included in the count. There were also those who could not choose between the factors in the first division and left this blank, but carefully indicated five factors in the second division. Then there were questionnaires on which this question was left completely blank. In total, there were 1255 questionnaires (92%) with a correctly handled first division and 1289 (94%) with a properly completed second division. In the calculations of the percentages, these differences have, of course, been taken into account.

2. The respondents were explicitly invited to indicate any extra factors that should be added to the list. This opportunity was taken in only a very few cases, and generally resulted in factors that had not been included in the list because they are basic conditions or because they are not sufficiently operational. Examples include good roads, better public transport, cleaner air, and quality of life. Sometimes a factor was added that was in fact already included in the

■

questionnaire or could be counted as being contained within a factor that had been included. It was interesting to note these additions, but they did not substantiate a need to extend the list with any extra factors.

3.The respondents were asked for their professional perception. In other words, they also had to give an opinion on the factor in which they are themselves professionally involved: for example, the director of a port on the factor International Seaport, the accountant on the factor Corporate Services, and the director of a Convention & Visitors Bureau on Congress Facilities. Bearing this in mind, it is not surprising that they generally valued their 'own' cluster more highly than did the respondents from other clusters. There is, therefore, some question of a 'professional component.' However, this has only a limited influence on the total picture.

4.The dividing line between the first and second division appeared to be quite sharp, in the sense that a factor had to acquire a substantial number of 'votes' in order to be upgraded or downgraded. When the watershed is set at 50%, the two factors Very Large Population and International Seaport are downgraded to the second division, while two others (Open to an International World and Good Public Safety) are upgraded. A couple of other factors also come close to this watershed level. Beforehand there had been some doubt as to whether the respondents would be able to choose from among 18 important factors a few that they clearly valued less. With hindsight these doubts were unfounded.

II.5.2 PLAUSIBILITY CHECK

As has already been explained in part I, the plausibility value (PL index) has been established for the total of all four questions, for each separate question, for the continents, for the clusters and (as desired) even for the separate elements (competitive factors, cities or concepts). In Figure II.4 the PL index is shown for the question on competitive advantages. In addition to the PL index for the total, the values for the separate clusters and for the continents are also shown.

The total line represents a PL index of 78%, equivalent to that for the whole survey. The PL indexes for the separate clusters are gathered around this average, there are no conspicuous deviations above or below. Per continent the differences are more noticeable. However, it must be remembered that the PL indexes for the whole questionnaire for North America and Asia+ were lower by, respectively, 11 and 7 percentage points. Taking this into account, the PL index for North America remains low in comparison to the other questions. Perhaps not spectacular, but enough to make one alert if results for North America deviate substantially from the total picture.

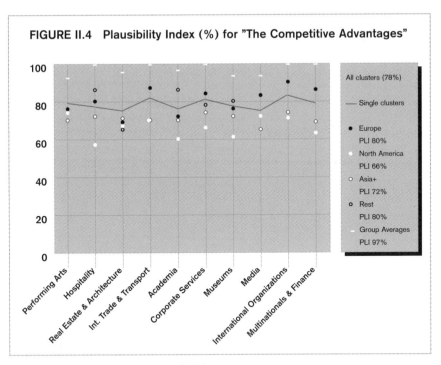

FIGURE II.4   Plausibility Index (%) for "The Competitive Advantages"

II.5.3 THE RESULTS IN TOTAL

The scores for each of the 34 competitive factors included in the research are shown in Figure II.5 (next pages). The black line connects the total scores, those of all the clusters and continents taken together. The scores of the four separate continents are also shown. It can therefore be seen how far the scores per continent deviate from the total picture and how much opinions differ between the continents.

It should be remembered that this represents the perception of almost 1300 'citymakers' spread across ten professional clusters and working in eighty cities around the world. After the reader has compared the scores for a number of factors with his/her own perception – there is no objective framework – and has recovered from the initial agreement, astonishment or disappointment, it will be swiftly noticed that the scores for the different continents lie particularly close to the average total line. For the top and bottom group that is not so surprising; with average scores of 96% or 8% no single partial score can be conspicuously different. This is not so self-evident when the scores are less extremely high or low. When, for the other factors, the scores are nonetheless also very close to one another – indeed, they are often exactly the same, so that a percentage point has had to be added or subtracted in order to make the scores visible – this indicates a high degree of consistency in the replies and therefore also a high degree of reliability.

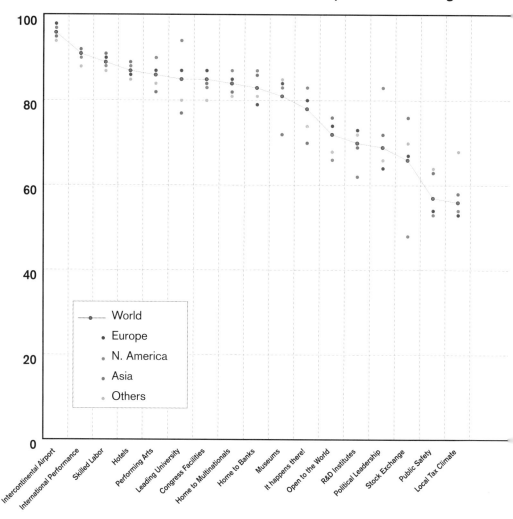

FIGURE II.5 The Competitive Advantages:

In the Figure, three groups can be distinguished. A top group with a score of between 75 and 100%; a middle group with a score of between 25 and 75% and a bottom group of between 0 and 25%. Significant deviations (10% higher or lower than average, for example) will be found especially in the middle group, in principle. In this example there are three. In the Asian world, the importance of an International Seaport is more highly rated. In North America more importance is attached to Political Leadership, while Stock Exchanges score less highly than on the other continents.

It is possible to examine the plausibility of these scores more closely, and this is not a superfluous exercise, especially for the scores from North America. For Political Leadership this delivers a PL index of 63%, and for the score for the Stock Exchange it is 68%. This deviates little from the average PL index of 66% that was calculated for North America for the question as a whole.

The results of the perception research speak for themselves. Little explana-

All Clusters (in % respondents selecting the factors)

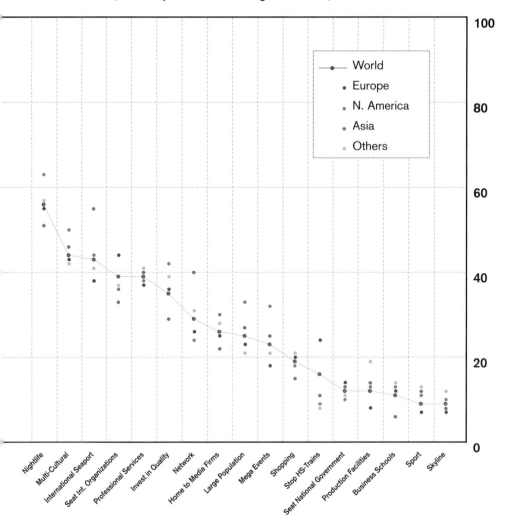

tion is required, particularly when they are collected together in easily surveyable graphics and personally tinted interpretations are of less relevance. It would be different if there was a frame of reference; a comparable study, for example, or existing literature on the subject. The research published here is – as far as can be determined – the first of its kind, so that there is no possibility for comparison in that sense. In Table II.2 a summary is, however, provided of competitive factors mentioned by more than twenty other authors. It may be that these selections depend on the personal analyses of these authors and give absolutely no insight into the relative weight of the factors, but from this quantity of literature it is nonetheless possible to deduce which factors are often mentioned or used. In addition there is also a substantial amount of literature that does not handle these factors as competitive elements, but instead as, for instance, significant to the economy of a city. Both of these contributions from the literature provide openings for some comparative comments.

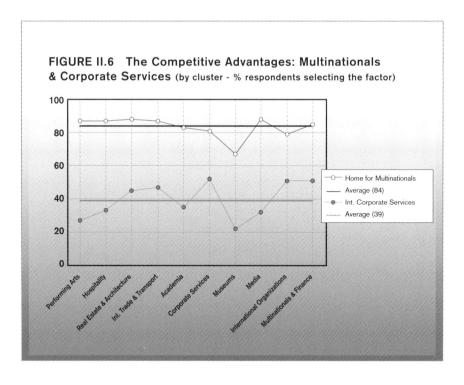

FIGURE II.6 The Competitive Advantages: Multinationals & Corporate Services (by cluster - % respondents selecting the factor)

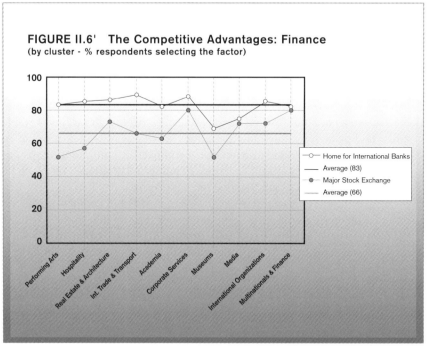

FIGURE II.6' The Competitive Advantages: Finance
(by cluster - % respondents selecting the factor)

II.5.4 THE RESULTS FOR THE DETERMINANT: CLUSTERS

CLUSTER: MULTINATIONALS, FINANCE, CORPORATE SERVICES
(Figures II.6 + II.6')

The most obvious lead is the proposition by Sassen that the headquarters of Multinationals and International Banks and the supporting Corporate Services are the most dominant factors in international competition between cities. This hypothesis has been adopted by many authors and has acquired a great deal of authority. So much so, in fact, that it has never been tested. Many publications on 'world city formation' use her theory as their starting point. It has meanwhile been established that simply adding up the number of headquarters of multinationals is a very limited approach (Nam & Semple and Godfrey & Yu, amongst others) and attempts have been made to widen or deepen the analyses by including regional or continental headquarters. In addition, the much broader factor 'Services' has been the focus of an increasing number of publications. This concept is not only multi-interpretational – does it include financial services or not? – but it is also fairly new as a competitive factor. In any case, it appears to be unavoidable that these treatments end up producing a ranking order or typology of cities or even networks of cities (Taylor et al.) All of this contributes further leads for part III, where the ranking of cities will be discussed.

The 'citymakers' agree with Sassen and all her followers, insofar as the headquarters of multinationals and banks do indeed score highly as a competitive factor, but they certainly do not enjoy the primacy and exclusivity that they have sometimes been awarded in the literature. They have to share their position at the top with at least ten other factors.

This relativization of the significance as a competitive factor of, in particular, the headquarters of multinationals can be further underlined using the Fortune Global 500 companies. This list is used by a number of authors in putting together a world ranking order of cities. As the table below shows, the headquarters of these giants is not the exclusive domain of the larger cities. Certainly not in North America, where less than half of these companies are based in one of the 19 cities in the study. In assessing this overview it should also be noted that around 100 companies on this list belong to the financial sector. These are almost all established in the cities.

Table II.7 Corporate Headquarters Locations of Fortune Global 500 companies (year 2000)

Continent	Total number of corporate HQ's	A. Corporate HQ's in cities covered by the research		B. Corporate HQ's in other cities	
		number	% of total number	number	% of total number
Europe	163	118	72	45	28
North America	191	79	41	112	59
Asia	139	122	88	17	12
Others	7	5	71	2	29
World	500	324	65	176	35

Considering the special importance that Sassen attaches to them, and their increasing popularity in the literature, the 'International Corporate Services' could also be expected to score highly. In this research they do not come any higher than a low to middle position. With such a classification it is usual for the scores to show a greater spread per cluster. It is not surprising that their 'own' clusters give them the highest score, whether it applies equally to the clusters Multinationals & Finance and International Organizations. Consistent with their scores for multinationals' headquarters, Museums again award a visibly lower score.

In her analyses of financial centers in the world, Sassen naturally gives a prominent role to trading in shares, and to stock exchanges in particular. Her opinion is supported within their 'own' cluster Multinationals & Finance and by the cluster Corporate Services. The other clusters judged this factor more variably.

Earlier, an interesting continental deviation downwards was noted for North America with regard to stock exchanges. From further analysis of the separate clusters it appears that this lower valuation is fairly general, with their 'own' cluster not excepted. An explanation could be that in most American cities, unlike in Europe and Asia, the stock exchanges have lost much of their power or have already gone under as the result of a powerful trend towards concentration at a single location.

Looking at the four factors together, it can be stated that Sassen's theory is largely supported by those directly involved, namely the clusters Multinationals and Finance and Corporate Services. Other clusters have somewhat more varied opinions, while the two cultural clusters clearly value them the least. This does not diminish the fact that the first two competitive factors are of the highest significance and should always form part of an analysis of the international competitive position of a city. However, they do make a very limited group. It is therefore recommended that, at a minimum, the Global 1000 of BusinessWeek should be taken as a starting point. Moreover, it would be worthwhile including the continental or regional headquarters, although there are practical objections to this. This will be discussed further in part III.

CLUSTER: PHYSICAL INFRASTRUCTURE (Figure II.8)
In the palette of competitive factors for cities, Sassen does not gives a special place to the physical infrastructure. She has gained fewer followers on this point; most authors add it to their list of relevant competitive factors. Unfortunately a number limit themselves to this not very operational concept and do not go deeper into which parts of the physical infrastructure are relevant in this context. However, there are enough authors who do go further, and they seem to have a reasonably good nose for what is important.

Publications about airports clearly dominate. They cover in particular the economic significance for city and country, whether they are comparative analyses of weaknesses–strengths, or an attempt at a ranking order of cities or a typology of intercity relations. The magnetic attraction for foreign enterprises is the subject

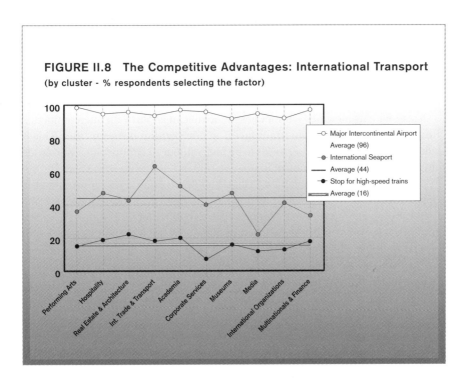

FIGURE II.8   The Competitive Advantages: International Transport
(by cluster - % respondents selecting the factor)

of just as many studies; these come somewhat closer to the aims of this research. An analysis of an airport as a factor in the integral international competitive position of a city is, however, not encountered anywhere.

From the literature it can be seen that seaports are distancing themselves from cities, also in metaphorical terms. When publications do appear on seaports in relation to the city they are now usually on the reallocation of disused docks to other municipal purposes.

These days, mountain climbers can phone home to announce that they have reached the summit of Mount Everest, passengers can send e-mails from their airplane seats, and 'explorers' can keep an eye on their stocks and shares while canoeing on the Amazon: facilities for telecommunication are taken for granted. Admittedly the capacity (glass fiber, broadband) and the costs (cable or satellite) continue to play a role, especially where establishing a new business is concerned, but telecommunication has pretty much disappeared from the literature as a general competitive factor. Publications on this have an increasingly sociological focus.

In her book 'Global Cities' Sassen describes, amongst other things, how Toronto and Sydney have achieved a prominent place on the world stage at the cost of, respectively, Montreal and Melbourne. The structural shift from industrial production to office headquarters and service industries is supposed to be the cause. Looking at the results of this questionnaire, the question arises of why precisely these cities have benefited from this shift? What role has the presence of an airport with worldwide connections played in this? It is probably a chicken-and-egg question, as one naturally influences the other. The unavoidable choice of a home carrier to concentrate its intercontinental connections at one airport in its home country is perhaps decisive. It deserves, in any case, further (historical) analysis, as all respondents indicated without hesitation that an airport with intercontinental connections is the most important factor in competition between cities. This is undeniable and nothing further needs to be said; without an airport with a worldwide network, a city simply cannot keep up.

The ports of Genoa, Venice, Lisbon and Amsterdam once represented the supremacy of their nations. That position has now been taken over by airports. The significance of an international seaport as a competitive factor is subject to varied opinions. It is even one of the two factors that could not maintain its position in the first division. This does not mean, let it be repeated, that the ports of New York or Tokyo are not important to these cities. At most it shows that they are not decisive in determining their international competitive position. For cities such as Hong Kong and Singapore it is probably somewhat different. It is then not surprising that this factor was generally more highly valued in Asian countries.

With the third element, a stop for high-speed trains, the differences in the valuations between the continents are again noteworthy. On average this factor scored low. However, once again, it must not be concluded that a high-speed train service is not important. A city in which this train does not stop feels passed by, literally and figuratively: apparently it is not considered important enough, internationally, to deserve a stop. This is the feeling in Europe in any case (it was seldom highlighted elsewhere), which is understandable as it is only in Europe that such a train connection is seen as being international. In Japan, the cradle of the high-speed trains, it is a national service, and in other countries, if it ever becomes a feature, it will not be much different. With hindsight, this could perhaps have been a reason not to include this factor. On the other hand, the shift method should sort out such 'mistakes,' as has been demonstrated once again.

In drafting a competitiveness analysis for cities, priority will therefore have to be given to the position of the airport and, if present, the home carrier. An international seaport is much less integrated with the city as a whole and does not necessarily have to form part of such an analysis. A stop for high-speed trains is only relevant for a competitiveness analysis at continental level and then only in Europe.

CLUSTER: CULTURAL FACILITIES (Figure II.9)

The cultural aspects of a city, such as symphony orchestras, opera and ballet companies, festivals and museums, are heavily underestimated in the literature on competitive factors for cities, you could almost claim they are ignored. Of course, museums and the performing arts are mentioned, but usually as part of an 'et cetera' or under 'quality of life.' No further study has been made of their real importance as a competitive factor, nor are there any ranking lists – apart

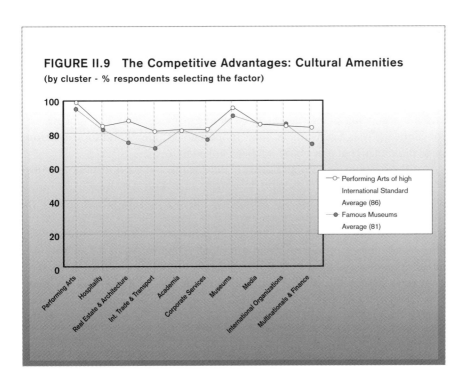

FIGURE II.9   The Competitive Advantages: Cultural Amenities
(by cluster - % respondents selecting the factor)

from overviews of the visitor totals for museums. This will not be the case much longer, as this subject has not been neglected in other literature. Back in 1988 a congress in Amsterdam concluded that culture, in its more limited definition, is one of the few ways that remain through which a big city can attract attention to itself. In the meantime it has been the focus of publications as a source of employment and economic growth, as part of the tourist product, as a means to revitalize a city or city neighborhoods and as an instrument for city marketing. "Cities: investing in culture is simply good business" was BusinessWeek's headline on 5 March 2001. It seems that city governments – in New York and Singapore for instance – are becoming increasingly aware that the 'Arts' are not one-dimensional.

There is even more good news for museums and the performing arts: both the Performing Arts and Museums are among the most important factors that determine the competitive profile of a city. With (average) scores of 86% for the performing arts and 81% for museums, the 'citymakers' have left no doubt about that. Admittedly they contributed heavily themselves by giving their own disciplines especially high scores, but the other clusters share that opinion, albeit at a slightly more modest level. It is therefore certain that in any study of the international competitive position of a city, the cultural aspects cannot be left out. From this moment on, the literature can no longer ignore cultural facilities as a competitive factor.

99

CLUSTER: ACADEMIA (Figure II.10)

The academic world also falls among the 'et cetera' in the literature; identified as a factor, but not recognized or valued. However, outside of this, it is the subject of other comparative studies. Annual ranking lists of universities, MBA courses and business schools are commonplace, especially in North America, and are a growing phenomenon in Western Europe as well. The ranking lists function largely as a consumers' guide for potential students and sources of funding; ranking lists of cities have not been linked to them.

Publications on the significance of universities and the research performed within them are mostly focused on the transfer of technical knowledge. Many an author has pointed out that expenditure on research and development delivers the greatest economic and social return within large conurbations. That is where the economic clusters are located, that is where networks can be constructed. This effect is even more important than the 'normal' economic input that a university already provides as a source of employment. These publications limit themselves in general, however, to the relationship between the university and the (high) technology industry in a city. This is only a (limited) part of the entire city's activities. The function of universities within a city network as a whole has been underexposed.

With a score of 85% the universities are placed, in a manner of speaking, at the top of the class. This score is relatively stable for all ten separate clusters.

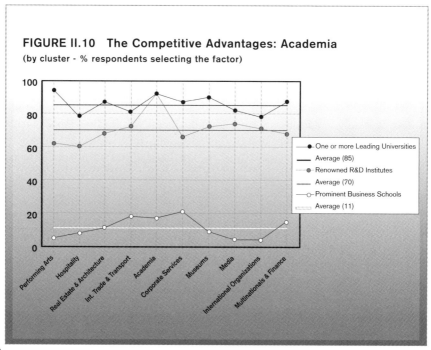

FIGURE II.10   The Competitive Advantages: Academia
(by cluster - % respondents selecting the factor)

With regard to the continents, North America values universities even more (90%) as a competitive factor; Asia, however, a little less, with 77%.

With this substantial high valuation, it can be concluded that universities, as a conglomeration of education, study and research, are considered more significant as a competitive factor than Research and Development as such. However much a city may pride itself on its prominent business school or management course, as competitive factors these remain stuck in the lower regions. This opinion is shared even in the cradle of such endeavors, North America.

The quality of the university or universities is a concrete part of the international competitive position of a city and must not be ignored in any analysis of competitiveness. The important factor Research & Development would appear to be covered sufficiently in such an analysis if, for universities, a special emphasis is placed on pure and applied research, and on the (international) networks to which the various academic disciplines belong.

CLUSTER: HOSPITALITY (Figures II. 11 and 11')

All the out-of-towners who visit a city are guests. They may be daytrippers just passing through, or overnighters who stay a little longer. The latter are of different kinds: visitors attending a congress, seminar or exhibition, visiting a company or coming for a business meeting, and of course the holiday-maker, the tourist. They all bring money into the city, some more than others, depending on

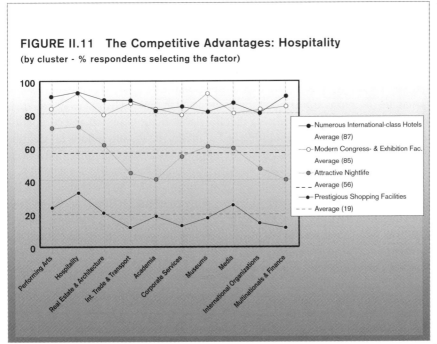

FIGURE II.11   The Competitive Advantages: Hospitality
(by cluster - % respondents selecting the factor)

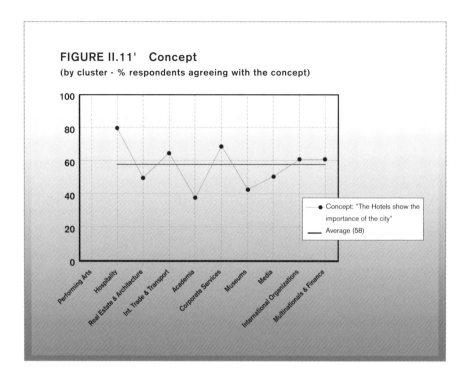

FIGURE II.11' Concept
(by cluster - % respondents agreeing with the concept)

Concept: "The Hotels show the importance of the city"
Average (58)

the transport they use, the hotels they stay in, and their pattern of expenditure. Small wonder then that plenty of literature can be found on the importance of visitors to the economy of the city. Everyone knows that this is a branch of industry with a great potential for growth. It is also common knowledge that, in the hotel world (as the result of international chains), new demand is created for a large part by the supply. It is a pure product of globalization. Various ranking lists of hotels are produced annually, on the basis of which ranking lists of cities can then be made. It is therefore surprising that hotels are not mentioned as a competitive factor in the literature. Shopping and nightlife, the top attractions for visitors, are encountered equally rarely in the literature, with a few exceptions. Conversely, congress facilities are often mentioned, as are the museums discussed earlier.

Hotels and congress facilities appear to be part of the package of facilities that a city must have in order to keep up internationally. Hotels score, in fact, even higher in the top group. All clusters agree on this to roughly the same degree. However, the 'citymakers' do not allow their judgement on a city to depend entirely on its hotels. This can be deduced from the response to the concept in question 3 of the questionnaire which read: 'the hotels show the importance of the city.' Half of the respondents did not agree, with a notable exception: those from the cluster itself. Of these, 80% support the concept (Figure II. 11'). The results for the various continents do not deviate markedly from the average and are therefore not included in the Figure. The concept had not yet been included in the questionnaires sent to the first two clusters, and there are therefore no results for these.

In addition to congresses, business meetings and the tourist sights, visitors to a city also seek out the shops and the nightlife. Enough reasons, therefore, to include these two less dominant factors in the same Figure. The relatively high score for nightlife is noteworthy. It can be confessed now that there was, in fact, no objective reason at all to place this factor in the first division originally. This was done only to make it easier for the respondents to choose five factors to downgrade. It turned out to be a poor prediction: with 56% this factor is a respectable middle-grouper. The score from the separate clusters, however, varies between 40 and 72%. It is not very surprising that the latter comes from the Hospitality cluster itself. The opinion from the continents, by contrast, varies little.

Shopping, as a factor, remained in the lower regions. It should be emphasized once more that this does not mean it is not an important factor. This will be shown again when we discuss the significance of the city center for the image of a city. Shopping is almost always an essential part of the city center.

In any case, hotels and congress facilities cannot be ignored in a competitiveness analysis of cities. The factors nightlife and shopping can be treated more optionally, but their importance should not be underestimated.

OTHER CLUSTERS (Figures II.12 and 12')

Seven clusters and a number of related factors have been addressed in the preceding sections. The results for the three remaining clusters are collected together in Figure II.12. A middle score can be observed for International Organizations, with two conspicuous deviations upwards: the votes from Academia and of course from the cluster itself. As the latter can be explained, the picture appears to be relatively stable. The PL index of 64%, however, indicates that there was no clear consensus among the respondents, which matches the impression from the literature. International organizations have been named as a competitive factor in four cases; other literature on this has not been encountered.

The Media score of 26% keeps them just in the middle group. There is much greater consensus on this. The score from the Performing Arts, their own score and that from the Multinationals/Finance deviate notably from the average. The modest attention that the media have been given in the literature as a competitive factor is somewhat justified. An image determinant is therefore quite different to an image maker).

The media are certainly the latter for cities. Two concepts were included in the questionnaire on that point.

• The first read: 'It is important for a city to be in the news.'

• The second referred especially to city marketing and was formulated as follows: 'The best way to promote a city internationally is to gain publicity in the media.'

In Figure II.12' the responses are summarized. For both concepts there is

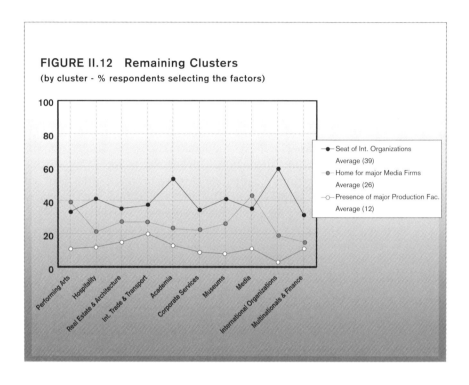

FIGURE II.12   Remaining Clusters
(by cluster - % respondents selecting the factors)

Legend:
- Seat of Int. Organizations — Average (39)
- Home for major Media Firms — Average (26)
- Presence of major Production Fac. — Average (12)

Clusters (x-axis): Performing Arts, Hospitality, Real Estate & Architecture, Int. Trade & Transport, Academia, Corporate Services, Museums, Media, International Organizations, Multinationals & Finance

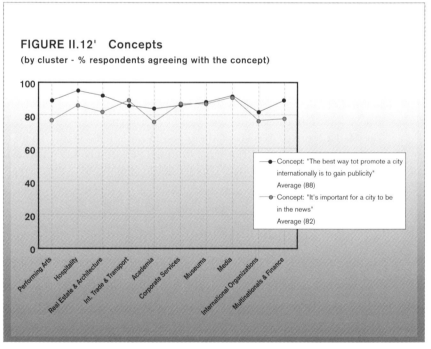

FIGURE II.12'   Concepts
(by cluster - % respondents agreeing with the concept)

Legend:
- Concept: "The best way tot promote a city internationally is to gain publicity" — Average (88)
- Concept: "It's important for a city to be in the news" — Average (82)

Clusters (x-axis): Performing Arts, Hospitality, Real Estate & Architecture, Int. Trade & Transport, Academia, Corporate Services, Museums, Media, International Organizations, Multinationals & Finance

notable consensus, which is also confirmed by the high PL indexes of, respectively, 87% and 91%. But how do you get the required publicity? That is a question which preoccupies many city leaders. Perhaps the greatest wisdom lies with the media themselves. They are all too familiar with the slogan 'The news is where the journalists are. Replace in this context 'journalist' with 'foreign correspondent' and the city leaders have pretty much got the answer to their question.

The respondents are quite unanimous in their judgement that the presence of major production facilities or factories as a competitive factor is an outdated notion. They thus confirm what has been recognized in the literature for some time. In practice this low score as a competitive factor is counterbalanced by its very high valuation as a source of local employment. This demonstrates how important it is to separate clearly these two judgements.

None of these three clusters can be considered as essential to the international competitive position of a city. However, in an analysis that goes further than the strict minimum of factors, a place should certainly be given to the cluster International Organizations.

II.5.5 THE RESULTS FOR THE DETERMINANT: THE HUMAN FACTOR
(Figures II.13 and 13')

In the 'City Diamond' (Figure II.3) four competitive factors are grouped in the determinant Humanities. The questionnaire has delivered interesting results for all four, which are briefly presented below.

Cities have always been magnets for people who want to make a living or practice their profession; from the least educated laborer to the most specialized professional. A phenomenon that has been described and analysed frequently in economic, geographical and sociological literature. The presence of a labor force is also mentioned as a competitive factor in much of the literature. The questionnaire confirmed the great importance of this, at least for a specific segment of the labor market: the highly skilled. With an average score of 89% it is certain that this factor must be included in any analysis of competitiveness.

Despite the focus on the highly skilled, it would not be easy to operationalize this factor in a study. The various trendsetters within the clusters will all have their own ideas on this. To give a few examples: a legal practice will consider potential lawyers, a hotel manager will think about potential floor-managers but also about chefs, while the management of a symphony orchestra will focus on experienced violinists. There are, therefore, many specializations. All research on this point will, however, end up analyzing the opportunities for training and the use made of those.

The next factor is probably more interesting: 'open to an international world.' This factor is seldom mentioned in the literature on competitive factors. Although everyone can imagine what it means, the description chosen is not very

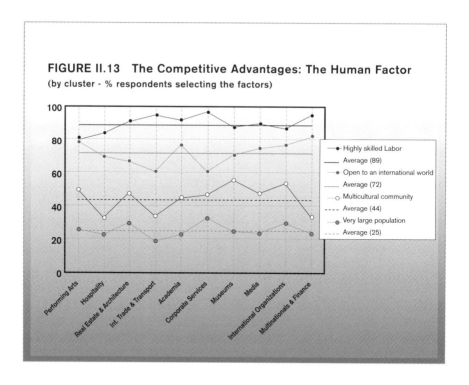

FIGURE II.13   The Competitive Advantages: The Human Factor
(by cluster - % respondents selecting the factors)

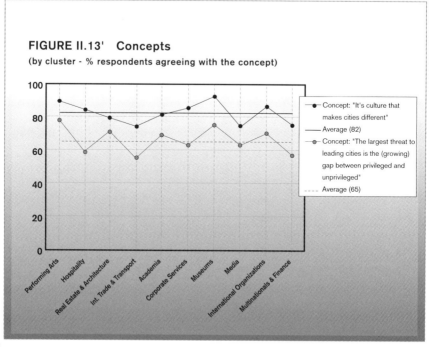

FIGURE II.13'   Concepts
(by cluster - % respondents agreeing with the concept)

operational. As explained earlier, it stands for openness to people and products from other countries and cultures. Foreigners have to be able to feel a bit at home in a city. This starts with understanding and support and is most powerful when people can communicate with one another. It also has to do with the cosmopolitan character of a city.

The results of the questionnaire mean not only that this factor should be a standard part of competitiveness analyses, but also that the literature needs to take a serious look at it, for example by operationalizing this concept. With an average score of 72% it is almost in the top group. This is even more significant as the factor was originally included in the second division and therefore had to, in a manner of speaking, climb up on its own. The scores per cluster vary from 10% above to 10% below the average. The four non-profit clusters all give scores above the average.

The required operationalization of the concept needs to provide a (limited) number of elements against which it can be tested. The national picture, even though that can differ not insignificantly from the city in question, will certainly have to be included.

A third factor is the 'multicultural community.' Again an element that is seldom encountered in the literature as a competitive factor. Only one author describes it as a "demographic indicator of world city status." The reason for this is presumably not the fact that it too is not very operational, as this is not normally considered an obstacle in this field. Perhaps the ambivalence of the factor plays a role. On the one hand, a multicultural community can be seen as an enrichment, on the other hand it can also be associated with less positive feelings. It is therefore all the more noteworthy that almost half of the respondents indicated this factor to be dominant for the international competitive position of a city. It is of less importance whether or not it should be interpreted as an enriching factor or as a factor – like public safety – that needs to be properly managed. Not surprisingly, the scores from the various clusters vary widely. From the continents the scores vary without any discernable pattern. This has, of course, consequences for the PL index, but for a middle group score it is not exceptional.

Two concepts related to this subject were included in the questionnaire. It can be seen that the respondents recognize the positive aspects of a multicultural society from their response to the concept 'It's culture that makes cities different,' as 82% agreed with this. North America and Asia gave scores of, respectively, 5% and 7% above this average. In addition, 65% are conscious of the threats posed by large differences in income, education and opportunity, through which minority groups are generally disadvantaged, as they endorse the concept that the largest threat to leading cities is the (growing) gap between the privileged and under-privileged. On this, the opinions from the various continents are pretty much the same (Figure II.13').

It is hoped that the above will mean that 'multiculturality' will lose its ano-nymity as a competitive factor and will become a structural part of competitiveness analyses for cities with a multiethnic population. And can you think of a city that does not have that? Further study is, however, required in order to map the most relevant elements of this factor. The results of this questionnaire only scratch the surface.

The factor 'very large population' can also be viewed both positively and negatively. A high number of residents does provide a broad support basis for large numbers of facilities. However, the respondents were apparently thinking more about the fact that in some parts of the world people live in enormous sprawling cities without sufficient means for existence, resulting in dreadful living conditions. For three-quarters of the respondents this factor did not belong in the group of most important competitive factors. No obvious differences can be seen among the responses from the clusters or the continents. If one thought that the positive side of a large population might be endorsed more in the western continents, then this is observed only for North America; there, taken as a whole, the factor was awarded eight percentage points more than the average score.

It could therefore be concluded that a 'leading city' does not have to have millions of residents. However, this would not recognize the fact that a large population strengthens the support basis for many facilities and initiatives. Improvements in the standard of living appear to determine the moment at which the balance shifts to the positive side.

Population size has enjoyed much attention as a factor in the literature, including its role in relation to competitive position. In the light of what has been established above, other characteristics of the city community may deserve this more.

II.5.6 THE RESULTS FOR THE DETERMINANT: INTERNATIONAL PROFILE (Figures II.14A, 14B, 14' and 14")

This is the name of the determinant that was constructed in the previous section from five competitive factors that had been included in the questionnaire. These were (positive) International Performance, It Happens There!, Mega Events, Sportlife (of high international standard) and (impressive) Skyline. In addition, four concepts relating to the international profile of the city had been included in the questionnaire, with the aim of learning more about some of the factors mentioned.

The first two factors in particular, International Performance and It Happens there!, are not very operational. Everyone can imagine what they mean, but that is not a guarantee that all those subjective interpretations can be brought together in one explanation and made objective. Before continuing it is necessary to establish how highly the respondents valued these concept packages. Very highly! (Figure II.14A) The factor International Performance in particular, with an average score of 91% and a second place up in the top group. The opinions on this, as shown by the exceptionally high PL index (90%), are close to unanimous.

The score for the factor 'It happens there!' is admittedly a little lower, but at 78% is still among the top group. The opinions per cluster are somewhat more diverse (PL index 76%), but do not exceed a ten percentage point difference with the average. It is a similar picture for the continents.

Such high scores indicate that both factors should be included in analyses of city competitiveness. They cannot be found in the existing literature, not even under a different definition. To operationalize both concepts, a number of leads have been sought amongst not only the other competitive factors but also some of the concepts that were included in the questionnaire, with partial success.

No leads could be found amongst the factors Mega Events, Sportlife and Skyline. That may seem paradoxical; the first two embody entrepreneurship and courage, while an impressive skyline also represents a certain grandeur. However none of these factors was highly valued: they earned average scores of 9 to 23% with one significant deviation for Mega Events in the cluster Performing Arts (Figure II. 14B, page 110).

Apparently strength should not be sought primarily in large-scale events that are, by definition, incidental. This is in accordance with the literature on these factors. Independent publications do not encourage city governments to invest in this kind of activity; or at least not if a financial return on their investment is desired. There can, however, be other aims in mind, such as urban renewal, modernization of the infrastructure or boosting the morale of the population. The effect is then

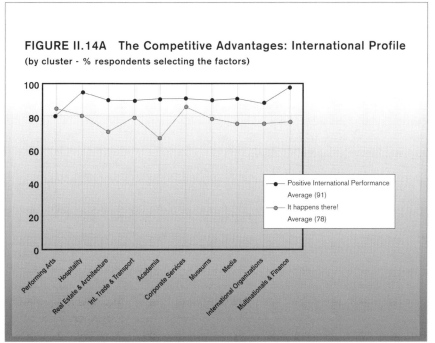

FIGURE II.14A   The Competitive Advantages: International Profile
(by cluster - % respondents selecting the factors)

■

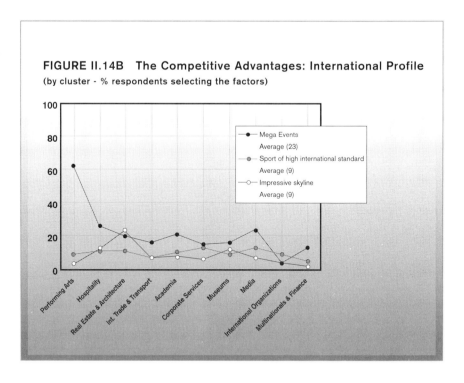

FIGURE II.14B   The Competitive Advantages: International Profile
(by cluster - % respondents selecting the factors)

rather difficult to measure. For New York, following the terrorist attacks of 11 September 2001, it is perhaps a small consolation that a skyline, however impressive it may be, does not greatly influence the competitive power of a city.

More important than the occasional spectacular project is the attention that a city regularly receives in the media. This has already been established in the discussion of the results for the cluster Media. In Figure 12' the positive agreements to the two concepts are shown graphically. First, it appears to be very important that a city is in the news. Around 80% of the respondents shared this opinion. It does, however, have to be positive or at least neutral news; only 15% found that the content of the news did not matter.

The second concept is admittedly connected to the marketing of the city, but just as clearly connected to the first. Almost 90% agreed that obtaining free publicity in the media is the best way to promote a city internationally.

Another lead can be found in two other concepts (Figures II.14' and 14"). The first says that the label 'leading city' gives prestige to a city and gives it a competitive advantage. This concept is a solid foundation for the part of the research that aims to select a group of 20 to 25 cities with this qualification. The 'citymakers' convincingly (89%) indicated that they do find such a label very important. In part III it will be reported which cities, in their opinion, fall into this category. The endorsement of this concept is so convincing that this qualification can be taken as a factor to be included in an analysis of international competitiveness.

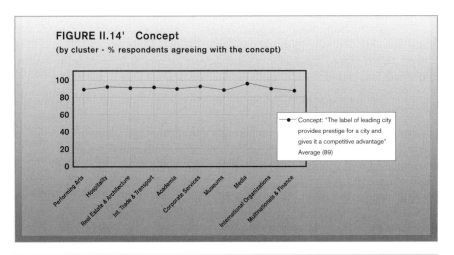

FIGURE II.14' Concept
(by cluster - % respondents agreeing with the concept)

Concept: "The label of leading city provides prestige for a city and gives it a competitive advantage"
Average (89)

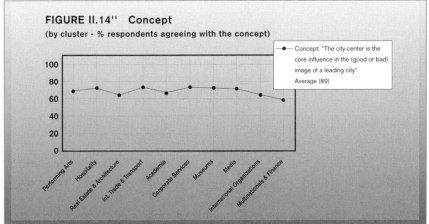

FIGURE II.14'' Concept
(by cluster - % respondents agreeing with the concept)

Concept: "The city center is the core influence in the (good or bad) image of a leading city"
Average (69)

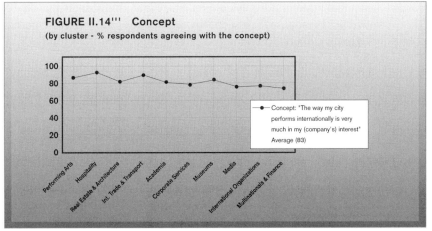

FIGURE II.14''' Concept
(by cluster - % respondents agreeing with the concept)

Concept: "The way my city performs internationally is very much in my (company's) interest"
Average (83)

From the response to the other concept it appears that the city center also has a real impact on the (good or bad) image of the city as a whole. Almost 70% agreed. This response is in line with expectations, because if 'it happens' anywhere, it tends to happen in the heart of the city. The clusters show great consensus in their opinions; the continents, however, show clear differences. Europe and North America, with, respectively, 74% and 78%, are above the average, while Asia and the other continents, with 60% and 55%, respectively, are substantially below it. This appears to be a structural difference in appreciation of the importance of the inner city. Despite this diverse appreciation, the support for it is sufficiently convincing that including the quality of the city center in an analysis of the competitiveness of cities deserves recommendation. With further operationalization of this factor, less significant factors such as shopping and nightlife can also be included in an analysis of competitiveness.

This section on the International Profile can be briefly summarized as follows. In the light of the results of the survey, and the fact that a number of factors were not formulated sufficiently operationally in the first instance, it is necessary to adjust significantly the determinant International Profile, or at least the factors that belong to it. The introduction of the factor 'Media Coverage' is aimed at making the very important factors 'International Performance' and 'It happens there' easier to handle in an analysis of competitiveness. Without going into more detail here, media coverage can be divided into integral and professionally oriented publicity. In part III, which will cover the ranking of cities, a number of examples of this are included.

In addition, two new factors make their debut: the position as leading city and the quality of the city center. Both come from the responses to the relevant concepts. The latter in particular will need to be further operationalized before it can be included in an analysis of competitiveness.

In this connection, the following is also of interest. The 'citymakers' find a positive international image not only important for the city but also for themselves. This is shown in the response to the concept 'the way 'my city' performs internationally is very much in my (company's) interest.' Around 83% of the respondents agreed (Figure II.14''', page 111). A city government therefore has a large number of potential partners when it comes to improving a city's international profile. There are differences per cluster, although not particularly large ones. It is not surprising that the cluster Hospitality gives the highest score with 94%; visitors, especially non-business ones, are naturally sensitive to image. It is equally unsurprising that the cluster Multinationals & Finance gives the lowest score of 75%. It is perhaps more surprising that the score was not even lower. Take, for instance, Coca Cola in Atlanta, Heineken in Amsterdam, or Woolworths in Sydney; their business success does not seem be directly related to the condition or international profile of the city. Perhaps a feeling of 'corporate citizenship' has played a role in this valuation.

II.5.7 THE RESULTS FOR THE DETERMINANT: CITY GOVERNANCE
(Figure II.15)

The literature on competitive factors, whether or not it covers these in relation to the ranking of cities, is not generous with factors that lie within the sphere of influence of city authorities. This is explicable, when one remembers that many of the publications in this field were initiated in North America. Porter, who originally (1990) also saw no important role for government, went back on this later (1998) by emphasizing the influence that governments, be it not exclusive, can have on the creation of clusters and networks. This role can be summarized under the fairly general term Political Leadership. However, it is Van Den Berg et al. in particular who have repeatedly brought forward the importance of this factor in their publications. For them it is a collective term for a number of characteristics, such as vision, strategy, creation and maintenance of networks, supervision of processes and organizational investment, which the city leaders – and those are certainly not only the politicians – must have at their disposal in order to keep up with the international competition. It could be an important competitive advantage for a city to have, in the first place, a mayor, plus captains of industry and other leaders, who can generate widespread political or social support, mobilize the business sector, combine the forces of originally opposed (political) trends within a conurbation, and obtain political support from higher

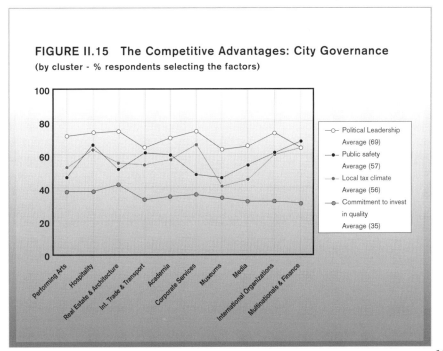

FIGURE II.15   The Competitive Advantages: City Governance
(by cluster - % respondents selecting the factors)

—○— Political Leadership
       Average (69)
—●— Public safety
       Average (57)
—●— Local tax climate
       Average (56)
—●— Commitment to invest
       in quality
       Average (35)

113

authorities. The results of the questionnaire endorse this. With almost 70% Political Leadership scores highly in the middle group.

To decide whether or not this score means that this factor should be part of a competitiveness analysis, the following should be considered. Both Porter and Van Den Berg et al. place great responsibility on the leaders (political and non-political) of a city for creating all kinds of relationships and interconnections between companies, institutions and the city government. In this way the leaders are responsible for an essential element in the competitive profile of a city. Again, it should be noted that while leadership may often be personified in the mayor, it is not limited to politics. The ambition and quality with which interest groups also work towards the development of their city should be included here. When this extra dimension of leadership is taken into consideration, the only possible conclusion is that this factor should be a structural part of an analysis of international competitiveness. That this means that one's own functioning would be subjected to a critical evaluation is merely a piquant matter of secondary importance.

Public safety is actually a basic condition that does not belong in this collection of specific competitive factors, and this is may be the reason why it is seldom mentioned in the literature on competitive factors. As explained earlier, this factor was nonetheless included because a basic condition could be a competitive advantage for a city when most other cities do not succeed in meeting it. From the average score of 57% it can be deduced that the opinions on this vary. There can be no doubt that the respondents find public safety to be extremely important; who doesn't? However, to what extent does that make it a factor, in their eyes, in being able to compete successfully? Not only the score but also the PL index shows that the opinions on this factor are very diverse. With this lack of clarity, further research seems to be required before this factor is included as a structural part of a competitiveness analysis.

The literature is ambivalent with regard to the local tax climate. On the one hand, much has been published on the effect of tax breaks on, for example, attracting new business, but it is not seen as a factor that influences, in an integral way, the international competitive position of a city. The results of the questionnaire on this point were equally ambivalent. It is a respectable middle-grouper without any noteworthy differences among the various clusters and occasional large differences between the continents. There is no solid indication from either this questionnaire or the literature that this is a factor that has to be included structurally in a competitiveness analysis of cities. It would appear to be more deserving of attention with regard to those specific questions which are clearly connected to it, such as the effect on visitors' overnight stays or the relocation of businesses.

Even less convincing is the response to the factor 'commitment to invest in quality.' With hindsight, it begs the question: what is quality in this context and

114

is such a commitment not self-evident? In other words, this factor was not for-mulated operationally and is in fact a basic factor. Interpreted in this way, the response is then convincing: it is very important, but not a factor that delivers a special competitive advantage to a city.

II.5.8 OTHER FACTORS   (Figure II. 16)

Two factors from the questionnaire have not yet been discussed: 'Large and richly varied network' and 'seat of the national government.'

With regard to the seat of the national government, the literature (which scarcely mentions this factor) is completely endorsed: the presence of the seat of the national government does not give a city any special advantage in interna-tional competition. Seven clusters are close to unanimous on this. With 12% the score is low and on average the different continents give pretty much the same score. The differences between the continents in the separate clusters are quite wide, however. Therefore the PL index (64%) is not especially high. The three clusters approached first were not included in the count as the formulation of the question had been changed in the meantime.

Perhaps this factor is the best example of the statement at the beginning of this section, that there are no unimportant factors. What would remain of

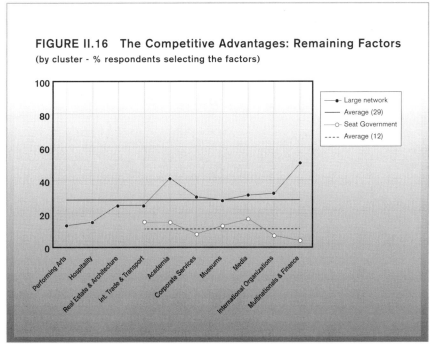

FIGURE II.16   The Competitive Advantages: Remaining Factors
(by cluster - % respondents selecting the factors)

Washington if the center of government moved? How will Berlin develop now that the federal government is located there? It is clear that Bonn is already old news; but before that it was no leading city. Has the significance of Rio de Janeiro, in an international context, changed since the government moved to Brasilia? More questions than answers on this point. Only the opinion of the 'citymakers' is certain.

The situation is different for the factor Network. In the first place it is not a particularly operational concept for relations and interconnections between all sorts of parties. In addition it is a concept that, as such, is fairly new, but this does not mean that the activities it covers are also new. It is quite common for activities to be undertaken on the basis of intuition and common sense at the time, and only later that an underlying strategy is discovered and defined. This seems to be the case for the formation of clusters and networks. It cannot then be ruled out that 'citymakers' did not associate this concept with what they have been doing in their daily lives for a long time, both within and outside their cluster.

From the response there appears to be a large discrepancy between theory (the literature) and practice. The average score of 29% relates poorly to what Porter would call "a fundamental role" (pp. 329). There are, however, two interesting exceptions: 44% from Academia and 62% from the Multinationals & Finance. Although the PL index for the cluster as a whole is fairly high, the PL indexes for the exceptions (55% and 50%, respectively) mean that one has to be a little cautious in drawing conclusions. At most, it can be said that these two clusters are more able to form a clear idea of what the concept 'network' means.

What can then be done with this discrepancy? The inclination is to choose the side of the literature. The analyses of Porter on this point are so sharp and based on practice that they cannot be ignored. The concept, the phenomenon, does not yet seem to be sufficiently familiar to the target group; in other words, it is difficult for 'citymakers' to imagine exactly what is meant. Perhaps it was too early to include the factor as such in the questionnaire, and the formulation could probably also have been improved.

What does this mean for the role that this factor could or should play in the drafting and use of a competitiveness analysis for cities? A solution could be the following. It was explained above that there is a close relationship between the functioning of city governments and the construction, maintenance and expansion of networks. This provides an extra argument to regard the factor Leadership as an essential factor in the competitiveness model for cities, particularly when structural changes need to be set in motion. An important part of the quality assessment attached to this will be the degree of success in bringing together more and less like-minded parties behind a common goal: strengthening the international competitive position of the city as a whole or in part.

* * *

II. 6 THE INGREDIENTS FOR ANALYZING A CITY'S COMPETITIVENESS

In the previous section, the perceptions of 'citymakers' were reported with regard to the competitive advantages of cities as listed in the questionnaire. Using the scores per factor and a number of concepts, plus the role given to them in the literature, a number of factors were selected that can be considered to be of overriding importance to the international competitive position of a prominent, international city – of a 'leading city.' These factors should form a standard part of any integral analysis of international competitiveness. Below they are briefly summarized once more, per determinant.

In the determinant CLUSTERS, six remained as fundamental. It would appear that a functional ranking order of cities for each of these clusters can best be based on the perceptions of professionals. Quantitative ranking lists can also be made, but, for the sake of comparability, strict and (especially) relevant criteria must be drawn up that do justice to the quality (international prominence), quantity (number, size, turnover) and coherence of the activities addressed. The 'Fortune 500' list is, in this context, too limited for Multinationals, and for the cluster Finance it means looking at more than the hundred largest banks or the number of enterprises listed on the stock exchange. An international standard for universities and museums, not to mention the performing arts, has not yet been invented either. The data for comparing cities on the basis of their hotels do not always seem to have been equally objectively collected and those for congresses even contradict one another. So far the statistics for air traffic and airports seem to be the best sources, provided that the relevant data are selected. In short, most data contain many "dirty little secrets" (Short J.R. 1996); research into perceptions is by far to be preferred. In part III this will be examined further.

The determinant INTERNATIONAL PROFILE contains three factors that are crucial for the international competitive position of a city: media coverage, the image of the city center and the qualification 'leading city.' These arose from the responses to the factors 'international performance,' 'it happens there' and four concepts.

For the factor 'leading city,' as for most clusters, worldwide perception-research is required. Internationally oriented people, such as the 'citymakers,' are willing and able to make a judgement on a city as a whole even if they do not know the city from personal experience; for a city center it appears to be more difficult. Adjusted perception-research would need to be developed for this. However, the degree to which a city is profiled in the media (media coverage) does not appear to be measurable through perceptions. This can be done better on the basis of observations. The demand for (international) comparability means the media must be very carefully selected, especially when it involves 'free' (in other words, not paid for) publicity.

117

■

Figure II.17

THE STANDARD FOR INTERNATIONAL CITY COMPETITIVENESS

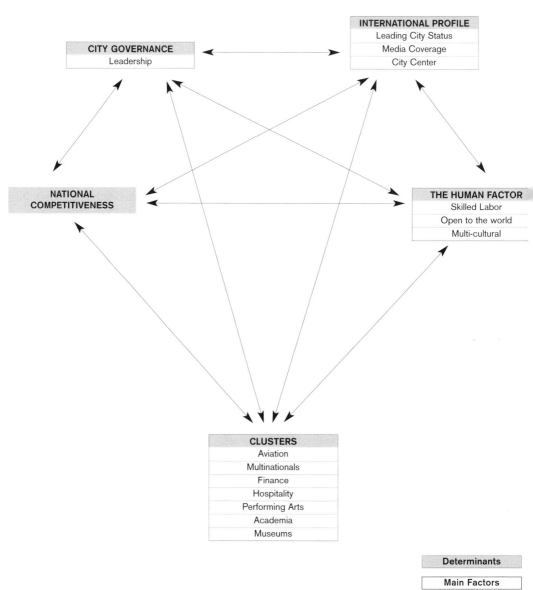

For the three factors in the determinant THE HUMAN FACTOR the research still needs to be developed. For perception-research this would seem to be least complicated for the factor 'skilled labor.' For the factors 'open to the world' and 'multicultural' any form of comparative research would seem to be experimental for the time being, whether it is qualitative, quantitative, or a bit of both. It is hoped that this challenge will be taken up within the academic world or elsewhere. In anticipation of this, the factor 'multicultural' will perhaps have to be put between parentheses as a standard part of a competitiveness analysis. For the factor 'open to the world' preliminary use could be made of the annual World Competitiveness Yearbook. Admittedly this gives a value on a national basis, but it is at least an indication. The same applies to 'skilled labor,' while there are no alternatives available that are based on perception.

For the determinant CITY GOVERNANCE only the factor 'leadership' remained. In this context leadership involves predominantly the power to develop and maintain networks. City governments have an initiating but not exclusive role in this. For this reason the original adjective 'political' has been left out. This factor can only be assessed qualitatively and then only by people who are in contact with this form of leadership or dependent upon it. When conducting perception-research among 'citymakers' for other factors, it is fairly easy to include a valuation of this leadership.

NATIONAL COMPETITIVE POWER is the fifth and last determinant. In section II.3.2 it was already established that this must be included in a competitiveness model for cities. It is also a given fact, because it cannot be influenced directly by the city. The influence of it on the other determinants is, however, high. When putting together an analysis for cities, a choice can be made from a couple of annual reports that are published on this subject.

Using the above, the 'city diamond' of section II.3 can now be further fine-tuned. In Figure II.17 the factors have been included that are of overriding significance to the international competitive position of a city. The factors that have been left out do not have such an impact or to a much lesser degree. In other words, the international competitive position of a city is not structurally influenced by them. This does not mean that they can be neglected, are not worthy of investment, need less attention or should not be periodically analysed. The model being constructed here is a standard or minimum one. It can be extended with other factors, as desired. However, the more factors that are included, the less operational it becomes.

A competitiveness model for cities à la Porter may have been the aim, but it must also be operational! For this, it is necessary to be able to put a value to the

■

factors in the standard model in an accountable way. The results from the research on the ranking of cities, integrally and for the various functions, are needed for this. The next part (III) covers these results. After that, in the concluding part IV, the manageability of the model can be tested.

◆ ◆ ◆ ◆ ◆

PART III
WORLD CITY FORMATION

"Hierarchical classification is less and less satisfactory. Cities hierarchical
positions may be reversed according to the kind of function considered"

(Paul Knox, "World Cities in a World System", 1995, p. 9)

III. 1 INTRODUCTION

"There is an ongoing competitive struggle for position in the global network of capitalist cities"
(John Friedmann, 1995, p. 36)

Hardly a month goes by without yet another study being published by some business consultancy or academic in which the competitive position of a city or country can be viewed in comparison to other cities or countries. It usually concerns a single aspect, such as the cost of living, economic growth, price of real estate, the most expensive shopping streets, or public safety. Occasionally it covers a wider spectrum, such as the best city in which to establish your business or the quality of life. In some other cases certain business sectors are compared (such as banks, airports, hotels) that are associated with cities. Just as businesses have stock market quotations as their indicators of performance, cities have their rankings.

Where does this huge drive for comparisons, studies and publicity come from? A comparative study gives the subjects of the research – such as cities or airports – a chance to ascertain their own position, to develop policy based on it and – if the results allow – to use it to enhance their profile. Geographers and economists look for structural change processes in cities, and the systematics or typology through which these changes can be analysed. In addition, the academic world needs to profile itself, and city rankings are always good for publicity. This is also common knowledge for all kinds of commercial research foundations, advice bureaus and business magazines. If they can demonstrate their expertise in this area, then they have a useful marketing instrument to boot.

The desire for publicity is also an important driving force for the noncommercial sector. There is nothing wrong with this in principle, it only becomes a problem when it affects the quality. This might be due to the research or the publication itself or to the publicity around it. In part I a number of examples were given of academic publications in which the 'ends' (a ranking and the resulting publicity) seemed to have become more important than the 'means' (solid research). The basic material was incomplete and/or used exclusively quantitative data, such as the number of establishments. Academics have managed to skirt around this problem by presenting the rankings together with indications of their implicit uncertainties. However, surely they must have realized by now that such nuances tend to get lost in the subsequent publicity? Publications from the more commercial world do not have to be quite so careful, but they are in turn more difficult to check.

There are, therefore, certain reservations about the various kinds of 'city rankings,' but on the other hand we have to accept the inevitability of this phenomenon. Without any possibilities for comparison, there can be no analysis of competitiveness. If, for this reason, it is decided to attempt to rank and list cities both functionally and integrally, then these reservations make very high demands on the quality of the research. It must address (1) relevant competitive factors, (2) these should be based on an integral evaluation not only of the city as a whole but also of the separate functions and (3) the results must be extremely reliable and accountable.

1. From part II we know which competitive factors are relevant to the international competitive position of a city. In that part, for the first time, the factors that should be a standard part of any competitiveness analysis for cities were selected on the basis of research into professional perceptions. An analysis of the position of the airport must not be omitted, for instance, but a comparison on the basis of the presence of international organizations is not strictly necessary.

2. In order to ensure an integral evaluation, the research sought the perceptions of professionals who (could) influence the international competitive position of their city through their business or institution. The selection of this target group (the 'citymakers') was described in detail in part I. The questions were constructed in such a way as to obtain their opinions on the cities both as a whole (integral perception) and in relation to their own professional field (functional perception). The latter is important because a good number of ranking lists have appeared in which cities are compared on the basis of a single element, such as the cost of office space or the number of banks. Sufficient safeguards were included in the research to ensure that the opinion on this point also had an integral character – in other words that it was for the cluster as a whole – as the target group comprises the 'magnets' of the various clusters and there is more than one magnet per cluster. The thrust of the questions was, in addition, explicitly focused on the cluster as a whole (the financial world, for example) and not on one or more subsection (such as the banks or stock exchanges).

3.Thirdly, the results must be reliable; one must be able to conclude with reasonable certainty that they truly reflect the opinions of the target group. Any reservations tend to become blurred further down the road; therefore any uncertainties can better remain unpublished. In part I it was explained in detail that, in order to assess the reliability of the results, a Plausibility check was developed. For each result, as a whole or in detail, a so-called PL index can be calculated and checked; it indicates what percentage of the observations lies close to the average. PL indexes were also calculated for this part of the research and will be reported not only for the integral ranking (the 'leading cities') but also for the ten functional rankings (the 'top cities').

With all due respect to the opinions of the professionals, the merit of their insights still needs to be checked. In principle one can use previous research and publications for this. However, if there are reservations about the way in which the various ranking lists have been constructed (and no secret has been made of these reservations in the preceding paragraphs), then they can hardly be used as a check. They can, however, be placed alongside the results of the survey for comparison or as a frame of reference. Therefore, while bearing these limitations in mind, one or more frames of reference were sought for both the integral and functional ranking lists, regardless of their intrinsic worth. Previously published ranking lists were used, plus lists put together personally on the basis of available material. In addition, the Free Publicity Index (FP index) was developed, which deserves further explanation.

In part II, an overview was made of the competitive factors for cities, and it was established that the International Profile is one of the most important. With regard to professional perception, this profile takes shape in a number of ways. Personal experience and information from one's network play a large role in this. The same applies to 'free publicity'; the 'citymakers' have clearly indicated it is the most effective way to place a city in the spotlight.

In anticipation of this opinion, a record has been kept over the last few years of the number of times that a city has attracted attention with, for example, a photograph, headline, inclusion in a calendar of events or a feature, when leafing through the pages of a number of renowned professional periodicals with a worldwide circulation. The periodicals had to meet certain requirements with regard to content and design; they needed to be more like a magazine than a journal. Such publications could be found for only a limited number of clusters: Performing Arts, Hospitality, Real Estate & Architecture. 'Free publicity' was also used to seek a frame of reference for the integral perception. After a number of attempts with other magazines (Fortune and Forbes), Time Magazine proved to be the most suitable. Admittedly this 'global magazine' has three editions, but the European edition of an American magazine seemed a reasonable compromise.

The FP index is calculated in the following way. The city that attracts the most attention becomes the standard. For example, if New York attracts the most attention over the whole period, say 150 times in total, then its score, its FP index, is 100. If Paris attracts attention 100 times over the same period, then its FP index is 67. A ranking list can be made using these values.

Finally, it should be noted that almost all the periodicals concerned were published from London. The impression is that this leads to a certain local distortion, in this case in that city's favour. However, this is not as much of a problem as it would have been if the city concerned was somewhere in the middle of the spectrum. In addition, it is no coincidence that the publishing houses have chosen this location.

In the following sections the results of the survey will be reported for both the opinions on specific functions (the Top Cities) and integrally (the Leading Cities). The former, the functional rankings, will be discussed first, if only to demonstrate that an integral valuation can be quite different to the sum of partial or functional evaluations. For consistency in the presentation, they will be handled in the order in which they were studied. Before turning to the results, a few technical observations are made with regard to the two questions (1-A and 1-B) on classifying the cities. (Those who wish to review the formulation of these questions can consult the questionnaire that is included as an appendix.) In conclusion, there is a short section in which both of the preceding sections are brought together and the various recommendations with regard to the classifying of cities are listed once again.

General observations

The experiences with completion of questions 1-A (the 'leading cities') and 1-B (the top cities for a certain function) were almost the same as for the question on competitive advantages (see part II). As the shift method was used for both, and they were therefore also split into two groups, this is not surprising. With regard to question 1-A, about the Leading Cities, the returned questionnaires were, in general, filled in correctly, although many respondents had to get used to using the shift method, as shown by the mistakes, corrections and annotations. There were, therefore, some questionnaires on which the five most important cities had been indicated in both columns. However, there were almost no questionnaires on which the first division had been left untouched, as had been the case for question 2. Apparently it was easier to choose a city to downgrade than a competitive factor. Overall, there were a few more imperfections than for question 2. For the first division there remained 1221 usable questionnaires (89%); for the second division 1263 (92%). There were many fewer rejects (5 percentage points) for North America than the average, which was fortunate as it was the weakest continent with regard to response.

It was reported earlier, in part I, section 3, that the response to the B question was lower than for the A question which preceded it.No matter what was done to the presentation in the questionnaire, it remained a weak point; there was some improvement only with the final versions. It may therefore have been due to the presentation, or to the fact that the respondents did not feel qualified to answer it, or perhaps some respondents did not want to come out into the open or did not want to answer the question for some other reason. Whatever the case, the result was a considerably lower usable response: 980 questionnaires were filled in correctly, 72% of the total. For this question the response from North America was once again clearly better: by 7 percentage points this time.

The respondents were explicitly invited to indicate which cities, in their opinion, should be added to the list and even upgraded. There seemed to be only a limited need for this opportunity, but, judging from the number of times that it was used, it was not overlooked. A pattern could be detected among the responses, with respondents feeling the need to add their own city when this had been omitted from the list. However, this commitment seldom went so far that it was

125

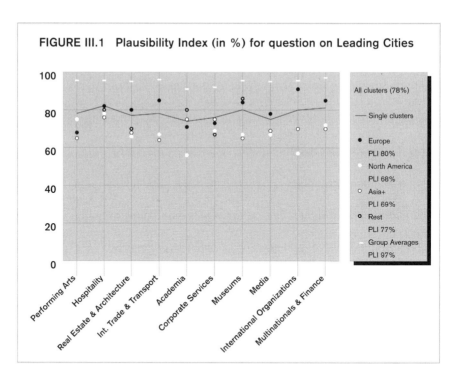

FIGURE III.1   Plausibility Index (in %) for question on Leading Cities

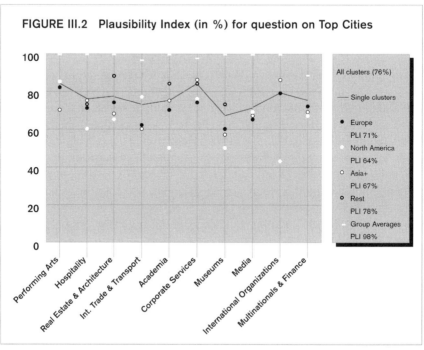

FIGURE III.2   Plausibility Index (in %) for question on Top Cities

also upgraded to a leading or top city. A second obvious pattern was when a certain city is very strong in a very specific function but does not appear in the pre-printed list. This was very clear in two cases: Geneva for all the executives in the cluster International Organizations and Rotterdam for the maritime executives in the cluster International Trade & Transport. The latter pattern strengthened confidence in the plausibility of the results to a not insignificant degree.

Of course, the separation of cities into a first and second division is of significance for the end result. It was explained earlier that this pre-selection was made on the basis of existing research, academic literature, other kinds of publications, and a certain geographical spread. Ultimately, it depended on the degree of unanimity of the respondents as to whether or not a city was upgraded or downgraded. For question 2 this had been the case for four competitive factors. For the question about the leading cities, the original doubts on whether the selection would be too fine to allow a clear choice and whether the original division would not be susceptible to change, or only barely, were once again unfounded: one city from the first division (Atlanta) remained below a score of 50% and one from the second division (Berlin) ended up above it, while around seven other cities came close to being upgraded or downgraded.

As with question 2, the professional and continental components must be considered. There is a professional component when a respondent judges a city as a top city in his/her professional field and then translates this opinion – against the general trend – into a vote for the city as a 'leading city' as well. Almost no such distortions were encountered. The reverse situation was observed, however: a city was chosen as a top city, but kept in the second division. A good example in this context is Boston in the cluster Academia. The continental component was more clearly observed, but affected primarily cities in the lowest regions. When, for example, Seoul or Taipei was put forward for upgrading to leading city, the vote usually came from Asia. A vote for one's own city was not included, unless at least 10% of the other respondents had also voted for that city.

Plausibility indexes

As with all the questions, a plausibility check was also performed on this part of the research. The PL index was calculated for the total, for the continents, for the clusters, and even for results from the separate cities. The PL index for question 1-A (the leading cities) is 78% for the total response; for question 1-B (the top cities) it is 76%. Figures III.1 and III.2 illustrate the PL indexes for both questions for the total, the continents and the ten separate clusters. The PL indexes for the separate cities will be mentioned later, when relevant.

With regard to the latter, the following should be noted. As explained earlier, the PL index is determined by the number of observations that fall outside the 10% margin, either above or below the average. This applies to the scores for a question as a whole. If the scores are examined for an individual city, then the observations that lie above the average are, in fact, only confirmations of that average. In other words, only the lower observations are relevant for the PL index of a separate city. In this way the PL indexes for the individual cities can be considerably higher than for the question as a whole.

The figures show almost the same picture as for the Plausibility check for the survey as a whole, as reported in part I: a score around the average for both Europe and (again a surprise) the remainder group and scores for North America and Asia that are visibly lower.

Finally, a few explanatory remarks on the figures and tables that have been produced for the various clusters.

The ranking lists include only those cities that received at least 10% of the votes. Lower scores are too insubstantial, or rather they are based on too few observations, to be included. For the functional rankings (the Top Cities) this means that the number of classified cities is limited to 10 to 15. Bar charts could therefore be made for this part, in which there was room for the columns of the continents next to the column of the total. For the 'Leading Cities,' however, use had to be made once more of the line graph.

The frames of reference for the functional rankings are given as overviews in table format. Each overview starts with the term 'WCR perception' with the scores from the research per city (to 10%) and the associated ranking. Imagine, for example, that there are 12. The classification for this Top 12 is sought in the frame of reference. This is printed in bold for both classifications. Each overview has gained, in addition, an appendix for the cities that are part of the Top 12 of the frame of reference but not included in the WCR Top 12. To make the comparison complete, the associated classifications from the WCR study and, if available, from another frame of reference are placed alongside one another. There is a conflict of interest here, as the WCR results that are below 10% are, in fact, too insubstantial for publication, as stated above. On the other hand, the frame of reference requires a comparison that is as complete as possible. Albeit with some hesitation, the latter has been given priority.

Classifications characteristically magnify differences. It is like sport, where whoever comes in second is quickly forgotten, even if the difference with the winner is only a split second, and there may also be only a few points difference between the third and eighth places. On the other hand, the differences can sometimes be greater than the classification implies. Nevertheless, the system has become so ingrained that it cannot be avoided; if you don't give a classification yourself, then others will do it for you. When it suits them, the cities themselves will also happily lead the way with such magnifications. That does not alter the fact that it is wise to emphasize the limitations of the rankings and the various overviews and to recommend that the numbers behind the classifications are always taken into consideration.

* * *

III. 2 THE TOP CITIES (FUNCTIONAL PERCEPTIONS)

III.2.1 TOP CITIES FOR THE PERFORMING ARTS

As described earlier, this is being used as a collective term for symphony orchestras, opera and ballet companies, international festivals and music centers. 320 'citymakers' were selected and written to, most of them in Europe and North America. The response rate of 50% was the very highest. There were 131 usable responses for this question.

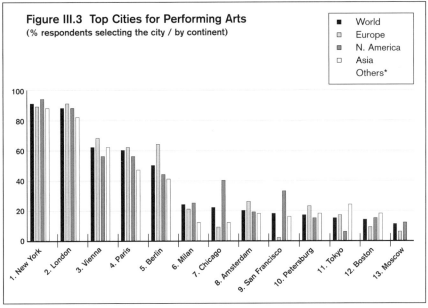

Figure III.3 Top Cities for Performing Arts
(% respondents selecting the city / by continent)

World
Europe
N. America
Asia
Others*

* Not included, owing to space limitations.

In Figure III.3 the cities are shown for which at least 10% of the respondents from this cluster indicated that they are the top cities in their professional field. New York and London are clearly at the top, which will not be a surprise. The cities that immediately follow them might be though. The fact that, from among the Asian cities, only Tokyo received a place in this list is undoubtedly due to the composition of this cluster being very much a product of western culture.

If one looks for continental distortions, then those of Berlin, Chicago and San Francisco attract attention. The valuation from Europe is also extremely low for both American cities, relatively speaking.

Plausibility indexes

The plausibility indexes for the results, which can also be seen in Figure IV.3, are high in relation to that for all the clusters taken together:

• Total 84% (+8)   • Europe 82% (+11)   • North America 85% (+21)   • Asia+ 70% (+3)

The numbers between parentheses are the number of percentage points by which the PL index for this cluster deviates, positively or negatively, from that for all the clusters taken together. In this context the whole cluster distinguishes itself positively, and the response from North America in particular. However, it should be noted that the total PL index for this continent is relatively low.

Breakdown per magnet

As stated earlier, the answers came from various quarters: symphony orchestras, opera, ballet and general. The latter included the directors of international festivals and concert halls. The response from this cluster was so good that the results could be further specified by professional background, as shown in Figure III.3'. Here one can see from which functions the votes for a certain city came, and therefore in which area of the Performing Arts the city is most valued. Thus Vienna and Berlin (unsurprisingly) had the most votes from the world of symphony music, Paris from the ballet and Milan from the world of opera. New York and London received votes from right across the cluster.

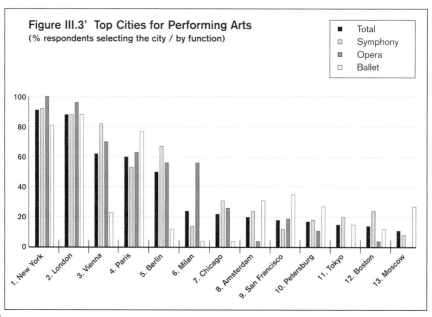

Figure III.3' Top Cities for Performing Arts
(% respondents selecting the city / by function)

Legend: ■ Total   □ Symphony   ▨ Opera   □ Ballet

Frames of reference

No quantitative or qualitative overviews could be found for this cluster that could be used as a frame of reference, nor even for parts of it. Two were therefore developed by the author. An FP index, first of all, for which the monthly periodical International Arts Manager Magazine was used, which is published from London. In addition it was possible to construct a ranking using the number of international competitions in the fields of music, singing and dance. In Table III.3" both of these frames of reference are placed alongside the results for the (func-tio-nal) WCR perception study.

As shown in the accompanying figure, a few cities were added in an appendix to the ranking list, as they did not score in the top 13 in both frames of reference. The top ten of the FP index shows a lot of similarity with the results of the study; after that, however, differences begin to appear. This is not so surpri-sing, as publicity is determined by other factors in addition to quality. Even if it does not remove all doubts about the results of the research, the FP index cer-tainly gives a little extra confidence. One thing does seem to be certain: however international a publication may be, in this case International Arts Manager Magazine, it is still a product of its city of origin. In this case London has a clear advantage as the home base.

Table III.3"   Top Cities for Performing Arts
with reference to Free Publicity and International Competitions

	WCR perception		Free Publicity (1)			Int. Competitions (2)	
	%	ranking	observations	FP-index	ranking	number	ranking
New York	91	1	72	55	2	25	1
London	88	2	131	100	1	11	4
Vienna	62	3	24	18	7-8	6	5-6
Paris	60	4	31	24	4	14	3
Berlin	50	5	39	30	3	1	*
Milan	24	6	3	2	*	5	7-12
Chicago	22	7	20	15	11	0	*
Amsterdam	20	8	23	18	9-10	5	7-12
San Francisco	18	9	23	18	9-10	1	*
Petersburg	17	10	14	11	16	4	13
Tokyo	15	11	12	9	21	16	2
Boston	14	12	14	11	16	1	*
Moscow	11	13	7	5	*	1	*
Frankfurt	8	14	10	8	20	0	*
Rome	7	15-17	8	6	*	5	7-12
Sydney	7	15-17	27	21	5	3	18
Toronto	7	15-17	25	19	6	2	*
Madrid	5	19	7	5	*	6	5-6
Brussels	3	*	24	18	7-8	3	18
Helsinki	0	*	19	15	12-13	5	7-12
Prague	0	*	3	2	*	5	7-12
Warsaw	0	*	3	2	*	5	7-12

(1) Source: International Arts Manager Magazine 1998 until 2000
(2) Source: International Arts Manager Magazine March 2000
* Not ranked anymore

The overview of international competitions gives approximately the same picture. It only covers one year, however, while similar overviews change from year to year, but no overviews from previous years were available.

In an attempt to clear up any lingering doubts, the plausibility value was examined for the last four cities of the WCR perception list or ranking. At 100% this is at a maximum for all four, which means that all of the observations per city (8) lie either within or above the margin of 10%.

* * *

III.2.2 TOP CITIES FOR HOSPITALITY

Hospitality is a top priority for hotels, congress centers and organizations that are involved in attracting foreign visitors to a city, which formed the target group for this cluster. The response, at 23%, was just a little above the average, but because of the large number of addresses selected (nearly 900) the number of forms returned was the largest; nearly 200. Of these, 147 (74%) could be used for this question.

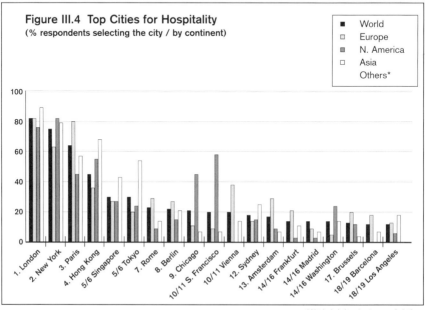

Figure III.4 Top Cities for Hospitality
(% respondents selecting the city / by continent)

■ World
□ Europe
▨ N. America
□ Asia
  Others*

* Not included, owing to space limitations.

In Figure III.4 the opinion from this sector is summarized. Again, London and New York stand side by side at the top. This time Paris is a respectable third, partly thanks to the contributions from Europe. The three Asian cities that follow also got a leg-up from their own continent, with Hong Kong, not Tokyo, leading the way. Chicago, San Francisco, Vienna and Amsterdam also received a little continental help. For Madrid and (to a lesser degree) Barcelona a completely different continental accent can be noted: the relatively strong preference from other continents comes largely from Latin America. For Rome this preference is much more mixed.

Plausibility indexes
The PL index of 76% is equal to the average for all clusters, and is as follows per continent:

• Total 76% (0) • Europe 71% (0) • North America 60% (-4) • Asia+ 75% (+8)

Breakdown per magnet
It was possible to make a professional division between the perceptions of the hotel managers and city promoters (Figure III.4'). This only provides the not so significant observation that the hotel managers gave a relatively higher valuation to the cities at the top of this classification, while the preference of the city promoters seemed to lie more strongly in the middle group.

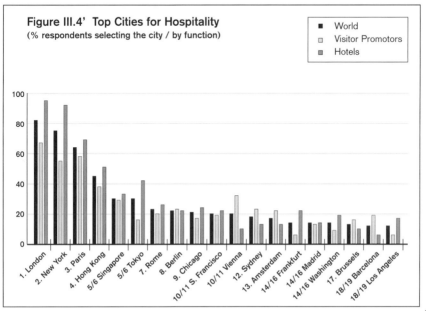

Figure III.4' Top Cities for Hospitality
(% respondents selecting the city / by function)

■ World
□ Visitor Promotors
▨ Hotels

133

■

Frames of reference

Finding frames of reference for this cluster is not difficult, there are numerous examples. Whether or not they are suitable is another question. For hotels there are a number of trade magazines that publish an annual ranking list of the best hotels in the world, usually based on a readers' survey. A place of honour on such a list is highly valued, as demonstrated by the fact that a good result is not seldomly framed and displayed at the hotel reception desk. There are also overviews of occupation rates and prices. The frame of reference chosen was the ranking list of Institutional Investor for the years 1998–2000.

The world of conferences has been wrestling for years with constructing a correct ranking list of cities for international congresses. Two institutes publish a ranking list annually – completely independently of one another and using different criteria for what qualifies as an international congress – one on the basis of the number of international congresses (ICCA) and one on the share of the city in the total number of all congresses (UIA). Small wonder that cities simply pick out the bits that suit them best. In order to demonstrate what such diverse criteria can lead to, both ranking lists have been included in the overview below.

For the cluster as a whole no existing frame of reference could be found, and the FP index was therefore used. Since 1998 it has been checked how often the cities in the WCR study have attracted attention in the magazine Business Traveller. The cradle of this publication is London once again, however, and that is very obvious. The size of the difference between it and the other cities should therefore be taken with a hefty pinch of salt.

In Table III.4" a comparison is first made with the cluster as a whole (overall picture). The similarity is striking: only four cities from the top 19 of the study are missing from the top 20 of the FP index. This is a powerful endorsement of the study.

The response can be split into that from the hotel managers and that of the city promoters (Table 4'). Although they deviate little from the total for the cluster, they have been included separately to allow the clearest possible comparison.

The first is compared with the number of hotels per city that appeared in the top 100 list of Business Traveller magazine over four years. This also provided a very recognizable picture, albeit somewhat less than for the FP index: six cities from the top 19 of the study are missing from this roll of honour. Rome and Berlin are the most conspicuous among the differences. In the appendix this is the case for Bangkok and Boston. It seems that the hotel managers base their functional opinion on a broader basis than just the qualities of the hotels themselves.

The comparison for congresses gives a chaotic picture. Looking at the differences between the two ranking lists from the congress world itself, this would not seem to be due in the first place to the WCR study. It is very clear here how different criteria, applied to the same subject and for the same aim, can lead to wildly different results. It is also clear that the perceptions of the city promoters are influenced by other criteria. The best advice seems to be not to take such rankings too seriously.

Table III.4" Top Cities for Hospitality
with reference to Free Publicity and Hotel and Congress Rankings

	Overall Picture					Hotel Rankings			Congress Rankings		
	WCR perception		Free Publicity (1)			WCR	Institutional Investor (2)		WCR	ICCA (3)	UIA (4)
	%	ranking	observations	FP-index	ranking	perception (a)	quotes(2)	ranking	perception (b)		
London	82	1	125	100	1	1	41	1	1	10-11	3
New York	75	2	83	66	2	2	32	2-3	3	*	10
Paris	64	3	50	40	4	3	26	4	2	6	1
Hong Kong	45	4	57	46	3	4	32	2-3	4	21	20
Singapore	30	5-6	44	35	5	6	22	5	6	7	11
Tokyo	30	5-6	27	22	6-8	5	11	13-14	14-15	27	*
Rome	23	7	17	14	16-20	7	8	16-19	10	23-24	14
Berlin	22	8	18	14	16-20	9-11	2	40-44	7-8	13	7
Chicago	21	9	18	14	16-20	8	10	15	13	35-38	*
San Francisco	20	10-11	18	14	16-20	9-11	13	10	11-12	*	*
Vienna	20	10-11	27	22	6-8	17-18	4	28-30	5	1	4
Sydney	18	12	27	22	6-8	15-16	8	16-19	7-8	10-11	12
Amsterdam	17	13	29	21	9	15-16	6	22-25	9	5	6
Frankfurt	14	14-16	24	29	11-12	9-11	9	15	18-19	*	*
Madrid	14	14-16	8	6	*	14	12	11-12	16	2	19
Washington	14	14-16	8	6	*	12	19	6-7	17	*	9
Brussels	13	17	11	9	13-15	17-18	1	45-55	14-15	23-24	2
Barcelona	12	18-19	12	10	*	19	1	45-55	11-12	9	16-17
Los Angeles	12	18-19	18	14	16-20	13	19	6-7	18-19	*	*
Bangkok	5	20-25	25	20	10	*	18	8	*	*	*
Zürich	3	*	11	9	24-28	*	11	13-14	*	*	*
Boston	2	*	8	6	*	*	14	9	*	*	*
Stockholm	1	*	19	15	13-15	*	4	28-30	*	4	18
Budapest	0	*	11	9	*	*	0	*	*	12	13
Copenhagen	0	*	9	7	*	*	1	45-55	*	3	5
Geneva	0	*	19	15	13-15	*	12	11-12	*	*	8
Jerusalem	0	*	0	*	*	*	1	28-30	*	19	*
Manchester	0	*	24	29	11-12	*	0	*	*	*	*
Melbourne	0	*	8	6	*	*	3	31-39	*	18	21
Prague	0	*	11	9	24-28	*	0	*	*	17	16-17
Helsinki	0	*	9	7	*	*	0	*	*	8	15
Lisbon	0	*	8	6	*	*	2	40-44	*	14	*
Rio de Janeiro	0	*	7	6	*	*	3	31-39	*	15	*
Seoul	0	*	7	6	*	*	8	16-19	*	16	*

(1) Source: Business Traveller 1998 - mid-2001
(2) Aggregated number of yearly quotes in The Institutional Investor Top 100 Hotels 1996 until 2000
(3) Source: International Congress & Convention Association (ICCA) publications 1998 until 2000
(4) Source: Union of International Associations (UIA) publications 1998 until 2000
(a) Hotel executives only   (b) Visitors promotors only   * Not marked anymore

Having established the substantial similarity between the results of the research and the FP index and/or the ranking list of Institutional Investor, there remain at most some doubts about the classification of Rome, Berlin, Chicago, Brussels and Barcelona. These doubts can be removed by considering the PL indexes of, respectively, 82, 100, 73, 91 and 100%.

* * *

■

III.2.3 TOP CITIES FOR REAL ESTATE & ARCHITECTURE

Within this cluster there are certain circles that like to use the height of buildings to measure the importance of a city. However, in part III it was already established that, while the skyline of a city may have a role, it is certainly not a decisive one. This does not mean that the opinions of globally operating architects, investors and developers are any less important. They know perhaps better than anyone else how well a city is doing, from the developments in the world of real estate. Around 800 were approached. The response rate (16%) was the lowest; the absolute number of replies (131) was, however, sufficient. Of these, 103 gave usable answers to the question on Top Cities.

Plausibility indexes

The PL index is a little higher the average for all clusters (76%), and is as follows per continent:

• Total 77% (+1) • Europe 74% (+3) • North America 65% (+1) • Asia+ 68% (+1)

Seventeen cities found a place in the top category for this cluster (Figure III.5). The scores from Asia for cities such as Hong Kong, Tokyo, Shanghai and Singapore give a, now familiar, continental distortion. Similar continental

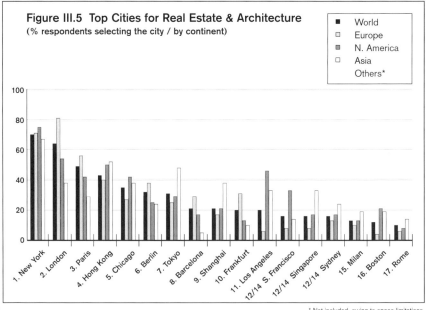

Figure III.5 Top Cities for Real Estate & Architecture
(% respondents selecting the city / by continent)

World
Europe
N. America
Asia
Others*

* Not included, owing to space limitations.

accents can be seen in the European and American scores. This partially explains the lower PL index for both continents. The opinion on the number one city (New York) is, in comparison to the rest, fairly consistent.

Breakdown per magnet

A breakdown was made of the data for architects and real estate specialists in order to see to what degree their perceptions differ from one another. The difference was, however, so insubstantial that a separate figure has not been included. If an observation has to be made, then one can note a light preference for London, Hong Kong and Frankfurt among the real estate specialists, while Chicago enjoys slightly more appreciation from the architects.

Frames of reference

There is no ready-made frame of reference for the cluster as a whole. However, the trade magazine World Architecture includes a monthly overview of new developments in cities, and an FP index for the past few years was made on the basis of these News columns. In addition, the magazine publishes an overview each year of the 300 largest architects' firms. It is interesting to put together a ranking list on this basis, even if only to see if there is any relationship at all between it and any others.

Overviews of the cost of renting office or retail space also appear regularly, and ranking lists can be made on this basis as well. The results of these studies, overviews and analyses are collected in Table III.5' (next page).

Of the four comparisons, the FP index is once again the closest match: it features 11 of the 17 cities from the WCR top group. The similarities in the top half are the most striking. In contrast, a city does not have to be the location of a large firm of architects in order to come high on their list. In this field this does not then seem to be a useful benchmark for classifying cities. To give a further example: a small Danish city like Aarhus, with three large firms, would score more highly than Los Angeles and many other 'leading cities.' Therefore it was not considered necessary to indicate all the cities with classification 13–20.

The ranking list for real estate prices is recognizable for the top part of the classification; however, after that it is hard to see any relationship. Very high prices sometimes have to be paid for office and/or retail space in cities that scored (extremely) low in terms of perception. Seoul, Manchester, Athens and Moscow are examples. The opposite can also be the case, as the data for Chicago, Barcelona and Shanghai demonstrate. Therefore, once again, these lists are only useful for the purposes for which they were made.

With the FP index in particular in mind, there is no reason to doubt the top part of the classification. The results for Chicago (90%) also encourage confidence.

137

Table III.5'   Top Cities for Real Estate & Architecture
with reference to Free Publicity, largest architectural firms, and office and retail rents

	WCR perception		Free Publicity (1)		Share in 300 largest architectural firms (2)		Occupancy costs for offices in best locations (3)		Retail rents in best locations (4)	
	%	ranking	FP-index	ranking	abs.	ranking	$/sf/year	ranking	$1000/sm/year $/sm/year	ranking
New York	70	1	100	1	10	4	65	7	6,5	1
London	64	2	98	2	37	1	157	1	4,5	4
Paris	49	3	42	6	6	10	84	4	4,9	3
Hong Kong	43	4	60	3	8	6-7	92	3	5,1	2
Chicago	35	5	15	18-19	8	6-7	38	*	2,2	16
Berlin	32	6	49	4	1	*	n.a.	n.a.	2,1	18
Tokyo	31	7	35	8	12	2	147	2	2,4	13
Barcelona	21	8-9	27	9	0	*	31	*	1,1	*
Shanghai	21	8-9	16	15-17	1	*	20	*	1,2	*
Frankfurt	20	10-11	9	*	1	*	58	10	1,9	19
Los Angeles	20	10-11	20	11-13	2	21	28	*	2,5	12
San Francisco	16	12-14	20	11-13	7	7-9	74	6	3,2	7
Singapore	16	12-14	13	20-22	5	11	52	14	1,6	23
Sydney	16	12-14	36	7	9	5	35	*	3,9	6
Milan	13	15	7	*	1	*	36	*	1,3	*
Boston	12	16	15	18-19	11	3	55	11	1,1	*
Rome	10	17	5	*	1	*	29	*	1,2	*
Beijing	8	18-19	18	14	1	*	41	25	1,5	*
Madrid	8	*	44	5	1	*	48	19	1,1	*
Moscow	7	20-22	13	20-22	0	*	62	9	3,1	8
Vancouver	6	23-25	2	*	3	13-20	18	*	n.a.	n.a.
Washington	6	23-25	24	10	0	*	45	20	n.a.	n.a.
Brussels	5	26-27	4	*	7	7-9	27	*	1,3	*
Toronto	5	26-27	16	15-17	2	20-26	38	*	1,1	*
Buenos Aires	3	*	2	*	0	*	50	16	1,3	*
Zürich	3	*	2	*	0	*	49	17	1,9	17
Mumbai	2	*	5	*	2	20-26	80	5	0,7	*
Stockholm	2	*	4	*	3	13-20	54	13	1,1	*
Seoul	2	*	7	*	0	*	62	8	4,2	5
Athens	0	*	2	*	3	13-20	n.a.	*	2,7	9
Glasgow	0	*	2	*	1	*	52	15	2,6	10-11
Johannesburg	0	*	3	*	4	12	11	*	n.a.	n.a.
Manchester	0	*	3	*	1	*	55	12	2,2	15
Melbourne	0	*	20	11-13	1	*	20	*	2,6	10-11
Munich	0	*	7	*	1	*	41	*	2,4	14

(1) Source: World Architecture mid-1997 until mid-2001
(2) Source: World Architecture January 2001
(3) Source: Richard Ellis January 2001 (costs are in square feet)

(4) Source: Healy & Baker 1999/2000 (costs are in square meters)
* Not ranked anymore
n.a. : Not available

In order to remove any lingering doubts about the rest of the top 17, the PL indexes for the scores of the remaining cities can be examined: Shanghai (100%), Frankfurt (78%), Sydney (90%), Singapore (78%), Milan (78%) and Rome (100%).

* * *

III.2.4 TOP CITIES FOR TRADE & TRANSPORT

It was established in part II, when discussing the competitive factors, that, of the three factors that belong to this cluster, one is of overriding importance: the intercontinental airport. The other two (international seaport and highspeed train service) cannot be considered as essential parts of a competitiveness analysis for cities. For this reason the frame of reference used later can be limited to aviation. In reporting on the top cities, however, the opinions of all the respondents within this cluster will count. They represent 35% of the total number approached (more than 400); a generous response from a comparatively small group. Of the 126 forms that were returned, 101 were usable for the question on the Top Cities.

Plausibility indexes
The following PL indexes were calculated for this cluster, on the basis of the usable answers:

• Total 73% (-3) • Europe 60% (-11) • North America 77% (+13) • Asia+ 60% (-7)

The percentages for Europe and North America deviate markedly from those for the other clusters, and require further explanation. In part I a figure was included (I.5) which illustrated how the PL indexes were calculated. The example looked at the responses from the cluster Trade & Transport for the question on the Top Cities in their field: the question currently being examined. The example was chosen, amongst other reasons, in order to demonstrate that a comparatively low PL index does not necessarily mean an inconsistent response. When this figure is examined anew, but now in the form of a bar chart, it is once again striking that North American and Asian cities are given values well below the average by respondents from Europe. This causes the unusually low PL index for this continent. In addition, on the higher side, the number of scores from Asia gives a second not insignificant continental distortion, with the same consequences for the plausibility.

Breakdown per magnet
Figure III.6 (next page) underlines again the dominant position of New York and London. The three cities that follow will also be no surprise, but perhaps Amsterdam in sixth place is, coming just ahead of Frankfurt, Paris and Chicago. The response can, however, be divided into two professional groups: aviation (41%) and other (trade 46% and sea traffic 13%). From Figure III.6' (next page) it can be seen that, in the eyes of the world of aviation, London has the top position and Hong Kong, Singapore and Amsterdam score less than Frankfurt and Paris. They therefore thank their higher position in the first figure to their (traditional) image as an international trading city.

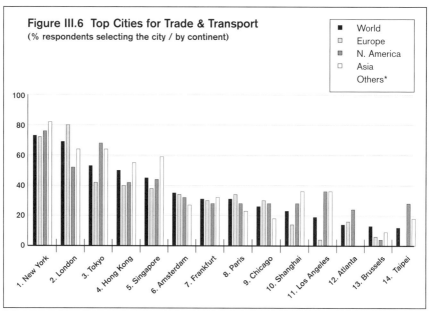

* Not included, owing to space limitations.

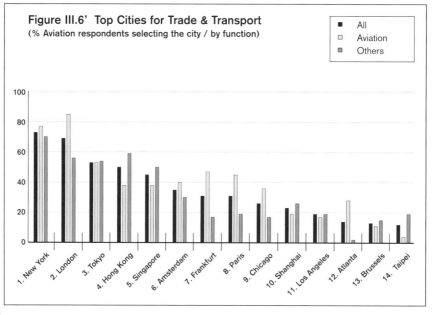

Frames of reference

The statistics that the Airports Council International (ACI) publishes on the number of passengers and amount of freight transported via airports can be used as a frame of reference. In addition, there are the annual publications in Business Traveller magazine on 'the best airports' and 'the best airlines.' The number of airports selected in these is, however, too small to allow a good comparison. In academic circles the realization is also growing that aviation can be an important indication of the international significance of a city. However, for the time being it is viewed more as an instrument to help portray the relations between cities ('network cities').

The passenger and freight statistics also have their "dirty little secrets," however. If the totals are taken, then this does give the best information on the total amount of traffic, and the American airports are then giants compared to most of the others. However, the total amount does not necessarily say anything about the international position of the city as a center for aviation, for which

Table III.6"   Top Cities for International Air Transport
with reference to passengers and cargo

| | WCR perception** | | Airports by passengers (in millions) | | | | Airports by international cargo | |
| | | | Total passengers | | International passengers | | (in metric tons x 1.000) | |
	%	ranking	abs.	ranking	abs.	ranking	abs.	ranking
London (5)	85	1	116,2	1	102,1	1	1.812	3
New York (3)	77	2	92,4	2	28,4	6	1.498	7
Tokyo (2)	53	3	83,8	4	24,9	8	1.907	2
Frankfurt	47	4	49,4	9	40,2	3	1.519	6
Paris (2)	45	5	73,6	6	52,4	2	1.319	8
Amsterdam	40	6	39,6	11	39,1	4	1.222	9
Hong Kong	38	7-8	32,8	20	32,1	5	2.240	1
Singapore	38	7-8	28,6	23	27,1	7	1.682	4
Chicago (3)	36	9	87,9	3	10,5	27	728	15
Atlanta	28	10	80,1	5	5,8	46	271	26
Shanghai	19	11	14,1	49	6,5	43	427	18
Los Angeles	17	12	66,4	8	16,6	15	911	12
Brussels	11	13	21,6	33	21,5	9	n.a.	n.a.
Bangkok	7	16-19	29,6	21	20,5	11	820	14
Zürich	7	16-19	22,6	31	21,2	10	387	20
Milan (3)	6	20-23	28,1	24	17,7	13	385	21
San Francisco	6	20-23	41,1	10	8,2	34	430	17
Seoul	6	20-23	36,7	14	17,9	12	1.597	5
Osaka (2)	4	27-29	36,8	12	11,7	24	890	13
Taipei	4	14	18,7	37	16,7	14	1.196	10
Dallas (2)	2	*	67,7	7	5,1	53	137	41
Miami	1	*	33,6	18	16,2	17-18	1.297	8
Copenhagen	0	*	18,3	39	16,2	17-18	1.192	11
Minneapolis	0	*	36,7	13	1,9	73	256	28

Source: Airports Council International 2000   *   Not ranked anymore
(.) More than one airport   ** Aviation respondents only

insight into international traffic is needed. Fortunately the ACI publishes statistics on this as well, and the picture is then completely different. Hong Kong, Singapore and a number of European airports make a huge leap. Not surprisingly, as the first two have no national air traffic at all, and in Europe there are alternative forms of transport because of the shorter distances. The best means of comparison for the purpose of this study would be intercontinental traffic, but sadly such statistics are not available. Therefore, in Table III.6"   page) two ranking lists for international passenger traffic and one for international freight traffic are used as frames of reference.

All three ranking lists support the results of the research to a significant degree, but they do not actually cover comparable areas. It cannot, therefore, be excluded that a match with the first (total number of passengers) and the third (international cargo) could be coincidental. The ranking list for international passenger transport seems, as explained above, to be the most obvious and suitable measure. The similarities with the WCR list are striking: only three cities score lower and two of these only slightly – Chicago, Atlanta and Shanghai. Any remaining doubts can be removed by examining the PL indexes for their respective scores: 88, 75 and 88%.

* * *

III. 2.5 TOP CITIES FOR ACADEMIA

For this cluster it is the universities in particular that can contribute inter-national prestige to a city. As a competitive factor they belong to the top and must therefore be included in any competitiveness analysis, as was established in part II. Subsequently, using this research, it can be determined which cities can count themselves among the top in the world in this field. Of the 151 respondents (43% of all those approached), 110 respondents correctly completed the question (1-B) on this.

Plausibility indexes
The PL indexes for this cluster are as follows:

• Total 75% (-1) • Europe 70% (-1) • North America 50% (-14) • Asia+ 75% (+8)

A very stable picture for the cluster as a whole and for the response from Europe; Asia even scores significantly higher. Only the American respondents have a lower score. It is also the smallest group, therefore it is better not to draw any conclusions for this part of the response.

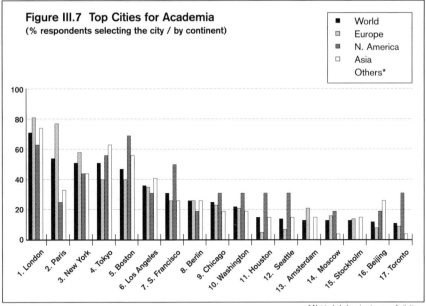

Figure III.7 Top Cities for Academia
(% respondents selecting the city / by continent)

■ World
▣ Europe
▨ N. America
□ Asia
Others*

* Not included, owing to space limitations.

Figure III.7 shows that the 'big two' (London and New York) are less dominant in this area. The differences with the cities that follow are also clearly smaller; New York is even overtaken by Paris. After these three and Tokyo, Boston appears as a true top city for the academic world. For insiders this will be, of course, no surprise; however, it underlines once again the plausibility of the results. The number of North American cities in the top list (9 of the 17) is conspicuously large. It should be noted that many prominent American universities are located on a campus on the periphery of cities and were therefore not included in the survey. In this context there remains the question of whether the respondents were thinking of Greater Boston, Los Angeles and San Francisco when making their evaluations. Cambridge will no doubt have been counted within Boston, but was San Francisco considered to cover the whole Bay area, including Berkeley and Stanford? Los Angeles is already a large city, but does it extend to Pasadena, and what about San Diego which is not so far away?

Frames of reference
This unanswerable question leads us to the frame of reference, where the same problem is faced. Matthiessen et al. (2000) resolved this by classifying so-called 'research gateways' instead of cities. This gave a large degree of flexibility in demarcating areas and therefore led to a ranking that is not always comparable to the cities in this study. For example, they not only plumped for the Bay area, but also for the 'randstad' conurbation instead of Amsterdam, for the combination Stockholm–Uppsala, and for the Ruhr region rather than Düsseldorf. More

important, however, is the question of whether the criterion they used – the number of academic publications produced – is a useful estimation of academic productivity. The opinions on this vary, according to the authors, but they come to the risk-free conclusion that it at least gives an indication.

This can also be said of another criterion that they use: the average number of times that a publication is cited, which leads again to a totally different ranking list. The authors themselves concede that there are countless factors that influence the number of cross-references and they certainly do not all have to do with academic knowledge. Nevertheless this does not prevent them from presenting the ranking list as an indication. This contains so many different cities in the top portion, however, that it is not possible to set up a good comparison.

Completely independently from these authors, and before their publication had even been encountered, but with similar feelings of doubt on the suitability of the criterion, a ranking list was developed by the author of this volume based on the number of times that authors had been cited. Just the number of cross-references – more than 11 million over the period 1984 to 2000 – is enough to make one hesitate. When there is no other possibility for comparison, however, one is quickly forced to lower one's standards.

The well-informed reader will point out that, just as for hotels, airports and airlines, ranking lists of 'the best universities' are made each year. This is true, but they are ranking lists exclusively for single continents (Asia and the USA) and for single universities, which may 'coincidentally' be located in a city. Decisive in the resolve not to make use of these lists was the fact that they are very controversial within the university world itself. Some very prominent universities even refuse to cooperate with them, or are considering refusing. It confirms, in fact, that for this purpose it is not feasible to contrive good criteria, to then attach weight to them and finally just to add them all together.

Against this background, the perception method does not seem to be such a bad idea for complicated institutions such as universities. If the right target groups are approached, then, on the basis of their professional perception, insight can be obtained into the centers of excellence in the world. This can be across the complete breadth of the university or for a specific professional area. The former was the concern of the WCR study; this was the reason for choosing university executives as the target group.

The consequence of these considerations is that two frames of reference are used in Table III.7': the ranking list of Matthiessen et al. with the number of publications produced, and the personally made list of the number of cited publications.

Table III.7' Top Cities for Academia
with reference to cited and produced papers

	WCR perception		Ranking by cited publications (1)		Ranking by produced papers according to Matthiessen et al. (2)	
	%	ranking	numbers (x1.000)	ranking	numbers (x1.000)	ranking
London	71	1	106	4	70	1
Paris	54	2	104	7	49	4
New York	51	3	105	6	42	8
Tokyo	51	4	100	9	68	2
Boston	47	5	107	3	43	7
Los Angeles	36	6	106	5	45	10
San Francisco	31	7	68	18	51	3
Berlin	26	8	84	13	25	12
Chicago	25	9	97	11	25	13
Washington	22	10	115	1	22	18
Houston	15	11	90	12	23	17
Seattle	14	12	77	14	20	21-22
Amsterdam	13	13-15	59	25	48	9
Moscow	13	13-15	114	2	46	6
Stockholm	13	13-15	55	26	23	16
Beijing	12	16	64	20	15	29
Toronto	11	17	75	15	19	23
Madrid	6	*	69	17	20	21-22
Osaka	5	*	102	8	48	5
Copenhagen	0	*	43	*	24	14-15
Munich	0	*	69	16	18	24
Philadelphia	0	*	100	10	29	11
San Diego	0	*	68	19	24	14-15

(1) Source: Science Citation Index Expanded 26-1-2000
(2) "Research Gateways of the World: an analysis of networks based on
   bibliometric indicators", Matthiessen, C. W. et al.
* Not ranked anymore

In both frames of reference 13 cities can be found that are also featured in the top 17 from the WCR study; admittedly not exactly the same and often with a different classification, but still easily recognizable. Cautiously formulated, it can be stated that the frames of reference certainly do not detract from the plausibility of the research, and even strengthen it. The reverse, however, cannot be said: as a result of this comparison, the numbers of cross-references and publications have not become better criteria for classifying universities. They remain instruments that are full of shortcomings, born out of necessity and, indeed, offering at most an indication.

* * *

■

III.2.6 TOP CITIES FOR CORPORATE SERVICES

This cluster may be of lesser significance than is usually assumed in the literature, in accordance with Sassen, but that is no reason to accord its input any less value. Advisors working in this cluster are involved in important decisions, and perception also plays a significant role in advising. Within this cluster 121 executives participated in the research. As a result of the low response rate (13%), many addresses were needed to obtain this. Fortunately, this was not a problem owing to the large number and variety of advisors. Of these respondents, 89 participated fully in answering the question on the top cities in their professional field.

Plausibility indexes

This modest number means that close attention must be paid to the PL index for the response. This more than compensates for the disadvantages of the small absolute number:

• Total 84% (+8) • Europe 74% (+3) • North America 76% (+12) • Asia+ 86% (+19)

It is a notably better score than for most of the other clusters for both the total and the separate continents, which means there was a high degree of unanimity in the response. Despite the limited number of respondents, the results can therefore be presented in Figure III.8 with the required confidence.

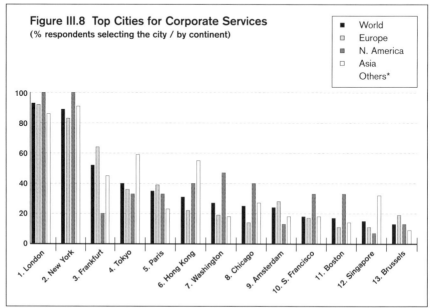

Figure III.8 Top Cities for Corporate Services
(% respondents selecting the city / by continent)

World
Europe
N. America
Asia
Others*

* Not included, owing to space limitations.

Frame of reference

After their 'dip' in the eyes of the academic world, London and New York are once again firmly at the top. The three cities that follow (Frankfurt, Tokyo and Paris) will not be a surprise, at least not for Beaverstock et al. (1999). These authors put together a ranking or typology based on the presence of corporate services in cities. Once again, as we have seen before for the headquarters of multinationals and financial institutions, the temptation could not be resisted to design a classification or typology of cities based on numbers of establishments. However, for such a simple listing, complicated analyses, lengthy calculations and computer models were used. This does not immediately strengthen confidence in the idea that this is the best approach. Research into perceptions, by comparison, looks very uncomplicated. Whatever the case may be, their efforts provided the only available frame of reference for the WCR study.

The authors cited above examined four different services – accountants, advertising agencies, legal services and financial services – and made an inventory of significant establishments. Sometimes, as they admit themselves, they had to be very imaginative. They then divided each category into three classes: prime, major and minor. Finally, the categories per city were added up and thrown into the hat, the prime centers with index 3, the major centers with index 2 and the minors with index 1. On the basis of the total number of points, the cities were then grouped into four categories: Alpha (A), Beta (B) and Gamma (C) world cities and a fourth category (D) of cities with clear characteristics of "world city formation." Earlier in this volume, in part I, hesitations were expressed about such an approach. However, the same applies here as with the universities: if there is no alternative, then there is no other choice. This is why space is given to this frame of reference in Table III.8'.

Table III.8'
Top Cities for Corporate Services

	WCR perception		A roster of world cities by corporate services criteria (1)	
	%	ranking	Category	ranking
New York	93	1	A	1-4
London	89	2	A	1-4
Frankfurt	52	3	A	5-10
Tokyo	40	4	A	1-4
Paris	35	5	A	1-4
Hong Kong	31	6	A	5-10
Washington	27	7	C	21-35
Chicago	25	8	A	5-10
Amsterdam	24	9	C	21-35
San Francisco	18	10	B	11-14
Boston	17	11	C	21-35
Singapore	15	12	A	5-10
Brussels	13	13	B	15-18
Los Angeles	8	14-16	A	5-10
Toronto	8	14-16	B	11-14
Zürich	8	14-16	B	11-14
Sydney	7	17-18	B	11-14
Sao Paulo	7	17-18	B	15-18
Madrid	6	19-21	B	15-18
Milan	4	21-23	A	5-10
Mexico City	2	*	B	15-18
Seoul	2	*	B	19-20
Moscow	1	*	B	19-20

(1) Source: Beaverstock J. V. , Taylor P. J. and Smith R. G.
"A roster of World Cities in: Cities, Vol. 16, No. 6, pp 445-458, 1999
* No ranking anymore

Placed next to one another, some similarities can be seen. However, the results differ conspicuously for four cities: Washington, Amsterdam, Boston and especially for Milan. The respondents are so clearly in agreement with each other on these cities, as shown by the PL indexes of, respectively, 89, 89, 78 and 100%, that there is no reason to doubt the results of the WCR study. In the case of Milan, none of the continents awards it a higher score than 7%, which does not in any way indicate a top position.

The conclusion must be the same as for the previous cluster (Academia): following a completely different route, a result has been reached that is quite similar to the results of the WCR study and encourages confidence. This does not mean that the quality of that other route has been endorsed.

* * *

III.2.7 TOP CITIES FOR MUSEUMS

The museums form, together with the Performing Arts, the culture cluster. The research has unequivocally underlined their significance to the international competitive position of a city. Great value must then be attached to the opinion of professionals from the museum world on the top cities in their professional field. Of the nearly 150 participants in the study, 112 answered the question on this issue.

Plausibility indexes
As shown by the PL indexes, these respondents are not pre-eminent in their unanimity:

• Total 67% (-9) • Europe 60% (-11) • North America 50% (-14) • Asia+ 57% (-10)

These values lie substantially below the total average, so conclusions must be drawn with great caution, particularly for the separate continents. In this context it is useful to recall the explanation of the calculation of the plausibility value given at the beginning of this part. For the question as a whole this is determined by the number of observations that lie either above or below the 10% zone around the average. The PL index of the separate cities, however, needs to be calculated using only the scores that are below the average, for ranking lists are about the height of scores. Observations that show a higher valuation than average do not detract from this; on the contrary, they only confirm the score. With this cluster there are markedly more observations above than below the average. The consequence is that the PL indexes for the separate cities turn out to be substantially higher.

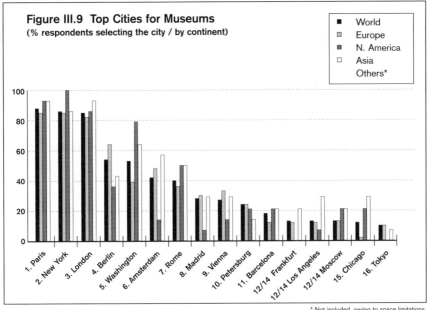

Figure III.9 Top Cities for Museums
(% respondents selecting the city / by continent)

Legend:
- World
- Europe
- N. America
- Asia
- Others*

* Not included, owing to space limitations.

In Figure III.9 a different city tops the list for the first time: Paris comes in just ahead of New York and London. Berlin and Washington are (surprising?) runners-up. The historic cities of culture in Europe score in the middle group. Cities such as Florence and Venice were, of course, added to the list many a time, but are not included in the research.

It was possible to divide the answers between museums for the fine arts and other museums. This showed, amongst other things, that Berlin and Madrid collected a clear majority of their votes from the world of fine arts, while Washington received most of its appreciation from the other museums.

Frames of reference

This breakdown is also of importance for the frame of reference. None could be found for the cluster as a whole. It would theoretically have been possible to make an inventory of the number of museums per city. However, this would have said nothing about their quality, sort or size, and it seemed to be going a bit far to start adding up unlike items oneself. Another possibility was to examine the number of museum visitors. This would have been interesting if it had been possible to look only at visitors from abroad, but such a division is not feasible in most cases. Then the idea came to make a frame of reference from the number of art galleries, antique dealers, auction houses and restorers. These kinds of businesses are not only part of the art cluster, but they are very similar all over the world and could, therefore, be added up with little hesitation. Just like the museums, they contribute to the image of a city as a center for fine arts. In order to make the comparison as close as possible, this frame of reference is placed in Table III.9' next to the perceptions of the respondents from the museums of fine arts. The other museums are therefore not included. They are representatives of the museum world, it is true, but not of the art trade.

Table III.9' Top Cities for Fine Arts
with reference to number of art galleries etc.

	WCR perception (1)		Art galleries, art & antique dealers, auctioneers, restorers, antiquarians	
	%	ranking	number	ranking
Paris	92	1-2	3.312	1
New York	92	1-2	2.000	3
London	89	3	2.257	2
Berlin	64	4	1.182	4
Washington	39	5-7	255	*
Amsterdam	39	5-7	569	12
Rome	39	5-7	983	6
Madrid	38	8	548	14
Vienna	30	9	1.080	5
Petersburg	28	10	83	*
Barcelona	20	11	464	20
Frankfurt	16	12	354	25
Moscow	15	13	195	*
Chicago	13	14-16	501	17
Los Angeles	13	14-16	565	13
Tokyo	13	14-16	207	*
San Francisco	7	19-20	605	10
Zürich	4	21-22	596	11
Houston	3	23-27	517	15
Milan	3	23-27	776	8
Munich	3	23-27	952	7
Stockholm	3	23-27	516	16
Hamburg	0	*	739	9

Source: International Directory of Arts 2000/2001
(1) Fine Arts respondents only
* Not ranked anymore

The match for the first four is perfect. The high classification of Berlin is confirmed in particular. This cannot be said for the (shared) fifth place for Washington. It is a reason to check the PL index, which at 67% is not particularly impressive. However, this is due exclusively to the low valuation from Europe. Against this background, the total result for the city certainly cannot be random. Then there are another four cities with a reasonably recognizable image, after which St. Petersburg is the next dissonant note. The PL index of 78% is quite high, and a tenth place is not surprising for a city with such a reputation. It is equally unsurprising that few signs of the art trade can be found, considering the limited local buying-power. Subsequently, Chicago and Los Angeles can be left in their places without any qualms, after which Barcelona, Frankfurt, Moscow and Tokyo need to be examined more closely. With PL indexes of, respectively, 100, 78, 89 and again 100% there is considerable unanimity on their place in the ranking list.

The list from the art trade shows a number of differences with the research. Many of these can be explained on the basis of history, the way in which the museums were founded, the local culture and especially the local buying-power. The differences are, however, too numerous and too large to allow conclusions to be drawn from one on the other. Nonetheless, the fact remains that many a city sees its position in the top 16 confirmed in the ranking list from the art trade.

* * *

III.2.8 TOP CITIES FOR THE MEDIA

The media cluster is much less decisive for the international competitive position of a city than the other clusters. The 'citymakers' were not shy in expressing this opinion. Apart from a few 'global players,' most of the companies in this cluster target a clearly demarcated market, either locally, regionally or nationally. Just the language issue alone forces this. The reason they are still considered 'citymakers' is the fact that they can influence the perception of not only their own city but also other cities to a significant degree. They are opinion-makers by profession. It was nonetheless difficult to pry that opinion out of them! The response of 92 was the lowest. On the other hand, all respondents except one answered question 1-B.

Plausibility indexes
The smaller the absolute number, the more critical the PL index becomes. For the cluster as a whole and for Europe this lies, respectively, 5 and 6 percentage points below the average for the total; for North America, 5 percentage points higher and for Asia+ it is equal:

• Total 71% (-5) • Europe 65% (-6) • North America (+5) • Asia+ (0)

However, because about half of the deviations lie above the average, the PL index for most of the separate cities will be substantially higher.

Figure III.10, with the top 13 for this cluster, shows once again the familiar

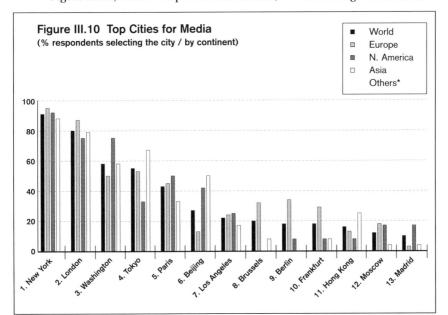

Figure III.10 Top Cities for Media
(% respondents selecting the city / by continent)

Legend: ■ World ▫ Europe ▪ N. America ▫ Asia Others*

picture of New York and London neck and neck, leading the field. Washington, Tokyo and Paris follow a little further behind. One can only speculate on the arguments that led the editors-in-chief of prominent newspapers and the correspondents of global press agencies to this choice. It seems very likely, however, that the place where the news happens would be decisive in their evaluation. This was the starting point in the search for a frame of reference.

Frame of reference

At first, nothing could be found for this cluster either. However, from the moment this research was begun a number of (trade) magazines were followed to determine how often the cities being studied were conspicuously featured. An FP index was calculated from this. Such an index was used above as a frame of reference for the clusters Performing Arts, Hospitality and Real Estate & Architecture.

An FP index was also calculated using observations from the European edition of Time magazine. As there was the impression that the list of top cities for the Media industry was comprised primarily of those which generate news, and no other frame of reference could be found, the idea came to use the Time FP index as a reference for this section as well. Originally however, this index was calculated with the intention of using it as a frame of reference for the list of 'leading cities,' and it will therefore be used again in the following part of this volume. After all, it shows the integral perception that the 'citymakers' have of the cities as well, and a magazine like Time covers all aspects of society and therefore also of the city.

Table III.10' Top Cities for Media
with reference to Free Publicity

	WCR perception		Free Publicity (1)		
	%	ranking	abs.	FP-index	ranking
New York	91	1	144	94	3
London	80	2	153	100	1
Washington	58	3	108	71	4
Tokyo	55	4	49	35	9
Paris	43	5	145	94	2
Beijing	27	6	53	35	8
Los Angeles	22	7	38	25	13
Brussels	20	8	32	21	15
Berlin	18	9-10	47	31	10
Frankfurt	18	9-10	19	12	29
Hong Kong	16	11	73	51	5
Moscow	12	12	62	41	7
Madrid	10	13	25	16	18
Sydney	4	19-20	46	30	11-12
Jakarta	2	*	46	30	11-12
Jerusalem	0	*	68	44	6

(1) Source: Time Magazine 1997-2000
* Not ranked anymore

Some further explanation now follows. In the introduction to this part it was explained why this magazine was chosen, and subsequently its European edition. The observations were started in the first weeks of 1997 and continued to the end of 2000, totaling about 200 magazines. Each observation was noted together with an indication of the kind of news it featured: political, social, war, academic, economic, cultural. However, no further use was made of this in the end. It was also noted if the news was explicitly negative, such as serious riots and criminality. The total of the observations is nothing more than the number of times a city was in the news, neutrally or positively.

It only says something about the newsworthiness of the city, in this case for the media and ultimately for the reader. In Table III.10' the WCR perception and the FP index are placed side by side.

The suppositions were correct: 11 of the 13 cities in the Top 13 of the study also have a relatively high FP index. Of course they are not all in the same sequence, but there is a strong similarity. Only two cities, Frankfurt and Madrid, are visible exceptions. The PL indexes of these cities of, respectively, 88 and 75% give sufficient confidence, however, that the list as a whole is a good reflection of opinions within the media cluster.

* * *

III.2.9 TOP CITIES FOR INTERNATIONAL ORGANIZATIONS

Although they are regularly referred to as dominant competitive factors in the literature, international organizations have not been confirmed as such by this research. With a score close to 40% they are no higher than the middle group. City governments, however – supported by their national governments – still attach great value to having such organizations established within their city. They are prepared to make great financial sacrifices to achieve this and the competition sometimes has to be settled at the very highest levels. For this reason alone there is cause to give special attention to their perceptions of the top cities for international institutions. Their viewpoint may also be completely different to that of the other clusters; their management team will often be international, for example, so there may be less chance of a continental distortion. Just over 100 participated in the study (25% response rate). Of these, 91 made a usable contribution to the construction of a ranking list.

Plausibility indexes
The PL indexes of the results lie well above the average, except for North America:

• Total 79% (+3) • Europe 79% (+8) • North America 43% (-21!) • Asia+ 86% (+19)

One can hardly regard the contribution from North America as 'seeming to be true,' all the more because it is a very small group (12). No conclusions can therefore be drawn from this response, and the score from North America will not be shown separately. In Figure III.11 (next page) the results are then shown for the total and for the continents Europe and Asia+. The replies from North America are, of course, included in the total.

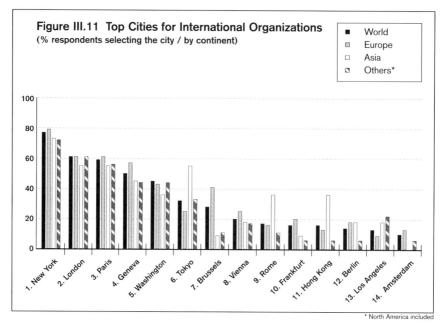

Figure III.11 Top Cities for International Organizations
(% respondents selecting the city / by continent)

■ World
▨ Europe
□ Asia
▨ Others*

* North America included

In this case, New York is more clearly in first place than London, which even has to share its second place with Paris. If the respondents felt that Geneva should not be left out of the list, then they had to add it themselves. This was frequently done, which contributes to the credibility of the results. A continental distortion can be observed for a few cities (Tokyo and Hong Kong), but, as stated above, it is not certain if this can indeed be traced back to the origin of the respondent.

Frames of reference

There is an extraordinarily precise record of international organizations available: the Union of International Associations publishes it every two years in its yearbook, comprising three enormous volumes. From one of the numerous overviews it appears that this is not a sector experiencing slow growth. While in 1985 there were over 24 000 registered, in 1999 this had more than doubled to over 50 000. How complicated this 'world' is can be seen in the number of types of organization that can be distinguished: three main groups comprise together 17 types and they can each be distinguished further into governmental (IGOs) and non-governmental organizations (NGOs). The editor of the yearbook admits in the explanatory notes that making the inventory is a hellish job, and acknowledges in advance the unavoidable shortcomings. Even so, it seemed at first to be quite simple to use the book to make a frame of reference by limiting it to "the central concern of the yearbook": the so-called 'conventional bodies' (types A–D). Altogether that is more than six thousand, but just a small part of the total. More important, however, was the feeling after a couple of test-runs that important institutions were being omitted: the Red Cross and the World Bank, for example.

This was sufficient justification for putting together a second list in which not only the 'conventional bodies' were included but also the type of organization (F) which, just like the first group, again covers many organizations that have little or nothing to add to the international profile and economy of a city. The classification generated by this second combination looks very different.

The two criteria mentioned above (the contribution of the organization to the international profile and to the economy of the city) were also used explicitly in the selection of the addresses for the research. That was exacting and time-consuming work which was aimed only at making a reasonably reliable selection of organizations that are truly of significance to a city (citymakers!). As one always strives for the largest possible list of addresses, the criteria were not applied too strictly. Even so, the total of more than 400 is in stark contrast to the 'official' numbers. Another reason to add to the frames of reference in Table III.11' a list with a completely different approach.

Table III.11' Top Cities for International Organizations
with reference to number of organizations located in city

| | WCR perception | | Number of International Organizations located in city | | | | | |
| | | | Combination A-D (1) | | Combination (A-D) + F (2) | | WCR-Mailing List | |
	%	ranking	abs.	ranking	abs.	ranking	abs.	ranking
New York	77	1	30	36-37	161	5	16	7
London	61	2	279	3	479	3	37	2-3
Paris	59	3	328	2	524	2	50	1
Geneva	50	4	96	4	212	4	34	4
Washington	45	5	36	19	141	6	21	5
Tokyo	32	6	44	13	71	14	13	9
Brussels	28	7	555	1	920	1	37	2-3
Vienna	20	8	72	5	109	8	12	10-11
Rome	17	9	51	9	133	7	5	20-25
Frankfurt	16	10-11	25	41-42	25	40-41	2	*
Hong Kong	16	10-11	12	>50	15	>50	4	*
Berlin	14	12	25	41-42	46	27	1	*
Los Angeles	13	13	8	>50	16	>50	4	*
Amsterdam	10	14	64	6	104	9	6	15-19
Bangkok	9	15	23	43-44	59	15	14	8
Singapore	7	18-21	41	15	53	21-22	7	13-14
Stockholm	7	18-21	59	7	84	12	0	*
Buenos Aires	6	22-24	46	11	56	16	5	20-25
Madrid	5	25-28	43	14	54	18-20	4	*
Nairobi	4	*	31	34-35	91	11	17	6
Mexico City	3	*	37	18	54	18-20	9	12
Cairo	2	*	45	12	53	21-22	12	10-11
Oslo	2	*	50	10	73	13	0	*
Copenhagen	1	*	52	8	97	10	2	*
Manila	0	*	19	49-51	33	35	7	13-14

(1) Conventional bodies; according to the UIA Yearbook 2000
(2) Conventional bodies + organizations having special form, including funds, foundations and financial institutions
* Not ranked anymore

All is well with respect to 10 cities from the top 14 of the WCR study; they are the first nine and the last one (Amsterdam). Only the position of New York is very high in relation to the number of establishments, and that of Brussels, on the other hand, comparatively low. Does the establishment of the United Nations have such an impact on perceptions that the number no longer matters? It seems to, as the PL index for New York is 100% in this case. Moreover, the IGOs do not form more than one-third of the response. A cast-iron image, apparently. That of Brussels is quite a bit lower on this point, especially outside Europe; not only because of the lower score, but also because the opinions differ quite widely (PL index 57%).

The other four cities are not recognized at all. It is noteworthy that they include two German and one American city, while it is precisely these countries that are relatively poor in international organizations. For Hong Kong it is equally difficult to think up any objective reason why it has fallen among the top 14. In addition, the PL indexes for these cities are certainly high: Frankfurt and Berlin 89% and Hong Kong and Los Angeles both 100%. Sometimes it seems better not to try and explain the perceptions. This does not detract from the fact that this part of the results must be considered as a weak point of the research.

* * *

III.2.10 TOP CITIES FOR MULTINATIONALS & FINANCE

The last and the best, if one believes the literature. No other cluster is mentioned or used as often as this one for determining the international competitive position and classification of cities; sometimes as if it were the only one. However, it has been established in part II of this volume that while it is indeed a very important factor, it is certainly not the only one and also not the most important. From another point of view it was even the worst one; the response rate of 11% was so low that 1200 addresses had to be used in order to make an analysis for this cluster possible. Of the 137 respondents, almost 100 correctly completed the question on the top cities.

Plausibility indexes
The PL indexes for the answers lie very close to the average for all clusters:

• Total 75% (-1) • Europe 72% (+1) • North America 67% (+3%) • Asia+ 67% (0)

Figure III.12 shows the nine cities that received 10% or more of the votes

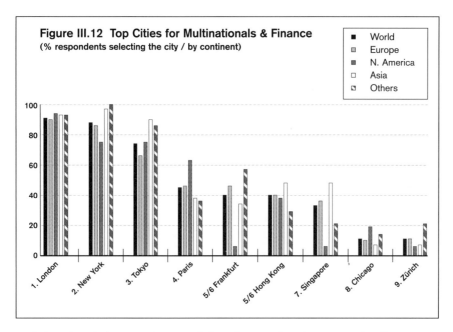

Figure III.12 Top Cities for Multinationals & Finance
(% respondents selecting the city / by continent)

and therefore belong to the top of this cluster. The cities seem familiar, owing partly to the abundant literature, and few readers will be very surprised by this result. For the research itself this is positive; confidence in all the results, not just these, can only be reinforced by this. However, there is still something noteworthy to mention. All the other clusters have a significantly broader top, varying from 13 to 19. It means that this cluster is indeed dominated by the 'big three' of Sassen, with a respectable middle group of four cities following behind, but after that there are only a couple more cities picking up the remaining crumbs.

Breakdown per magnet

This figure shows a combination of two groups: financial and non-financial multinationals. If it is divided into these two groups (Figure III.12', next page) then Paris clearly drops three places as a financial center and Frankfurt becomes the number four in the world. At the back Chicago and Zurich swap places. Frankfurt is overtaken by Hong Kong and Singapore, however, when only the non-financial companies are considered. Zurich's place is then taken by Atlanta. All of this is also very familiar.

Frames of reference

There are more than enough frames of reference in the literature. The only problem is that most publications date from the first half of the 1990s. Sassen's theory (1991) that cities with headquarters of MNCs (multinational corporations) in combination with MNFIs (multinational financial institutions) and MNCSs (multinational corporate services) are the 'command centers' of the world economy

157

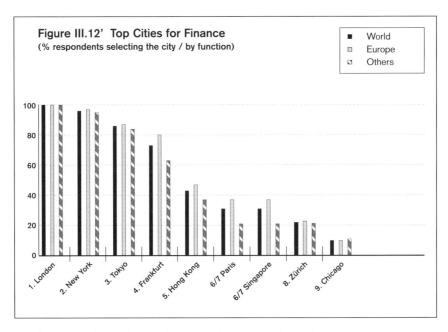

Figure III.12' Top Cities for Finance
(% respondents selecting the city / by function)

– only New York, London and Tokyo in fact, according to her – is not contradicted in that period; on the contrary, many articles use this 'triad' as their starting point. From 1995 there is a shift, however: the realization grows that a somewhat one-sided image of 'world city formation' has been created by this overaccentuation. Godfrey and Zhou (2000) miss Hong Kong and Singapore, in particular, in the well-known lists and advocate that, in addition to the 'corporate headquarters,' the important regional offices of these companies – the headquarters for Europe, Central America or South-East Asia, for example – should be included in the rankings. On this basis they make a list that looks somewhat different to the usual one. Because of its broader (or less narrow) point of view and because the list from these authors is still reasonably recent (the database is from 1997), the list of Godfrey and Zhou has been chosen as the frame of reference for the current cluster. Its shortcomings just have to be accepted – the regional headquarters of no more than 100 multinationals were covered, and for western companies the regional headquarters were very difficult to determine.

Finally, the temptation to include a recent list from Fortune could not be resisted; even if only to demonstrate where a ranking list based exclusively on the location of multinationals can lead. A similar exercise was undertaken for the financial world, but then on the basis of the ranking lists that The Bankers Magazine publishes each year of the (1000!) largest banks in the world. Table III.12" places all these side by side.

For the top of the classification, numbers 1 to 5, there is very little difference between the ranking lists at first sight. The sequence is also important, however, considering the differences between them and and the prestige attached to the

Table III.12" Top Cities for Multinationals and Finance
with reference to location of corporate headquarters in cities

Top Cities for Finance only
with reference to location of corporate HQ's

	WCR perception		Godfrey & Zhou (1)		Fortune 500 (2)		WCR perception !		The Bankers' 100 (3)	
	%	ranking	number	ranking	number	ranking	%	ranking	number	ranking
London	91	1	50	3	27	2-3	100	1	11	2
New York	88	2	69	1	20	4-5	96	2	10	3
Tokyo	74	3	66	2	73	1	86	3	17	1
Paris	45	4	29	7	27	2-3	31	6-7	6	4
Frankfurt	40	5-6	22	15-16	5	16-17	73	4	5	5-7
Hong Kong	40	5-6	40	4	1	*	43	5	0	*
Singapore	33	7	35	5	0	*	31	6-7	0	*
Chicago	11	8	22	15-16	2	*	10	9	1	*
Zürich	11	9	*	*	7	13-14	22	8	2	10-19
Washington	9	10	*	*	2	*	4	12-13	0	*
Atlanta	8	11-13	*	*	8	10-12	2	14-17	0	*
Amsterdam	7	13-15	18	24	4	18	6	11	2	10-19
Brussels	7	13-15	22	15-16	3	19-24	2	14-17	1	*
San Francisco	7	13-15	22	15-16	8	10-12	2	14-17	1	*
Houston	6	16	14	34-37	9	8-9	0	*	0	*
Los Angeles	5	17-19	20	21-22	5	16-17	2	14-17	0	*
Sao Paulo	5	17-19	25	11	0	*	8	10	0	*
Osaka	4	20-21	24	13	20	4-5	0	*	5	5-7
Munich	3	22-23	14	34-37	8	10-12	0	*	3	9
Dallas	2	*	11	42-44	6	15	0	*	0	*
Madrid	2	*	28	8-9	4	18	0	*	0	*
Toronto	1	*	18	24	7	13-14	0	*	5	5-7
Beijing	0	*	23	14	9	8-9	4	12-13	4	8
Düsseldorf	0	*	*	*	12	6	0	*	1	*
Mexico City	0	*	28	8-9	2	*	0	*	0	*
Milan	0	*	30	6	3	19-24	0	*	2	10-19
Seoul	0	*	26	10	11	7	0	*	2	10-19

(1) Godfrey, B.J. and Zhou Y in Ranking World Cities: Multinational Corporations and the Global Urban Hierarchy (in Urban Geography, 1999, 20, 3, pp. 268-281)
(2) Fortune Magazine July 2000
(3) The Bankers Journal July 2000
* Not ranked anymore   ! Financial Executives only

classification. The perception of Tokyo and Paris is then clearly lower, in this regard, than the positions which they are accorded on the basis of the ranking lists of both Fortune and The Bankers. After the first five, the glow of recognition swiftly fades: scarcely any relation can be detected between the perceptions and the locations of corporate headquarters or regional head offices.

Godfrey and Zhou were indeed successful in bringing Hong Kong and Singapore into view, but their ranking list does not otherwise contribute to a more comparative picture. The reader cannot avoid using his or her own perception when considering whether cities such as Osaka, Dusseldorf, Seoul and Beijing, with all due respect, do indeed belong to the top of the world in this field simply and solely because a larger number of multinationals are located there. To ask the question is also to answer it. The 'citymakers,' in any case, leave us in no doubt about it.

* * *

FIGURE III.13   The Leading Cities of the World

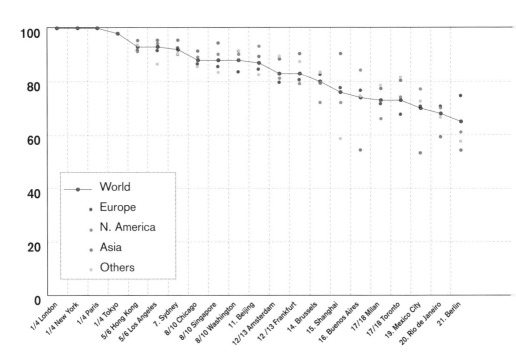

III. 3 THE LEADING CITIES OF THE WORLD (INTEGRAL PERCEPTION)

In the previous section a report was made of the functional perceptions of the 'citymakers.' For each of the ten different city functions, the cities were mapped that, in the perception of this target group, can be counted among the top in the world. In addition, the plausibility values of the results of the research were reported and a large number of sources were used as frames of reference in order to probe these functional perceptions further, to demonstrate how different methods can lead to different results and to reinforce – where necessary and possible – confidence in the plausibility of the results.

A city is more than the sum of its parts, and therefore an integral perception was also requested in the survey. In this section a report will be made on which

All Clusters (in % respondents selecting the city)

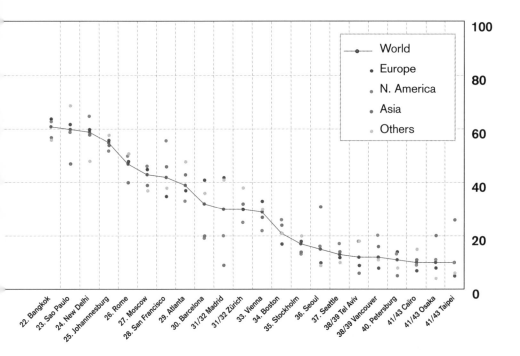

cities, in the opinion of the 'citymakers,' qualify for the label 'leading city of the world.' In part II, section 4 (Figure II.14') it has already been established that, in the eyes of the 'citymakers,' this qualification gives not only prestige but also a competitive advantage.

In Figure III.13 the 44 cities are shown that scored at least 10% on this question. It is recommended to pause and take some time to absorb the figure. Each reader will have his or her own personal perception on this question, and, in accordance with this, will find that s/he agrees with, doubts, or dismisses this overview. In the context of this personal reaction, the reader should remember that the figure reflects the opinion of more than 1200 diverse professionals ('citymakers') who show a high degree of unanimity. After a first acquaintance, an opportunity is taken for a few observations.

The first four cities are, of course, no surprise; such comprehensive research is not needed to establish those – although there are a number of academic publications, including some of the most renowned (Hall, Sassen), which do not include Paris in the absolute top; they speak regularly of the 'triad,' the three cities that form the world hegemony. The 100% score does not have to mean, however, that these four cities are all valued equally. For that, the functional valuations have to be consulted and especially those for the functions that are decisive for the international competitive position. This will be addressed in the final part of this volume, when the integral and functional valuations are brought together in a competitiveness model for cities.

The aim of the survey was to select a group of around 20 cities that could qualify for the label 'leading city in the world.' Introducing a cut-off point is somewhat arbitrary, as the line of the average score descends quite gradually. If the watershed is a score of 75%, then there are only 15 cities that qualify. If it is 50% then 25 cities can claim the title. A score of 2/3 of the votes (66%) seems to be a reasonable compromise; 21 cities then deserve the title, with Berlin as the last. This seems very reasonable, as not only was this city the only one to be upgraded from the second division, but it was also pronounced a top city by the 'citymakers' in a number of specific functions. Figure III.13 has been divided for practical reasons; the 21 'leading cities' are included in the first part and the other 23 in the second.

Even though the line of the average score only descends gradually after the 'big four,' a number of other small groups can still be identified among the 'leading cities.' These are first of all Hong Kong, Los Angeles and Sydney with scores of 92 to 93%. Then there is a quartet of cities with scores in the high 80s: Chicago, Singapore, Washington and Beijing. Then there are three European cities that have remarkably equal scores in the low 80s: Amsterdam, Frankfurt and Brussels. The cities Shanghai, Buenos Aires, Milan and Toronto score around three-quarter of the votes, while Mexico City, Rio de Janeiro and Berlin form the last small group.

As stated before, there is the possibility of a continental component. This makes the results extra interesting. This component is strongest in the response from Asia. Cities such as Singapore, Shanghai, Seoul, Osaka and Taipei receive conspicuously more votes from that continent than from the other continents. Latin American cities, on the other hand, receive a clearly lower valuation from Asia. These cities are also affected, however, (just like Madrid and Barcelona) by a distortion from their own continent. This cannot be seen in the figure because this preference is itself neutralized by the response from Africa and the Middle East, the two other continents in the group 'other.' For that matter, Madrid and Barcelona also receive many preferential votes from Europe; and the same applies to Berlin. The only continental component from North America affects San Francisco.

Plausibility indexes

The outcomes of the Plausibility check for the results of this section were already reported in section III.1. For all ten clusters these were very close to the average of 78%. The PL indexes for the separate continents, as was the case with the other questions, lie a little further apart: Europe reasonably close to the average and North America and Asia+ about ten percentage points below.

Frame of reference

Although one can have confidence in the plausibility of one's results, the need for at least one frame of reference continues to nag. The literature comes to mind first of all, for example the second version of the 'world city hypothesis' of John Friedmann (1995) or the research of Reclus/Datar (1989), although that is also from some years ago and only covers Europe. However, it is precisely these publications that exhibit the shortcomings which partly led to this research being undertaken in the first place: no research into the relevance of the competitive factors, and the functions are simply added together in order to reach an integral evaluation. In addition, the overview of Friedmann is something in between a ranking order and a typology of cities, and this also makes comparisons difficult. It therefore seems best to go no further than stating that of the 30 'world cities' selected by Friedmann, 19 can be found in the first 30 of the WCR study.

The annual publications of Fortune Magazine ("best cities for business") and Cushman & Wakefield/Healy & Baker ("the best cities to locate your business") were considered as frames of reference. They are the only ones which have the massive advantage of an integral design and being (at least partially) based on research among those involved. As their titles suggest, however, they are exclusively focused on the qualities of a city as a place to locate a business.

Some shortcomings can be overlooked, if one keeps certain reservations in mind. Use can then be made, for example, of the overview constructed by Beaverstock et al. (1999) using 16 studies (including that of Friedmann) which awarded the qualification of world or international status to a number of cities, each from their own starting point or angle. If the city with the most qualifications (15) is ranked number one, the one with 14 number two, and so on, then a ranking list can be created from the overview which can then be compared with that of the WCR study.

The reservation is that all 16 studies are quantitative in nature – based on the number of establishments, for example – and often take a very limited number of functions into consideration. It was pointed out earlier that functional ranking lists must be clearly distinguished from integral ones, that this is not always done and also that integral conclusions are sometimes drawn on the basis of a very limited number of functions or on the basis of functions for which the relevancy for the international position is not known. The comparison of the results of the research with those of the world literature has therefore been undertaken mainly to demonstrate the similarities and differences generated by the different approaches.

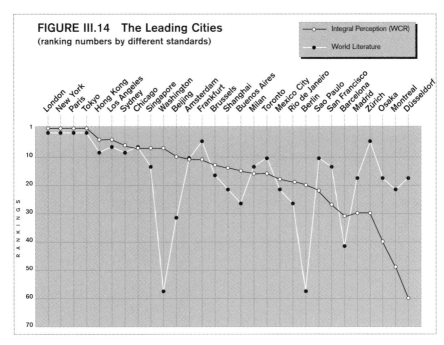

FIGURE III.14 The Leading Cities
(ranking numbers by different standards)

Figure III.14 illustrates this comparison. The cities that score highly in the collected world literature but did not qualify as a 'leading city' have been added to the figure. The ranking from the world literature is indicated with a white line; the 'leading cities' with a black one.

From this comparison it can be seen that, once again, the differences only start after the 'big four.' It is very obvious that Sao Paulo, San Francisco and Zurich clearly lag behind in the perception of the 'citymakers' compared to their ranking based on the world literature. On the other hand, cities such as Washington, Beijing and Berlin score much much higher on the basis of perception. A number of other differences are also noteworthy; what, for example, should we make of the high valuation for Osaka, Dusseldorf and Miami in the world literature?

The differences are too numerous and too large to allow conclusions to be drawn from this comparison. The WCR research will therefore have to be judged on its own merits as a new addition to the literature 'family.' The comparison does underline the fact that very different conclusions can easily be reached, depending on whether the research is based on perceptions or data. The most important reason for this seems to lie in the 'overvaluation' of the functions multinationals and finance in the literature.

A self-made frame of reference is also available. In the previous part of this volume, which handled the competitive factors, 'Free Publicity' was indicated as a factor that cannot be omitted from an analysis of the international competitive position of a city. In recent years the frequency with which cities have profiled themselves on various subjects has been followed in an international magazine such as Time. On this basis an (integral) Free Publicity Index has been constructed. It is integral because this index, in contrast to the functional one, covers the city in all its facets. In the introduction to section III.1 the method used for this was explained. This FP index has already been used, with the overview of top cities for Media in the previous section. Now there is an opportunity to use the index for its original purpose: as an integral frame of reference for the integral perception. In Table III.15 the two are placed side by side. As the underlying numbers have already been reported in the earlier section (Figure III.10'), the overview contains only the ranking from the FP index.

Around half of the 'leading cities' also belong to this elite group on the basis of the 'FP ranking,' albeit in a different sequence in most cases. A number of the 'leading cities' have, however, a conspicuously low FP index; highly placed cities such as Chicago, Singapore, Amsterdam, Frankfurt and Shanghai are notable examples. From the overview it cannot, therefore, be positively concluded that the FP ranking provides a firm basis for an integral ranking of cities; at most, it gives extra certainty for a limited number of 'leading cities,' while at the same time raising some doubts on the position of others. This is why the PL index for the score as 'leading city' has also been included in the overview. From this it can be seen that there is no doubt about the opinion of more than 1200 respondents from 80 cities in six continents.

However, it is interesting to turn the argument around; it should not be forgotten that, for the functional perceptions, the FP index was established as a reasonably reliable measure. If this is taken as the starting point for the integral perception, then the differences remain but a different conclusion can be drawn: the five cities mentioned clearly have a publicity problem. As this involves an important competitive factor, this could damage their international competitive position in the long term.

Finally

It is interesting to place the list of 'leading cities' side by side with two other competitive factors from the study: population and seat of government. In Table III.16 the population size is indicated in cate-

Table III.15 The Leading Cities of the World
with reference to Free Publicity

| | WCR-results | | Free Publicity |
	ranking	PL-index (%)	ranking (1)
London	1-4	100	1
New York	1-4	100	3
Paris	1-4	100	2
Tokyo	1-4	100	9
Hong Kong	5-6	94	5
Los Angeles	5-6	98	13
Sydney	7	92	11
Chicago	8	91	50
Singapore	9	95	34
Washington	10	97	4
Beijing	11	97	8
Amsterdam	12-13	92	47
Frankfurt	12-13	94	29
Brussels	14	90	15
Shanghai	15	88	53
Buenos Aires	16	85	22
Milan	17	81	29
Toronto	18	87	34
Mexico City	19	81	20
Rio de Janeiro	20	83	38
Berlin	21	78	10

(1) Source: Time Magazine 1997-2000

Table III.16 The 'Leading Cities' of the World
with reference to Population and Seat Government

Leading Cities	> 20 mln.	10-20 mln.	5-10 mln.	2-5 mln.	< 2 mln.	Population Ranking for the 80 researched cities	Population Ranking for for all cities
1-4 London		11,8				16	16
1-4 New York	21,4					2	2
1-4 Paris			9,7			21	21
1-4 Tokyo	34,8					1	1
5-6 Hong Kong			7,3			27	29
5-6 Los Angeles		16,6				8	8
7 Sydney				4,2		47	67
8 Chicago			9,3			22	24
9 Singapore				3,3		55	92
10 Washington			7,7			24	26
11 Beijing			8,5			23	25
12-13 Amsterdam				2,1		69	164
12-13 Frankfurt				2,1		71	177
14 Brussels				2,5		65	133
15 Shanghai		11,7				17	17
16 Buenos Aires		13,4				11	11
17 Milan				3,8		48	76
18 Toronto			5,2			40	50
19 Mexico City	20,3					4	4
20 Rio de Janeiro		11,2				18	18
21 Berlin				4,2		46	66

Source: "The Principal Agglomerations of the World" (UN publication 2001)

gories, and the 'leading cities' with a seat of government are printed in bold.

The conclusions that can be drawn from this correspond with the comparatively low valuations (25 and 12% respectively) that both elements received as competitive factors. It is not necessary to be a megalopolis in order to be seen as a 'leading city': seven of the 21 'leading cities' belong to the category of smaller conurbations (2 to 5 million inhabitants). However, when two-thirds have 5 million inhabitants or more, it can equally be concluded that a large population does have some advantages. This was referred to earlier in the discussion of the results for this factor in part II.

It is even less necessary to be the seat of government. Only 11 of the 21 'leading cities' have this quality. If we look at the larger group of 43 cities (cities with a score > 10%), then there are 21. However, as stated earlier, although it may not be a decisive factor for the international competitive position, it remains an important one. The degree of importance appears to depend on the international significance and the political structure of the country. On this basis it can be explained, for example, why Beijing has a superior position to Shanghai, although the latter, on the basis of functions, should clearly have been placed higher.

* * *

III. 4 THE PERCEPTIONS FACE TO FACE

Ranking lists of cities appear with great regularity on a variety of subjects. Originally a field for academia, it now receives attention from commercial institutions as well – the fact that a fair amount of publicity can be attracted by it undoubtedly plays a role. This publicity influences the formation of perceptions; and as perception plays an important role in all kinds of decisions, it is necessary for the ranking lists to be based not only on correct data but also on relevant data. The latter in particular is sometimes lacking, with the result that cities are judged on aspects that are of lesser significance to their international competitive position. The crucial factors were mapped earlier, in part II.

Ranking lists are also sometimes misleading because a lower or higher classification can suggest a much larger difference than is actually the case. On the other hand, a small difference in classification can sometimes disguise a large difference in size or quality.

Finally, most ranking lists are constructed on the basis of quantitative data, for example a number of establishments. A cluster, let alone a city, cannot be judged on one single aspect. If more aspects are considered, however, it is very tempting to base the classification on the (indexed) mathematical sum. The academic world, especially, is still struggling with this issue; the more commercial publications handle it better.

Nonetheless, rankings are a vital instrument for cities in the analysis of their (international) competitive position. However, the classification and handling of the data must be done in an accountable way. The academic world is ideally qualified to take a pioneering role in this.

In this third part a report has been given on the research results concerning the ranking of cities. First, the classifications for the ten different clusters of functions were addressed. The 'citymakers' indicated which cities are among the top in the world for their own cluster, according to their (functional) perception. On the basis of this, a ranking list of Top Cities was put together for each cluster. In addition to this functional perception, the 'citymakers' also evaluated the cities as a whole: the integral perception. This resulted in a list of 21 'leading cities.'

No other example is known of a study of perceptions of this size and diversity. In Table III.17 (next page) the functional classifications for the ten clusters and the integral one are summarized in a clear overview.

New York and London are at the top in almost all the functional ranking lists, with the number one spot being claimed in one by New York and in another by London. The differences between them are almost always quite small. In two cases (academia and museums) Paris joins them. Together with Tokyo, the 'city of light' is always to be found among the top cities, usually very high in the ranking

Table III.17   Rankings for Integral and Functional Perceptions

Rankings based on integral perception Cities with 'Leading City' status	Rankings based on functional perceptions ('Top City' status) *									
	Performing Arts	Hospitality	Real Estate & Architecture	Int. Trade & Transport	Academia	Corporate Services	Museums	Media	International Organizations	Multinationals & Finance
1-4 London	2	1	2	2	1	1	3	2	2	1
1-4 New York	1	2	1	1	3-4	2	2	1	1	2
1-4 Paris	4	3	3	7-8	2	5	1	5	3	4
1-4 Tokyo	11	5-6	7	3	3-4	4	16	4	6	3
5-6 Hong Kong	-	4	4	4	-	6	-	11	10-11	5-6
5-6 Los Angeles	-	18-19	10-11	11	6	-	12-14	7	13	-
7 Sydney	-	12	12-14	-	-	-	-	-	-	-
8-10 Chicago	7	9	5	9	9	8	15	-	-	8
8-10 Singapore	-	5-6	12-14	5	-	12	-	-	-	7
8-10 Washington	-	14-16	-	-	10	7	5	3	5	-
11 Beijing	-	-	-	-	16	-	-	6	-	-
12-13 Amsterdam	8	13	-	6	13-15	9	6	-	14	-
12-13 Frankfurt	-	14-16	10-11	7-8	-	3	12-14	9-10	10-11	5-6
14 Brussels	-	17	-	13	-	13	-	8	7	-
15 Shanghai	-	-	9	10	-	-	-	-	-	-
16 Buenos Aires	-	-	-	-	-	-	-	-	-	-
17-18 Milan	6	-	15	-	-	-	-	-	-	-
17-18 Toronto	-	-	-	-	17	-	-	-	-	-
19 Mexico City	-	-	-	-	-	-	-	-	-	-
20 Rio de Janeiro	-	-	-	-	-	-	-	-	-	-
21 Berlin	5	8	6	-	8	-	4	9-10	12	-

Other Important Cities

26 Rome	-	7	17	-	-	-	7	-	9	-
27 Moscow	13	-	-	-	13-15	-	12-14	12	-	-
28 San Francisco	9	10-11	12-14	-	7	10	-	-	-	-
29 Atlanta	-	-	-	12	-	-	-	-	-	-
30 Barcelona	-	18-19	8	-	-	-	11	-	-	-
31-32 Madrid	-	14-16	-	-	-	-	8	13	-	-
31-32 Zürich	-	-	-	-	-	-	-	-	-	9
33 Vienna	3	10-11	-	-	-	-	9	-	8	-
34 Boston	12	-	16	-	5	11	-	-	-	-
35 Stockholm	-	-	-	-	13-15	-	-	-	-	-
37 Seattle	-	-	-	-	12	-	-	-	-	-
40 Petersburg	10	-	-	-	-	-	10	-	-	-
41-43 Taipei	-	-	-	14	-	-	-	-	-	-
56 Houston	-	-	-	-	11	-	-	-	-	-

* Scores of 10% and more only

or otherwise high in the middle group. Tokyo drops to the tail of the classification in just the two cultural functions (Performing Arts en Museums). Only these four cities operate at a high international level for all ten clusters. They are the most complete and that will be why they received the full 100% as 'leading city.' Nevertheless, the differences in valuation of functions for London and New York on the one hand, and Paris and Tokyo on the other, are not small. This can be seen better, however, in the separate scores (percentages) than in the classifications. In the final part IV these scores will be portrayed once again, but in a different and easy to compare format. The differences between Tokyo and Paris are also clear in a number of cases; usually to the advantage of the latter. In general, this research shows that the so-called 'triad' of Sassen, Hall et al. must be enlarged with the addition of Paris, or perhaps it can better be reduced to a pair. Only New York and London are, after all, "true global cities of the world"; they are not only complete but also the top in everything.

Nevertheless, the conclusion cannot be drawn that there is a connection between a functional valuation and the valuation as 'leading city.' To name just a few examples: a city such as Sydney only scores in two functional classifications and then very low; as a 'leading city,' however, it scores particularly high. Berlin scores reasonably high in as many as seven functional classifications, but only just scrapes through into the classification 'leading city.' San Francisco scores in five functional classifications, but does not make it in the integral perception; while Beijing only scores twice functionally and then low, and still becomes number 11. Finally, Buenos Aires, Mexico City and Rio de Janeiro do not score in any of the functions, but nonetheless maintain their position as 'leading city.'

The message from the 'citymakers' to the academic world is clear: you cannot determine whether or not a city is 'leading' by just adding up functional scores. Apparently there are other issues to be considered. Might it be the power, the size, the potential or the image of the country in which the city is located? Whatever the case, they are close to unanimous. This is shown by the plausibility values that were calculated for all the answers together, for the clusters and, as necessary, even for the separate cities. It is a convincing demonstration that the research does indeed reflect, even in detail, the opinions from the clusters as well as those of all the 'citymakers' taken together.

In addition, a large number of frames of reference have been collected or constructed against which the results can be checked. First, this enhances the insight into the various methods that can be used to rank cities. From this a general rule has emerged that the many kinds of rankings must be very strictly interpreted. Whether they are based on the level of rent, or the quality of hotels, the number of conferences, or the largest banks, they mean just that and nothing more; no further conclusions can be drawn about a city. In addition, the relevancy of the factor concerned for the international competitive position of a city must always be questioned. There are rankings that cities can acknowledge fairly laconically.

A second function of the frames of reference was to help remove any doubts on a certain ranking, should there be any. In some cases, especially in the case of rankings based on the free publicity index (the frequency rate at which a city makes it into 'the news'), this has been fairly successful. The use of this approach to gain further insight into the competitiveness of cities certainly deserves further exploration. With most of the other methods all went well for the four top cities, but after that the similarity with the research results rapidly decreased or even disappeared. In those cases, the PL index had to be examined in detail in order to remove the doubts that had crept in. In nearly all cases it was then found that the citymakers fully agreed on the position the city concerned had been given on the ranking list. Only in one case (International organizations) was it ultimately concluded that even perceptions have their "dirty little secrets."

◆ ◆ ◆ ◆ ◆

PART IV
CITY PROFILES

"It is the layering of urban functions, in different proportions, in different cities,
that makes the analysis of world cities so complex"
(Ann Markusen and Vicky Gwiasda 1994, p. 169)

IV.1   A BRIEF REVIEW

IV.2   APPLYING THE CITY DIAMOND

IV.3   OBSERVATIONS

IV.1 A BRIEF REVIEW

In part II, section 1, the first aim of this research – designing an operational competitiveness model for cities – was discussed in the context of Porter's national model. The conclusion was drawn that this national model cannot be used unaltered to portray the international competitive position of a city. A number of adjustments appeared to be necessary, and were facilitated by the changes in emphasis that Porter himself advocated in the 1990s.

In the second section, using the existing literature, a selection and valuation was made of competitive factors for cities that would need to be presented to the target group of the research (the 'citymakers') for their appraisal. In the third section these competitive factors were grouped in five determinants. Together they form the ingredients for a competitiveness model for cities. A number of issues were visualized using an actual 'city diamond.'

Subsequently, a comprehensive report was made of the results of the research in which the 'citymakers' were asked for their opinion, their perception, of the local factors that make a city prominent or 'leading.' Using these results, a model for an analysis of competitiveness for cities was constructed with the factors that are crucial for the international competitive position of the city. It is a basic model; it can be expanded with other factors as required. However, it cannot be emphasized enough that all factors are important, even if they are not part of the basic model.

In part III a report was made on the second aim of the research: the ranking of cities both functionally (per cluster) and integrally (for the city as a whole). The research has provided a classification of Top Cities for each of the ten clusters. The integral perception was also requested, alongside the functional perception. More than 1200 'citymakers' have indicated, with great unanimity, which cities they perceive as so prominent that they qualify for the label 'leading city of the world.'

In this way, each city has a (functional) score, varying between 100 and 10%, for each cluster. Scores under 10% are also available, but are based on very small numbers. Each city also has an integral score. For the 'leading cities' (21) this varies between 100 and 65%, and for the other important cities from 61 to 10%.

* * *

172

IV.2 APPLYING THE CITY DIAMOND

Available data

In this final part, the basic competitiveness model will be applied to a number of cities, using the scores mentioned above – at least, as far as that is possible! Of the (minimum) total of 15 factors, the research provides a score for eight: all seven factors in the determinant 'clusters' and the factor 'leading city' from the determinant 'International Profile.' The research does not provide data for the other factors, therefore it remains to be seen if other sources can be found for these, or some other kind of next-best solution. If not, then it must be accepted that the factor cannot be filled in. This will now be examined for the following determinants and factors:

1. Determinant/factor National Competitiveness;
2. Determinant International Profile: the factors Media Coverage and City Center;
3. Determinant City Government: the factor Political Leadership;
4. Determinant The Human Factor: the factors Skilled Labor, Openness and Multicultural;
5. Optionals.

1. National competitive power is a special determinant in the competitiveness model. In part I it was explained that the competitive power of a city is influenced or determined in a number of areas by the national environment of which the city is a part. As such, it must be included as a given in the model. Models exist that, inspired by Porter's theories to a lesser or greater degree, map national competitive power either partially or integrally. The most detailed and comprehensive is probably "The World Competitiveness Yearbook (WCY)." Since 1994, this study has classified and analyzed the business climate in 49 industrialized and fast-developing countries, using data and opinion studies on more than 250 criteria, spread across 20 factors and four determinants. Results are given for each determinant and also integrally. The latter can be used to fill in the factor national competitiveness in the city model, albeit with a somewhat heavy heart. For in the end this calculative model, no matter how carefully the factors have been selected and weighed, is once again nothing more than a mathematical addition of disparate quantitative and qualitative quantities.

2. The determinant International Profile includes, amongst other things, the factor Media Coverage. In part III the Free Publicity Index was used as a frame of reference, based on four years' issues of Time magazine, and it can also be used as a score for this factor. This is the only index available, which does not mean that there is no other or better way of expressing a score for the media coverage of a city as a whole. That alternative route has simply not yet been developed,

and, if/when it is, it will be essential that it covers the whole world and that, in principle, all cities have a realistic chance of obtaining publicity.

The quality of the city center is the third factor in the determinant International Profile, alongside Free Publicity and Leading City status. New comparative research also needs to be developed for this, and research on the basis of perceptions would be ideal; however, a different kind of survey should be used. Citymakers may have a professional perception on many cities, but that is not to say they also have a perception of the city center. That requires more detailed knowledge, and personal experience plays a large role. A perception study should therefore be tailored to that experience. On-the-spot research would seem to be, therefore, the best guarantee that the correct target group will be reached (the 'citymakers') and that their personal experiences are explored. There are cities that conduct this kind of research themselves. If the results are to be compared, then a uniform design (target group, place, frequency and questions) is required.

3. In the basic model for an analysis of city competitiveness, a full place has been allocated to local governance, under the title Political Leadership. This is not exclusively the elected city government, but also the various authorities which, through the interests that they represent, are (partially) responsible for the international competitive position of the city. With regard to city government, this refers in particular to the power to mobilize various private and public organizations for a joint operational goal. No study is known which provides measurable results for this which could then be included as a score in an analysis of competitiveness. It would have to be some kind of internal study of satisfaction; outsiders would find it difficult to judge the 'internal business strategy of a city.' Clearly, such a study should also involve the professional interest groups that represent the various clusters.

Once again, perceptions on this point could be the key to and also the results of the research. What may start as a fairly spontaneous perception, should, in a well-managed process, develop into a carefully considered standpoint. The results must be comparable to those of other cities; therefore the same benchmarks must be used. This process also has an important secondary aim: the parties involved are drawn into discussion with each other, where that may not have been the case before or not sufficiently, and thus one basic condition for partnership has already been fulfilled.

4. Of the three factors in the determinant The Human Factor, 'highly skilled labor' is by far the most important. The demand for highly skilled labor is, however, extremely diverse. For many activities it depends on local and regional availability. The greater the specialization or expertise required, then the greater the demand for mobility of the labor force when the local market cannot adequately meet these needs. In most countries the next limit will be the national market, but in special cases it does not stop there and becomes international. The greater the

radius of action, the more important it becomes to offer not only good working conditions but also good living conditions. The many different qualities of a city play a large role in this. It is not for nothing that 'Quality of Living Reports' are among the most noticeable ranking lists produced for cities. In fact, a high quality of living is complementary to the factor 'labor force.'

For the WCR perception study it could not be anticipated that 'highly skilled labor' would be signalled as one of the most important competitive factors. No further questions were therefore asked about it, not even to the executive search firms (part of the cluster Corporate Services) who are ideal examples of experts in this field. A perception study on this point, particularly where they are part of a worldwide office network, could provide excellent insights into the qualities of a city with regard to the availability of highly skilled personnel or, perhaps more importantly, the power to attract them to the city and to ensure that they stay.

While no such insight is available, we will have to make do with a 'next best' solution. One of the eight determinants of the WCY gives each country a score for "the availability and qualifications of human resources." Keeping the mobility of specialised labor in mind, it seems justifiable to use these national scores for the city model as well. However, as stated before, the professional perception of those with experience at local, national and international level is much to be preferred.

It will require quite some research before the factor 'Open to the World' can be operationalized. Emphasis can be placed on the economic side, the human side, or on a combination of both. Even when one has reached a conclusion for one city, it will be difficult to do the same with other cities – and that is essential if one wishes to compare the results of research on this point. A rigorously coordinated process will be unavoidable. The very first question to be addressed must be: what is already known? The answer will probably be that much work remains to be done in operationalizing the entire scope of the factor, and especially the human side. The following question will then be: which target group can give the most expert opinion? The most obvious is the group of 'expatriates' who have worked and lived there for a number of years. Then there is the question of how to select and approach such a diverse group. Only once all this has been agreed upon, can a start be made with implementation.

Until then this important factor will remain blank, unless it can be covered temporarily by an emergency measure. Once again the World Competitiveness Yearbook offers a way-out. Among the many factors one also finds 'openness.' This factor is made up of five elements, four of which have to do with attitudes towards globalization and its consequences. The fifth is more general and refers to the image that exists abroad about a country's attitude towards the business sector. This does focus on the economic side, but surely the human factor will be involved in one way or another in such a judgement. Out of necessity, and with much greater hesitation than was the case for the previous factor Skilled Labor, the result of the last element has been included in the competitiveness model.

175

Once more: the result is for a national factor and is based on opinions from the business sector.

All large cities are melting-pots of races, cultures and nationalities, to a lesser or larger degree. In part II it was established that this great variety of people offers both opportunities and threats to a city. A city that succeeds in using it as an enrichment adds an important plus point to its international competitive power. Having established this, the question that immediately follows is how this success can be measured in a way that allows the result to be compared with that of other cities. It does not seem very likely that rigid standards can be developed for this. Again, one might come a long way with perceptions. However, it is once more a factor on which comparative outsiders, the 'citymakers' of other cities for example, may find it difficult to give an opinion. Thus the perception of insiders from within their own city would have to be used. Obtaining an objective professional opinion from them, which can also be compared to that from other cities, is an extraordinarily difficult task. A completely separate study would seem to be necessary. Reason enough to refrain from trying to give any indications here for such a perception study. Also sufficient reason to realize that, for the time being, this factor will have to remain blank in competitiveness analyses.

5. While three of the factors have to remain blank, there are factors that can be added to the model, if desired, as long as one remains constantly aware that these factors may be important but they are not crucial to the international competitive position of the city. This is the reason why space has been created in the model for a number of 'optionals.' Each city can add these at its discretion.

A possibility that may be attractive to many in this context is the factor 'Quality of Life.' This factor was not included in the research because no-one quite understands the same thing by it, and it is not an operational concept. However, that does not have to stand in the way of including this factor in the model, if accountable comparative research has been undertaken. Even if it is not possible to base operational policy on it, the result still gives an indication of how living in the city is evaluated – with respect to international standards, of course, for that is all that counts in this context.

The annual study of William M. Mercer Companies is probably the most authoritative. It gives an inventory of perceptions for 40 factors that are relevant in the opinion of international executives. These perceptions and the relevant criteria are the strongest points of this research. Another strong point is that the executives are asked to indicate how important they consider the diverse factors to be. A weak point is once again that the factors, after they have been given a weighting, are added together to give a single final total. This is unavoidable, considering that the aim of the research is to function as an aid in determining compensation packages for expatriates. However, it is also to be regretted, as 'quality of life' is an integral concept that cannot be captured in a mathematical addition, however carefully the factors may have been weighed. Bearing this comment in mind, and especially with an eye to its internationally established authority, this study (2001) has been used to fill in one of the variable factors.

The research into perceptions which is the subject of this volume also provides data for four clusters that are considered less essential to the international competitive position of a city: Corporate Services, International Organizations, Media and Real Estate & Architecture. Of these four, the first two received the highest scores as competitive factors, which is sufficient reason to include them among the 'optionals.' Of course, the other two could also have been included. Omitting them emphasizes, however, the discretionary character of this part of the competitiveness model. The relevant results were given earlier, in part III.

With the above data, the competitiveness model for cities can be completed for the cities studied, and their international competitive profiles can be portrayed. Of the 15 basic factors, eight can be filled in using the WCR perception research, three using the World Competitiveness Yearbook, and one using self-made Free Publicity research, while the other three have to be left blank. Of the three 'optionals,' two can be filled in using the perception research and the third using an annual worldwide study. Table IV.1 gives a summary.

Table IV.1

Determinants	Factors	WCR Perception	WC Yearbook (national data)	Other data	No data available
Clusters	Multinationals	+			
	Finance	+			
	Aviation	+			
	Hospitality	+			
	Academia	+			
	Performing Arts	+			
	Museums	+			
National Competitiveness	National Competitiveness		+		
The Human Factor	Highly Skilled Labor		+		
	Open to the World		+		
	Multicultural Society				+
City Government	Leadership				+
International Profile	Media Coverage			+	
	Leading City Status	+			
	City Center				+
Optionals	Cluster Corporate Services	+			
	Cluster Int. Organizations	+			
	Quality of Life			+	

■

The model has been completed for the 21 'leading cities' and also for a limited number of other cities that may not have achieved that status but still received a good score for a number of functions: Rome, San Francisco, Barcelona, Madrid, Vienna and Boston.

It should be mentioned that the scores from both the WCY and the FP index (Media coverage) are related to the country or city with the highest score (= 100%). For uniformity, the scores from the WCR study have been adjusted accordingly. The city with the highest absolute score received 100% and the other scores have been related to this. This provides different, somewhat higher, percentages to those in the figures in part III, but in relation to each other they remain, of course, the same. The scores from the research that were lower than 10% have also been included in the models. Admittedly it involves very small numbers, but 8% or 0% still indicates some difference in appreciation and that is what it is all about.

CITY PROFILES

<table>
<tr><td>

'BIG FOUR' (p.180 -181)

London
New York
Paris
Tokyo

</td><td>

ASIA (p.188 -189)

Hong Kong
Sydney
Singapore
Beijing
Shanghai
Bangkok

</td></tr>
<tr><td>

NORTH AMERICA (p.182 -183)

Los Angeles
Chicago
Washington
Toronto
San Francisco
Boston

</td><td>

LATIN AMERICA (p.190 -191)

Buenos Aires
Mexico City
Rio de Janeiro
Sao Paulo

</td></tr>
<tr><td>

EUROPE (p.184 -187)

Amsterdam
Frankfurt
Brussels
Berlin
Milan
Rome
Vienna
Moscow
Zürich
Madrid
Barcelona
Stockholm

</td><td></td></tr>
</table>

Legenda City Profiles

| Determinant Nation | Determinant International Profile | Determinant The Human Factor | Determinant Clusters | Optionals |

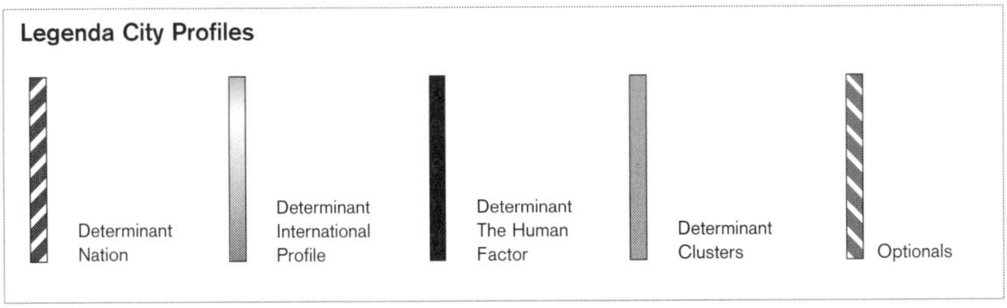

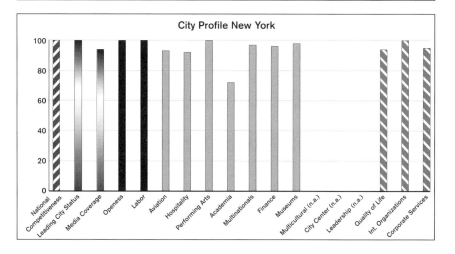

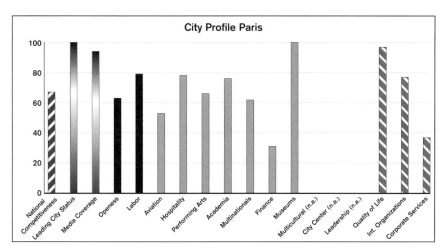

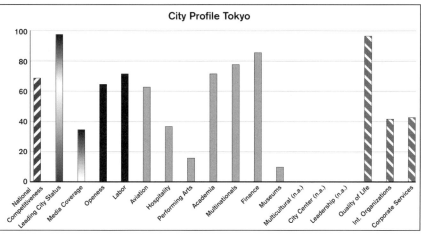

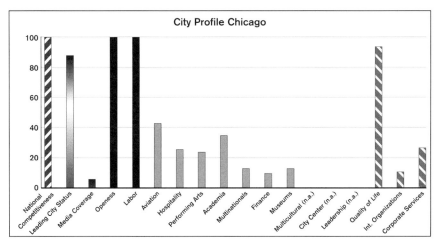

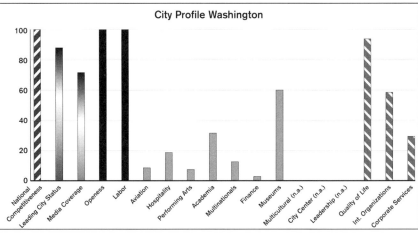

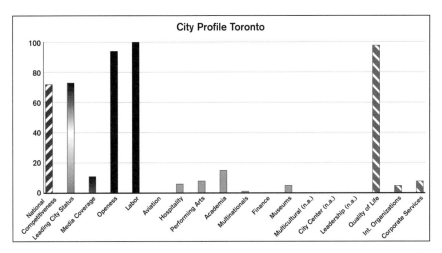

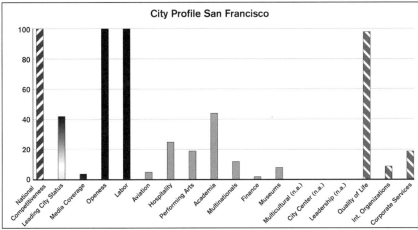

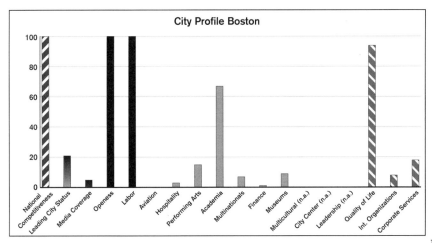

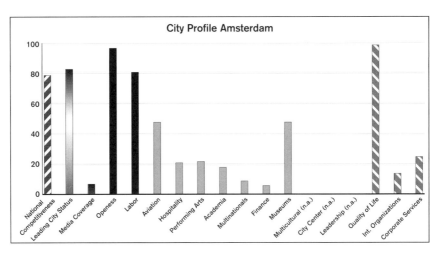

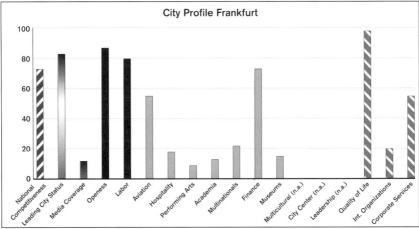

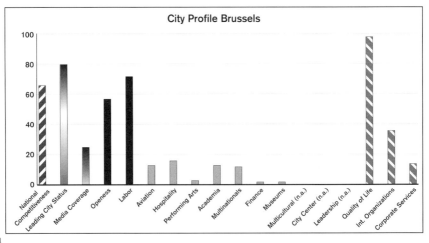

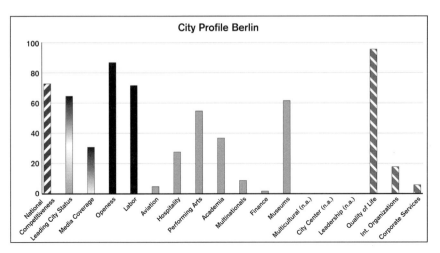

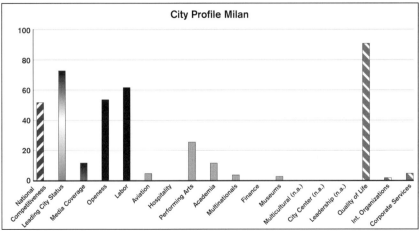

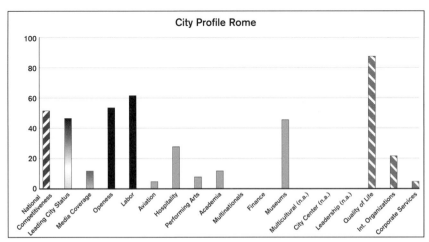

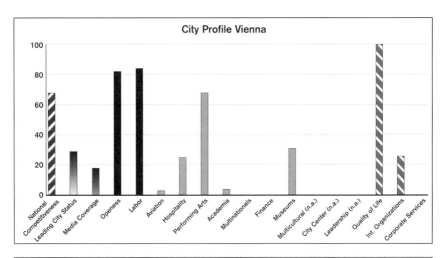

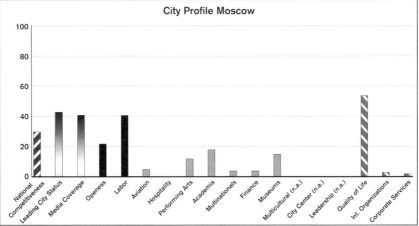

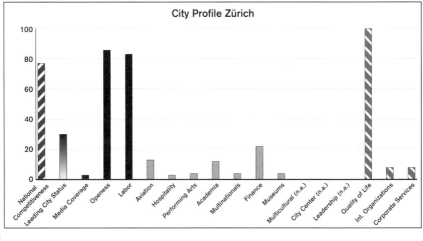

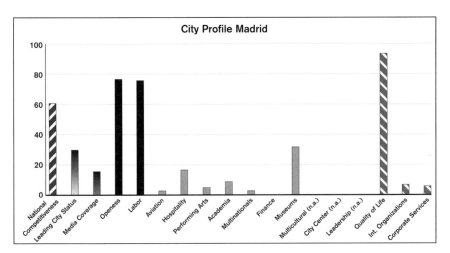

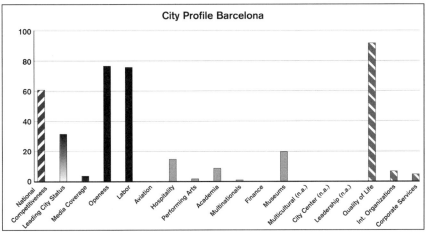

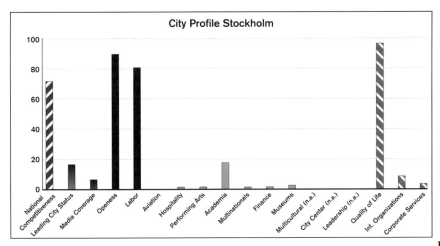

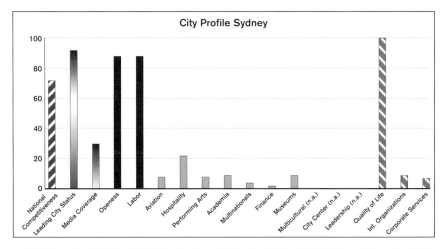

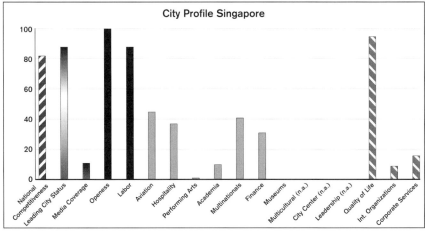

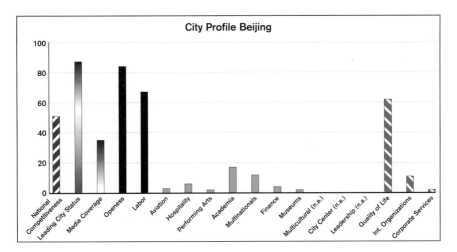

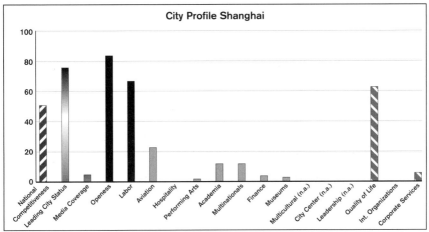

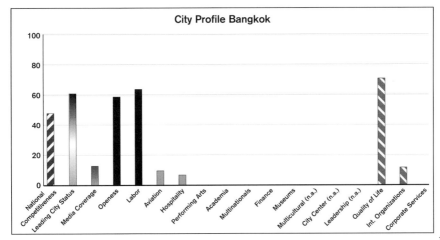

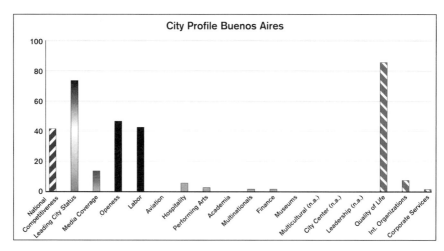

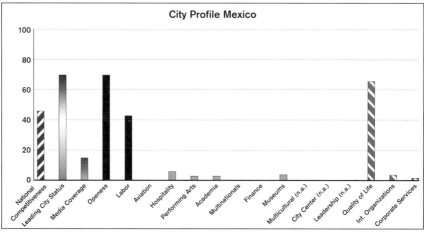

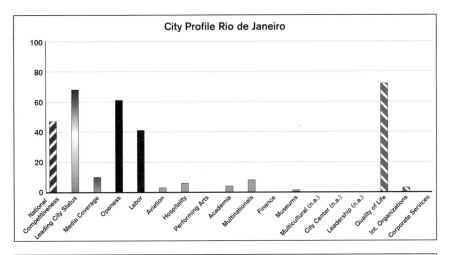

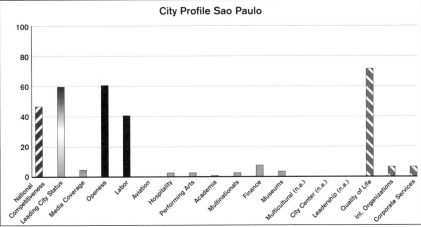

IV.3 OBSERVATIONS

A number of observations can be made on the basis of these profiles of competitiveness, starting with the profiles of the 'Big Four' as they are a group apart. The profiles of the other cities will then be grouped by continent, as competition between cities, or rather between the businesses and institutions established there, takes place more on a continental scale than a global one. John Friedmann undertook a similar exercise when, in 1995, he retrospectively assessed his original 'World City Hypothesis' of 1986 and at the same time looked to the future. Occasional reference will be made to this in the following.

'The big four'
As had already been established in section III.4, the similarity between the

■

IV.3 OBSERVATIONS

A number of observations can be made on the basis of these profiles of competitiveness, starting with the profiles of the 'Big Four' as they are a group apart. The profiles of the other cities will then be grouped by continent, as competition between cities, or rather between the businesses and institutions established there, takes place more on a continental scale than a global one. John Friedmann undertook a similar exercise when, in 1995, he retrospectively assessed his original 'World City Hypothesis' of 1986 and at the same time looked to the future. Occasional reference will be made to this in the following.

'The big four'

As had already been established in section III.4, the similarity between the profiles for **London** and **New York** is striking. The differences are minimal and all factors score exceptionally high so that both profiles are almost completely filled. If differences had to be found, then London scores a little better on the separate functions, while New York has the advantage that the US scores the maximum with regard to national competitive power, highly skilled labor force and 'openness.' However, these are small differences and should certainly not be further exaggerated. These are two world cities who are a complete match for each other!

For some time now there has been confusion in the literature on the position of **Paris** as a world city. The number of true world cities is supposed to be limited to New York, London and **Tokyo**, the "command centers of the world" (Sassen). Hall has also contributed to this image by not including the 'city of light' as a study subject in his standard work "The World Cities." This City profile shows that Paris is, at the very least, equal to Tokyo. There are noteworthy differences: Tokyo is stronger in the 'profit' functions and Paris in the 'non-profit' ones. The profiles of both cities are, however, clearly inferior to those of London and New York. On the other hand, they are conspicuously more complete than the profiles of all the other 'leading cities.'

Continental observations

In **NORTH AMERICA**, five cities have received the status 'leading city.' One of these, Toronto, lies in Canada. New York, of course, stands alone at the top. The fact that Los Angeles and Chicago have joined it in the list boosts confidence in the research; in the literature these three cities are frequently mentioned as the top ones in the United States, although this usually refers to national competitive positions rather than international ones. Washington is usually seen more as an outsider, and the high position of this city will probably raise questions. Those who think that its high score is due to its position as the capital of the 'world's leading nation' have lost sight of the fact that its City profile is not inferior to that of Chicago and certainly not to that of Los Angeles.

The competitive profiles of San Francisco and Boston are scarcely inferior to those of the cities already mentioned, and clearly better than that of Toronto. Even so their score for 'leading city' status is substantially lower. San Francisco did stay ahead of Atlanta, but no less than 61% of the respondents indicated that the latter is not a 'leading city.' A remarkable score when one considers that Atlanta contains two highly developed functions: after New York it is the center for multinationals and Hartsland Atlanta International Airport is a distinct 'hub'; in addition it was selected as the host city for the Olympic Games not so long ago. All to no avail. More interesting than this statement is, however, the question of why all of this was not able to prevent its downgrading. On the basis of the research, no other explanation can be found except a lack of image, at national and international level.

Seattle and Vancouver just made the 10% cut-off, thus the highly placed expectations of Friedmann for this pair located on the North East Pacific coast have not (yet) been realized. Cities such as Houston and Dallas failed to reach even the lowest cut-off, although both are locations for a large number of multinationals, and Houston also has a worldwide reputation as a center of academic knowledge, as shown in the relevant functional perception. A city that does not appear at all, although it was high on the list in Friedmann's analyses, is Miami. Even in the cluster trade and transport it was seldom mentioned by the respondents.

EUROPE can rejoice in seven 'leading cities.' Two of these, London and Paris, are among the absolute world top. Authors who did not believe or could not imagine that two world cities could be located so close to one another will have to adjust their imaginative faculties. John Friedmann even placed Paris in a third category: "cities with important national articulations."

Amsterdam scored well for the non-profit functions; however, so did other cities, such as Rome, Vienna, Berlin, Madrid and, to a lesser degree, Barcelona. The difference with these lower placed cities is that Amsterdam also scores highly as a 'hub.' It is therefore probable that it thanks its high classification as 'leading city' largely to Schiphol Airport and the home carrier KLM.

Frankfurt certainly thanks its status to its economic functions. Where it lacks cultural functions, Berlin shines; on the other hand this city lacks the economic functions of the Manhattan on the Main. If Berlin and not Frankfurt had been chosen as the location for the European Bank in the 1990s, then that decision might have laid the basis for a fifth world city.

German cities face heavy competition in the home market; an excellent starting point to be able to handle international competition, Porter would say. However, neither the functional nor the integral perceptions give any indication of this. Although, for example, Munich and Dusseldorf are both centers for impressive industrial and financial conglomerations, they do not generate that association with the 'citymakers.' Friedmann's prediction that Dusseldorf would become a prominent world city within ten to twenty years does not seem likely

193

to be realized. Even though it is centrally placed in an impressive economic region, the city lacks the required international profile and especially an airport with a sufficient frequency of intercontinental connections.

The latter draws one's attention back to Berlin, another city where the most important competitive factor has not been realized. Efforts towards this begin, of course, with the construction of an adequate airport, but the real fight starts afterwards: the battle for intercontinental connections. Further development of Berlin as a 'leading city' would seem, therefore, to lie largely in the hands of Lufthansa.

Although the profile of Brussels, compared to that of Frankfurt or Amsterdam, is low, the city scores equally high for the status of 'leading city.' While the high position of Washington could be explained on the basis of the functional scores, in the case of Brussels there remains only the question of whether, after all, its function as European capital was decisive. The collapse of Sabena raises serious questions on the future development of Zaventem Airport and, as a consequence, on the development of the city as a whole.

Milan and Rome seem to be a fairly good match, even if not at a particularly high international level. Did Milan perhaps have the (imaginary) advantage of being placed in the first division in the pre-selection, and Rome the (equally imaginary) disadvantage that it had to work harder to get itself upgraded? The difference in economic valuation (or image?) seems to have been decisive, to the advantage of Milan. From a functional point of view, however, these two cities are more closely matched than is expressed in the scores for 'leading city' status.

Madrid and Barcelona are a similar rival pair. Although they score in a number of functions, they do not come near to achieving the status of 'leading city.' It is striking how evenly the respondents valued both cities on almost all issues. In the eyes of the 'citymakers' they are a complete match for one another, both functionally and integrally. The only significant difference is the higher score of Barcelona for Architecture, while Madrid has a higher valuation from the cluster Museums. The latter cluster is a very important competitive factor, as has been demonstrated by the research. However, once again it has been shown that it leads to a higher integral score only when in combination with other factors.

The City profile of Vienna has strong similarities to the Italian and Spanish cities mentioned above. It distinguishes itself only in the area of Performing Arts; there the city belongs to the absolute world top. This distinction, however, is equally poorly translated into its score for 'leading city' status. In that regard, it scores conspicuously less than Milan and Rome and about the same as the Spanish pair and Zurich. The latter could only distinguish itself somewhat as a financial center.

There is another pair of rivals: Moscow and St. Petersburg. This rivalry also takes place largely at national level. Internationally, both cities score in the cultural arena, and Moscow also in the academic world. Economically, however, neither plays an international role, which can be attributed to the unfavorable competitive position of the Russian state. The fact that Moscow still scores more than 40% for 'leading city' status then probably reflects its position as the political center of a weakened superpower.

Then there are the Scandinavian cities. Of these, only Stockholm appears in the scores, albeit very modestly. Functionally, it distinguishes itself at the level of Amsterdam and Moscow as a center for academia. The score for 'leading city' status was, at 17%, well below that of the other European cities mentioned above.

ASIA, including Australia, has six 'leading cities,' of which Tokyo belongs to the 'Big Four,' behind New York and London and also a little behind Paris. It is not lonely at the Asian top however, or not any more. Not only does Hong Kong score almost as highly as 'leading city,' but it also approaches Tokyo's level in the valuation of economic functions.

However, in the non-profit clusters Hong Kong still has a long way to go; from an international point of view they are very underdeveloped. Whether or not they will make progress in the future seems to depend largely on how China develops as a nation and on the development of two competitors: Beijing and Shanghai. Taking their low City profiles into consideration, both of these cities, and especially Beijing, score remarkably high as 'leading city.' Once again, being the capital city of an influential nation pays off; in this case with an extra 11 percentage points.

The United States and Germany are two countries with several competing cities that have significant City profiles. In the US, New York is the undoubted number one; in Germany the struggle is still undecided. In China a similar situation is developing, but it is not likely that everything will be staked on a single city, as in England, France and Japan. With this in mind, one wonders whether Hong Kong will be able to continue successfully in its race with Tokyo. It will probably have to turn its attention to maintaining its position as a co-center in the basin of the South China Sea.

Singapore, the only remaining 'city state,' is lying in wait there, as always. Its competitive profile is pretty much equal to that of its great rival, Hong Kong. Its position as economic center in South East Asia also seems to be invulnerable. This title reveals that its position as a city is based primarily on economic functions. However, the city has proved itself capable of meeting many challenges. Bringing its non-profit functions up to an international level is yet another one, albeit of a very different nature.

Bangkok and New Delhi have both disappeared from the original list of 'leading cities.' With their lack of competitive profile, and considering the enormous tasks facing their home countries, it seems unlikely that they will be able to distinguish themselves further internationally in the immediate future.

In the City profiles of Osaka and Seoul, the large number of head offices of multinationals is the only noteworthy item. Even so, both cities are towards the bottom in the classification of 'leading cities.' The comparative examples from the

United States and Europe are thus confirmed. Friedmann's expectations for Seoul also seem to be realized. However, he was rather more optimistic for the position of Osaka.

Finally there is the special case of Sydney. A reasonably big city in a large country with a low population, a long way away from other economic and population centers and without any noteworthy scores in any function. A city that, in the opinion of Friedmann, is of a similar class to Seoul, Mexico City or Sao Paulo. The city must then have a terrific image in order to score so highly for 'leading city' status. If anyone is thinking that the successful Olympic Games may have given it a helping hand, they should remember that the research was completed well before that event took place. It is good example of the enjoyable side of research into perceptions: it can deliver surprises!

Another surprise is the result for **LATIN AMERICA**: three cities (Buenos Aires, Mexico City and Rio de Janeiro) with 'leading city' status and without any competitive profile. This is in very sharp contrast to Friedmann's statement that he did not wish to give Rio de Janeiro and Buenos Aires a place even in the third category any more, but that Sao Paulo would naturally continue to fulfill its role as "principal articulator" of the Brazilian economy and that the future of Mexico City was "far from clear" (p. 38).

We now know that no link can be made between functional scores and the integral score as 'leading city.' This is clearly illustrated by the profiles of these cities: they do not score above 10% in any function. Do we just have to accept that perceptions can be inscrutable, or does this come from having a position in the first or second divisions of the questionnaire, or a combination of both? The respondents had no doubts, even if others do. Unless the contrary can be proven, their opinions should be respected. They gave their professional preferences, and are close to unanimous in their opinions. The results cannot, however, be rationalized. From the results it can also be seen that no single city sets the tone for this continent. With their more national than international competitive profiles, they are perfectly matched.

AFRICA was represented with two cities in the questionnaire. Johannesburg, which was included in the first division, did not manage to achieve 'leading city' status. Cairo, in the second division, received just enough votes to cross the 10% cut-off. Friedmann had already pointed out in 1995: "Johannesburg will find it difficult to win back its old position as the only world city in Africa." In subsequent years it seems to have become, if anything, even more difficult.

Concluding remarks

If the functional scores were added up, another list of 'leading cities' would be created. Cities such as Beijing, Shanghai, Buenos Aires, Mexico City, Rio de Janeiro and probably also Milan, Sydney and Toronto and maybe even Los

Angeles would lose this status. Their place would be taken by cities such as San Francisco, Rome, Madrid, Barcelona, Vienna and Boston. The higher functional scores of the latter cities are only for non-profit functions, however. Apparently this is not sufficient for 'leading city' status. Considering the positions and profiles of Hong Kong, Singapore and Frankfurt it seems that economic functions are more of a guarantee for this.

A city can be one of the top world cities, can be 'leading,' without distin-guishing itself in any functions. Even a relatively unfavorable national competitive position and/or moderate Quality of Life do not stand in the way of this status. Beijing and Shanghai and the Latin American cities are examples of this. The competitive factors may have been mapped as thoroughly as possible, but the integral perception apparently involves quite different considerations. Perhaps the function as capital city of a large or important country? New Delhi did end up with more than 50%, while Atlanta – a city with a large number of headquarters – fell from the first division with 39%. One can only speculate.

It is unsatisfactory, particularly for academics, to find that the results of research, especially research into perceptions, sometimes cannot be explained. The temptation is then to question its validity. In this case there is little reason for that, considering the results of the Plausibility check. This does not mean, howe-ver, that the list of 'leading cities' given here is the last word on the matter. It is very possible that research on a differently structured target group, using an adjusted questionnaire or other method, would give a slightly different list that would appeal equally to the imagination. Each study must therefore be judged on its individual merits. With this in mind, it is recommended that no more value is attached to the status of 'leading city' than that given in one of the concepts: "The label of 'leading city' provides prestige for a city and gives it a competitive advantage."

◆ ◆ ◆ ◆ ◆

EPILOG

"In general, a city has to understand why it is not competitive,
second where it can be competitive and finally what it can do
to become competitive".

(Jan van den Berg and Ilaria Bramezza, 1991, p. 14)

I

Have the original objectives of this project been achieved? This question cannot and should not be avoided, now that it has been completed. Let us remind ourselves once more of the aims, before turning to the answer:

1. To make an inventory of the factors that make a city internationally competitive, prominent, 'leading,' and to use this to design an operational model of competitiveness for cities, à la Porter's national model;
2. To rank the cities, both integrally and functionally;
3. To realize both these aims through research among the parties most involved, in accordance with Porter's recommendation.

1. First, in order to be able to portray the international competitive position of a city, an inventory was made, with the help of the literature, of the factors that play a role in the international competitiveness of cities. These factors (34) were included in the questionnaire. In addition, they were used in an attempt to apply the Porter model to the city. This proved to be somewhat more complicated than suggested by Porter himself when he proposed that, "the theory can be readily extended to explain why some cities or regions are more successful than others" (p. 158). Ultimately, the analysis resulted in a 'city diamond,' which one naturally associates with Porter's 'national diamond.' The determinants and their associated factors, however, differ significantly. Therefore there is a question of whether it can properly be called a model à la Porter, but it was certainly inspired by it.

On the basis of the results of the survey, it was possible to select 15 factors that are most relevant for the international competitive position. As such, they should be a standard part of any analysis of competitiveness of cities. This smaller number of factors brought the practical application of the 'city diamond' somewhat closer, but are the factors measurable and comparable?

This was the subject of another part of the survey: the question about the integral and functional valuation of cities. Using these results it was possible to fill in eight factors of the standard competitive profile. Data for a further four factors could be found via an alternative route; admittedly, not a completely satisfactory one, but justifiable at this stage. For the three remaining factors, however, a practical method still needs to be developed. This will be a particularly challenging task for the factor 'multicultural.'

With 12 of the 15 crucial factors filled in, plus another three 'optionals,' it has been demonstrated that the main part of the competitiveness model is indeed operational. In addition, it proved to be straightforward to compare the profile of one city with that of another by use of graphical figures; it was not necessary to add up the scores to do so. One can look back with satisfaction on the achievement of this particular objective. At most, it is pity that it was not possible to fill in the competitive profiles completely. The 'citymakers,' however, made it clear that it is too soon for that; further study is still required on some factors.

2. The questions about the 'leading cities' and 'top cities' had more than one aim. On the basis of the answers it was possible, as stated above, to fill in the competitive profiles to a substantial degree. In addition they provided a single ranking list of the 21 'leading cities' and 11 ranking lists of the 'top cities' of particular clusters. It therefore goes without saying that, on this point, the original aims of the research were more than met.

3. If one recalls yet again that the results given above were obtained from a survey of around 6500 'citymakers' in more than 80 cities across the world, of whom the vast majority believe themselves to be involved in the international profiling of their city, then one can look back with some sense of satisfaction on a project which covered a period of more than five years. Knowing that, with a response rate of 21%, all eyes would be on the validity of the results, a check was developed to determine their plausibility; in other words, the likelihood that a subsequent group of answers would give a comparable result. The plausibility value of 78% for the results as a whole shows that this is, in fact, highly probable.

II

Quite unexpectedly, a fourth objective crept in. During the project, the author became increasingly aware of the shortcomings inherent in the current ranking lists of cities – more so in the academic literature than the more commercial studies and publications. This feeling began when the Reclus/Datar report was consulted, one of the fundamental studies in this area. Within it, the most disparate factors are simply added together like a grocery bill in order to create a classification of cities. Sadly, this continues to happen to this day. Although most authors recognize that the underlying data do not in fact lend themselves to this, they nonetheless do not flinch from basing classifications and typologies upon them.

A city is, however, much more than the sum of a number of factors. Even a single factor, such as an international financial center, is itself an ensemble of various kinds of activities that do not lend themselves to being valued on the basis of, for instance, the number or size of banks or the number of funds on the stock exchange. When evaluating a city, either integrally or functionally, many aspects must be taken into consideration. Similarly, you cannot simply calculate which is the best bank or the best university. No wonder it is the universities, or at least their executives, that are starting to object to the kinds of evaluations which take a number of arbitrary factors, award them a plus or a minus, add them all up in some fashion, and then churn out a classification. These kinds of organizations are far too complex for such treatment; and so are cities. Only the experts on the inside are capable of weighing all the relevant interdependent aspects. It is therefore better <u>and</u> more effective to tap into their professional perceptions.

From the start, the author had the impression that the valuation of a city should only be done on the basis of perceptions, while a functional valuation could also be possible on the basis of data. Later, having applied a number of frames of reference, he came to the conclusion that even functional ranking lists can be justified only on the basis of perceptions. However, let it be quite clear: there should be absolutely no objections to the classification of cities on the basis of, for example, the cost of real estate, the quality of hotels, the number of congresses, the crime rate, the size of banks or on the number of headquarters of multinationals. These kinds of overviews can be exceedingly instructive. What must be avoided, however, is attaching far-reaching conclusions about a city to them. Academics know this very well, and attempt to take refuge with the term 'indicators.' The caution built into this term is swiftly forgotten, however, and work then continues unperturbed on a "city ranking," "typology" or "formation."

This was the most important motivation for seeking frames of reference for all the results of the research, so that the results from different methods could be compared to each other. These comparisons show more differences than similarities; apart from the 'big four,' often there was scarcely a likeness. Moreover, a few frames of reference even contradicted one another. *"L'art de grouper des chiffres"* has in this sphere indeed been elevated to an art form. The conviction was confirmed that it is much better to base this kind of classification on a study of perceptions.

The impression that cities should preferably be evaluated on the basis of perceptions was also confirmed through a quite different route. The research has shown that there is not necessarily a connection between the functional scores and the integral score of a city. Particularly striking was the fact that a city can receive an exceptionally high score as a 'leading city,' while barely scoring at all at a functional level. This means that no conclusive 'world city formation' can be determined on the basis of functional valuations. There are factors playing a role in perceptions of which, apparently, even the 'citymakers' are not consciously aware. Their choices do not always, therefore, appear logical. 'Feelings' may then be 'facts,' but it is troublesome, especially for academics, when the choices do not appear to be explicable in all cases.

Of course, it is for others to judge whether data research or perception research, or a combination of the two, will lead to the best results. Perception research could be the best route, but it is not the easiest one, for it makes high demands on the professionality of the target group. The 'citymakers,' such as those selected for this study, have to combine their experience and knowledge on all the relevant aspects. These must be taken together in order to reach a weighed, integral judgement on a certain function or as a whole. However, they will also have their personal and local preferences, and therefore high demands must also be made on the scope and geographical spread of the target group.

III

Together, these 'citymakers' have ensured that a competitiveness model for cities could be designed and then substantially filled in for more than twenty cities. Before a city is tempted to initiate a similar study itself, only to discover after a time that it is a hopeless task for a city alone, let us remind ourselves of an important experience gained from this research.

While a feeling of satisfaction accompanies the end result of the research, nevertheless it would not lend itself to a repeat effort; at least, not in this format. There is an impression that with less effort an even better result could be reached.

The most important lesson learned was that one needs a network of people in the relevant cities who feel personally responsible for the success of the study. This need had, indeed, been anticipated, and a contact person had therefore been sought in each city; successfully in 40 cases. However, they were only asked for assistance, and only then when it was strictly necessary. It has been shown that this did not create a lasting bond, or it was only a personal relationship and not a connection with the institutions for which they worked. For a worldwide study, a network is needed of institutions which have an affinity with each other, are striving for the same objectives, who continue to feel responsible for this objective and are conscious that it can only be reached in cooperation with others.

When this condition is met, the target group ('the citymakers') can be approached much more effectively, the response rate will be markedly higher, it will be possible to get even more information through personal interviews, and a local component can even be added to the research.

As a network is a primary condition, such a worldwide study can only be undertaken by an institution that has a worldwide network of offices (such as a consulting firm or bank), or by an institution which can create such a network on the basis of a common goal (a city or a university, for example). The initiative and coordination will need to be centralized at a single point, where the project will be analyzed and evaluated in consultation with the network.

Of course, it will also be necessary to publish the results. Perceptions on these issues are not very susceptible to change, and neither are the competitive profiles, so for the sake of all the parties involved – initiator, network and especially for the target group – it would be better not to strive for too high a frequency for the main publication. Once every three years, with intermediate publications, seems reasonable. Considering the great interest worldwide for the competitive position of cities, success would seem to be guaranteed. The gauntlet has been thrown down; the question is, who will pick it up?

◆ ◆ ◆ ◆ ◆

EXECUTIVE SUMMARY

INTRODUCTION

"No company, and no country, can afford to ignore the need to compete.
Every company, and every country, must try to understand and master competition"
(M. Porter, 1998, p.1)

And what about cities? In a globalizing world, with borders becoming blurred and international competition increasing, cities also need to be constantly aware of their own international competitive position. Whereas enterprises can strengthen their position through takeovers, mergers, or joint ventures, cities cannot. Cities can only try to make the most of their competitive advantages. A city with international ambitions has to be able to face the challenge of international competition, and therefore must have insight into its international profile.

Which *local* factors make cities important, prominent, trend-setting, leading? One should be able to find the answer to this question in the academic literature, and, indeed, there are many publications dealing with the competitive factors of cities. However, at best they are based on the researchers' personal analyses. Even influential professors such as Sassen, Friedmann and Hall do not explain how the key elements they selected relate to other, non-selected elements. For the national level, Michael Porter paved the way with his standard work The Competitive Advantages of Nations (1990), in which he introduced his famous 'national diamond.' Surprisingly, though, at the level of the city no such substantial research exists, let alone that a 'city diamond' has been developed. Based on these findings, the aims of this volume are:

1. To map the key local factors that determine the international competitive position of a city: the competitive advantages (Part II).
2. To map the cities that are the leading cities of the world:
   integral ranking (Part III).
3. To map the cities that are at the top with respect to the most relevant functions: functional ranking (Part III).
4. To outline the international competitive profile of the world's leading cities (Part IV).

PART I - THE RESEARCH

This part addresses the local factors of competitiveness as described in numerous academic and other publications, and explores the extent to which these selected factors are based on fundamental research. For that purpose, 23 publications of an academic or more commercial nature have been analyzed. The findings of this section can be summarized as follows.

In order to be able to get a good impression of a city's international competitive position and, subsequently, to develop meaningful policy, it is necessary to map the relevant competitive factors, including the relative importance of each factor. As far as can be determined, this has never been done before.

Ranking and classifying cities is a popular and useful occupation that can be approached in several ways. The most obvious are through integral or functional rankings. However, it is also a delicate business. If the starting points are not carefully defined, the results will be inaccurate and thus unreliable. In both the academic literature and commercial publications there seems to be an irresistible urge to classify cities (and countries) by just adding up individual factors, even though the authors know very well that a city is much more than the simple sum of its parts. This is why it was decided to construct, separately, both integral and functional rankings.

The research into perceptions

It is true that decision-makers want to know all the facts. Yet they also give plenty of space to their own intuitive feelings about and evaluations of the object of their decisions, which in this case is the city. Decisions can relate to the city as a location for enterprises, as a location for an annual international conference, as a candidate for an international sports event, as a stopover during an international tour, as a place for developing, buying or selling real estate, as a hub in an international network, as a background for commercials, and so on and so forth. This intuitive, subjective feeling, this perception, can become a decisive element in itself.

The individual's perception of a city is distinguished into an integral and a functional perception. The former relates to the overall picture of the city, which may be built up from numerous impressions, sometimes very personal ones. The functional perception relates to one single part and usually stems from one's professional background. For instance, an architect, the conductor of an orchestra, and the director of the tourist information board will each have his or her own functional perception of one and the same city.

Porter stated (1990, p. 545), "The ability to upgrade an economy depends heavily on the position of a nation's firms in that portion of the economy exposed to international competition." In this study, the citymakers have become the target group: ten clusters of enterprises, organizations and institutions, all working in an internationally competitive environment, and contributing through their qualities to the international profile of the city. Table I.1 (p. 16) presents these clusters, including their 'magnets' around which the others group themselves.

A second selection that had to be made involved the cities. In which cities should the 'citymakers' be approached? Using five criteria, including, of course, the literature, more than 80 cities were selected, spread across six continents (Table I.2, p. 18).

The research was carried out in the period of January 1998 through March 2001, by means of a questionnaire sent by mail.

Evaluation of the research

This section presents a detailed account for each of the ten clusters regarding the addresses selected for the questionnaire, the number of questionnaires sent, and, of course, the response received. The results, per continent, are summarized in Table I.4 (p. 28), which also includes the dates on which the study was started and closed.

To be absolutely clear, this research is tentative; an exploration into the perceptions of 'citymakers'. A statistically accountable result was not aimed at because of the complexity of the target group. Instead, an approach was chosen which would lead to plausible conclusions. In order to measure the plausibility of the responses a special (plausibility) check was developed; not as a statistical test, but as a tool to verify sufficient consistency in the responses registered. On this basis it can be stated that the results of the survey give a reliable picture - both for the total and for the separate clusters - of what the 'citymakers' perceive as important with regard to competitive factors and the ranking of cities, the two aims of the research.

PART II - THE COMPETITIVE ADVANTAGES

Based on the results from the research explained above, in this part an attempt is made to realize the primary aim of this thesis: to develop a model that will provide an insight into the competitiveness of a prominent international city. A model like Porter's 'diamond,' but in this case for a city instead of a country.

The City Diamond

In Table II.2 (pp. 60 and 62) a survey, based on the literature, has been presented of the factors influencing the international competitive position of a city. The survey makes a rather chaotic impression and it could not be established that any of the selections were based on fundamental research. Nevertheless, an emphasis on certain factors could be clearly observed.

This section examines how the selected factors can be allocated under the four determinants of Porter's model. This was only partially successful, which shows that the national model cannot be applied to the city without some adjustment. Porter's four basic determinants have been reshuffled and transformed into three new ones, with different names and new content. In addition, governance is no longer on the sidelines but has been incorporated into the model as a fully fledged determinant. Last but not least, the national competitive power has also been incorporated as a separate determinant, in line with the fact that the national competitiveness has to be seen as a given for the competitive power of a city.

Porter contends that, in practice, any factor can influence another factor, but the interaction between some factors is stronger than that between others. The interactions of the five determinants and their factors are therefore described. Following this, a 'diamond' can be drawn for the city, although it is now a pentagon as there are five determinants: clusters, the international profile, governance, the human factor, and national competitiveness (Figure II.3, p. 77). However, this is merely a theoretical model, based on factors largely selected from the existing literature. In order to make the model operational it is necessary to get an insight into the extent to which each factor contributes to the subject of this study: the international competitive power of a city. This was precisely the aim of the research among the citymakers. These professionals were asked to indicate which of these 35 factors, in their opinion, are the most important for the international competitive power of a city.

Findings of the research

This section first reports on the experiences gained through the question mentioned above. Then an insight is presented into the PL index for this question, which was 79% for the total of all answers.

Figure II.5 (pp. 92 and 93) presents the scores for each of the factors involved in the research. Such a table of results contains the risk that low-scoring factors are discarded as being unimportant. However, all competitive factors are important, it is just that one may be more important than another. The aim was to select those factors that are of crucial importance for the international competitive position of a city and therefore should not be left out of any analysis of competitiveness.

This resulted in 15 factors. In Figure II.17 (p. 118) these factors have been incorporated into the 'city diamond,' which constitutes an important step in the effort to arrive at an operational model. In order to be able to apply this model, the research results for the ranking of the cities will be needed, both integral (the leading cities) and functional (the top cities). These results are addressed in Part III.

PART III - WORLD CITY FORMATION

In this third part a report is given on the research results concerning the ranking of cities. First, the classification of ten different clusters of functions is addressed. The citymakers have indicated which cities are among the top in the world for their own cluster, according to their (functional) perception. On the basis of these data, a ranking list of top cities for each cluster has been composed.

In addition to this functional perception, the citymakers have also evaluated the cities as a whole, the integral perception. This has resulted in a list of 21 leading cities. No previous study of perceptions of this size and variety is known. Figures III.3 to III.12 (p. 129 onwards) summarize the functional classifications per continent and for the ten clusters, as does Figure III.13 (p.160 - 161) for the single integral classification per continent (the 'leading cities of the world').

Almost all the functional rankings place New York and London in the top two places, sometimes with London as number one and sometimes with New York. The differences between them tend to be very small. In two cases (Academia and Museums) Paris joins this select company. Both Paris and Tokyo are always among the top cities, usually very high in the ranking or high up in the middle section. Tokyo is in the bottom section for only the two cultural functions (Performing arts and Museums). Only these four cities function at a high international level for all ten functions. They are the most complete, and that is probably why a full 100% of respondents refer to them as leading cities.

However, this does not justify the conclusion that there is a direct relationship between the functional valuations and the valuation as 'leading city.' To mention but a few examples, a city like Sydney scores in only two functional rankings, and then very poorly, but as 'leading city' it scores very highly. Berlin scores relatively highly on no less than seven functional rankings, but it only just makes the qualification of 'leading city.' San Francisco scores on five functional rankings, but does not get the qualification of 'leading city,' whereas Beijing scores on only two functional rankings (and poorly), but it still scores an eleventh place as 'leading city.' Buenos Aires, Mexico City and Rio de Janeiro, finally, do not score on any functional ranking, but they nevertheless consolidate their positions in the ranking of 'leading cities.'

The citymakers' message to the academic world seems to be clear: whether or not a city is 'leading' cannot be determined by adding up the functional scores. Other issues clearly matter as well. Is it the power, the size, the potential, or the image of the country where a city is located? Whatever the case, they generally agree with one another. This is clear from the PL index that has been calculated for all the responses taken together, for the clusters and, when necessary, even for individual cities. It is a convincing demonstration that the research does indeed reflect, even in detail, the opinions from the clusters as well as those of all the citymakers taken together.

In addition, a large number of frames of reference have been collected or constructed against which the results can be checked. First, this enhances the insight into the various methods that can be used to classify cities. From this a general rule has emerged that the many kinds of rankings must be very strictly interpreted. Whether they are based on the level of rent, or the quality of hotels, the number of conferences, or the largest banks, they mean just that and nothing more, and they do not allow further conclusions to be drawn about a city. In addition, the relevancy of the factor concerned for the international competitive position of a city must always be questioned.

A second function of the frames of reference was to help remove any doubts on a certain ranking, should there be any. In some cases, especially in the case of rankings based on the free publicity index (the frequency rate at which a city makes it into 'the news'), this was fairly successful. The use of this approach to gain further insight into the competitiveness of cities certainly deserves further exploration. With most of the other methods all went well for the four top cities, but after that the similarity with the research results rapidly decreased or even disappeared. In those cases, the PL index had to be examined in detail in order to remove the doubts that had crept in. In nearly all cases it was then found that the citymakers fully agreed on the position the city concerned had been given on the ranking list. Only in one case (International organizations) was it ultimately concluded that even perceptions have their "dirty little secrets."

PART IV - CITY PROFILES

In this final part the international competitive profile of the leading cities of the world was completed using the standard model from Part II and the rankings from Part III (page 179 onwards). At least, as far as was possible! For eight out of the fifteen factors from the standard model, scores were available from the research. For four other factors a 'next best' solution was found, using national data and the free publicity index. For the remaining three factors (City center, Multiculturality, and Governance) there was no alternative but to accept that they could not be filled in. In order to arrive at a design that will deliver data of practical use, much work still needs to be done. Three other factors, not being part of the standard model (Quality of Life, International Organizations and International Corporate Services), have been added to the profile as 'optionals.' The model explicitly leaves room for this.

Of course, this summary is not the place to elaborate on these profiles. As would be expected, the profiles illustrate the special place held by the 'Big Four.' In addition they clearly show that a city can belong to the world top, can be 'leading,' without excelling in certain details. Even a relatively unfavorable national competitiveness and/or a relatively mediocre level of 'Quality of Life' do not stand in the way of reaching such a position. Beijing, Shanghai and three of the Latin American cities illustrate this. The competitive factors may have been mapped as carefully as possible, but it is clear that other considerations also determine the integral perception.

For the academic world in particular it is very unsatisfactory to have to conclude that the research results sometimes cannot be explained. In those cases, the immediate temptation is to doubt their validity. However, according to the results of the Plausibility check, there are no grounds for such doubts. That does not necessarily imply, however, that this ranking of 'leading' cities is the ultimate one. It

211

is quite possible that research among a differently structured target group, with an adjusted questionnaire or using a different method, could lead to a somewhat different list that would also appeal to the imagination. Therefore, all research has to be evaluated on its own merits. With this qualification in mind, it is recommended that the status of 'leading city' is awarded no greater value than that given in one of the very widely supported concepts from the research: that the label of 'leading city' provides prestige to a city and gives it a competitive advantage.

EPILOG

First, the extent to which the original aims have been realized must be checked: to make an inventory of competitive factors and to compose a functional and an integral ranking of cities, using a questionnaire for citymakers. It can be concluded that the results have amply met the original expectations. Moreover, the international competitive profile of more than twenty important cities could be completed.

It must also be noted that, quite unexpectedly, a fourth aim has crept in. During the project the conviction has grown that the current city rankings have many shortcomings. Although authors are aware of the fact that the underlying data are insufficient, they are nonetheless not afraid to base their rankings or typologies on these data. Every single specific function, e.g. the financial function, is an ensemble of various kinds of activities which cannot be explained or evaluated simply on the basis of the number or size of banks, or the number of funds listed on the stock exchange. It is equally impossible to calculate, for instance, the best university. No wonder that the universities in particular object to the kinds of evaluations that award pluses or minuses to a number of arbitrarily chosen factors, add up the data in some way, and then churn out a classification. These kinds of organizations are too complex for such treatment, and cities are even more complex. The ranking of a city and its functions should therefore be left to the experts, as only they are in a position to weigh all the relevant and interdependent aspects. Perception research also has its unsatisfactory side: choices cannot always be explained logically, and academics do not like that.

The present research should be repeated some years from now, but in a different form. There is an impression that with less effort even better results could be achieved. However, this would require a global network. There are some institutions (such as consultancy firms) that have such networks, and those (such as cities or universities) that could easily build them. It is hoped that this research will inspire such initiatives.

◆ ◆ ◆ ◆ ◆

THEMATICAL
BIBLIOGRAPHY

■

A. BASICS

- **Gottmann, J. & Harper, R. (eds.) (1990),** *Since Megalopolis.*
  Baltimore: The Johns Hopkins University Press
- **Hall, P. (1966),** *The World Cities.*
  London: Weidenfeld and Nicolson
- **Hall, P. (1998),** *Cities in Civilization.*
  London: Weidenfeld and Nicolson
- **Jacobs, J. (1961),** *The Death and Life of Great American Cities.*
  New York: Random House
- **Jacobs, J. (1984),** *Cities and the Wealth of Nations.*
  New York: Random House
- **Knox, P.L. & Taylor, P.J. (eds.) (1995),** *World Cities in a World-system.*
  Cambridge University Press
- **LeGates, R. & Stout, F. (eds.) (1996 and 2000),** *The City Reader.*
  London: Routledge
- **Porter, M. (1990),** *The Competitive Advantages of Nations.*
  London: The MacMillan Press Ltd.
- **Sassen, S. (1991),** *The Global City: New York, London, Tokyo.*
  Princeton N.J.: University Press
- **Sassen, S. (1994),** *Cities in a World Economy.*
  Thousand Oaks (CA): Pine Forge Press

B. GLOBALISATION AND THE CITY

- **Clark, D. (1996),** *Urban World / Global City.*
  London and New York: Routledge
- **Cohen, M.A., Ruble, B.A., Tulchin, J.S. & Garland, A.M. (eds.) (1996),**
  Preparing for the Urban Future: Global Pressures and Local Forces.
  Washington DC: Woodrow Wilson Center Press
- **Gravesteijn, S., Griensven, S. van & Smidt, M. de (eds.) (1998),** *Timing Global Cities.*
  Utrecht: Netherlands Geographical Studies (NGS)
- **Harris, N. (1997),** Cities in a Global Economy.
  Urban Studies, 34, No. 10, pp. 1693-1703
- **Lo, F. & Yeung, Y. (eds.) (1998),** *Globalization and the World of Large Cities.*
  UN University Press
- **Moss Kanter, R. (1995),** Thriving locally in the global economy.
  Harvard Business Review, September/October, pp. 151-160
- **Shachar, A. (1990),** The Global Economy and World Cities.
  In: Shachar, A. & Öberg, S. (eds.), *The World Economy and the Spatial Organization of Power.*
  Aldershot: Avebury
- **Seabrook, J. (1996),** *In the Cities of the South; scenes from a developing world.*
  London, New York: Verso
- **Short, J.R. & Him, Y.H. (1999),** *Globalization and the City.*
  Longman Harlow

- **Short, J.R. et al. (2000)**, From World Cities to Gateway Cities; extending the boundaries of globalization theory. *City, 4,* No. 3, pp. 317-340

C. WORLD CITIES RESEARCH AND PERCEPTION

- **Friedmann, J. & Wolff, G. (1982)**, World City Formation; an agenda for research and action. *International Journal of Urban and Regional Research, 6,* pp. 309-343
- **Driehuis, W. (1992)**, *The Competitive Advantages of Ten Major European Cities.* Amsterdam: Interview
- **Meester, W.J. (1999)**, *Subjectieve waardering van vestigingsplaatsen door ondernemers.* Utrecht/Groningen: NGS
- **Meyer, P. (1995)**, Measurement, Understanding and Perception: The Conflicting Realities. In: Hambleton, R. & Thomas, H. (eds), *Urban Policy Evaluation,* pp. 89-99 London: Chapman
- **Pellenbarg, P.J. (1985)**, *Bedrijfsrelokatie en ruimtelijke kognitie.* Groningen: NGS
- **Pred, A. (1967)**, *Behavior and Location.* Lund: Gleerup
- **Short, J.R. et al. (1996)**, The Dirty Little Secret of World Cities Research: data problems in comparative analysis. *International Journal of Urban & Regional Research, 20,* No. 4, pp. 697-717
- **Taylor, P.J. (1997)**, Hierarchical Tendencies amongst World Cities: a global research proposal. *Cities, 14, No. 6,* pp. 323-331
- **Tuan, Y-F. (1977)**, *Space and Place; the perspective of experience.* London: Arnold

D. CITY RANKING FORMATION AND TYPOLOGY

- **Abu-Lughod, J. (1999)**, *New York, Chicago, Los Angeles: America's global cities.* Minneapolis: Minnesota University Press
- **Friedmann, J. (1986)**, The World City Hypothesis. *Development and Change, 17,* No. 1, pp. 69-84
- **Friedmann, J. (1995)**, Where we stand; a decade of world city research. In: Knox, P.L. & Taylor, P.J. (eds.), *World Cities in a World System,* pp. 21-47 Cambridge University Press
- **Fortune Magazine (2001)**, *Best Cities for Business* (yearly survey)
- **Healy & Baker (2001)**, *Europe's Top Cities Monitor* (yearly survey)
- **Savitch, H.V. (1996)**, Cities in a Global Era: a new paradigm for the next millennium. In: Cohen, M.A. et al. (eds.), *Preparing for the Urban Future: Global Pressures and Local Forces,* pp. 39-65 Washington DC: Woodrow Wilson Center Press
- **Shachar, A. (1996)**, European World Cities. In: Lever, W.F. & Bailly, A. (eds.), *The Spatial Impact of Economic Change in Europe,* pp. 145-177 Aldershot: Avebury

- Taylor, P.J. (2000), World Cities and territorial states under conditions of contemporary globalization.
  Political Geography, 19, pp. 5-41

E. FACTORS AND COMPETITION

- Begg, I. (1999), Cities and Competitiveness.
  Urban Studies, 36, No. 5-6, pp. 795-809
- Berg, L. van den & Bramezza, I. (1991), *The competitiveness of the European Metropolitan Area in the European Metropolitan System of Tomorrow.*
  RSA Congress Paper
- Brotchie, J., Batty, M., Blakely, E., Hall, P. & Newton, P. (eds.) (1995), *Cities in Competition; Productive and sustainable cities for the 21st century.*
  Melbourne: Longman
- Buursink, J. (1991), Europese Steden tussen idee en competitie.
  KNAG Tijdschrift, No. 5, pp. 427-433
- Chereque, J. (1989), *Les Villes Européennes.*
  Reclus Datar report
- Cheshire, P. (1990), Explaining the Recent Performance of the EC's Major Urban Regions.
  Urban Studies, 27, No. 3, pp. 311-333
- Cheshire, P. (1999), Cities in Competition.
  Urban Studies, 36, No. 5-6, pp. 843-864
- Conti, S. & Spriano, G. (1990), *Effeto Città.*
  Fondazione Agnelli
- Jensen-Butler, C., Schachar, A. & Weesep, J. van (1997), *European Cities in Competition.*
  Aldershot: Ashgate
- Kresl, P. (1995), The determinants of urban competitiveness.
  In: Kresl, P. & Gappert, G. (eds.), *North American American Cities and the Global Economy,* pp. 45-68
  Thousand Oaks: Sage Publications
- Kresl, P.K. & Singh, B. (1999), Competitiveness and the Urban Economy: 24 Large US Metropolitan Areas.
  Urban Studies, 36, No. 5-6, pp. 1017-1027
- Krugman, P. (1996), *Pop Internationalism.*
  Cambridge (MA): The MIT Press
- Lever, W. (1999), Competitive Cities in Europe.
  Urban Studies, 36, No. 5-6, pp. 1029-1044
- Lippman Abu-Lughod, J. (1995), Comparing Chicago, New York and Los Angeles: testing some world hypotheses.
  In: Knox, P.L. & Taylor, P.J. (eds.), *World Cities in a World System,* pp. 171-191
  Cambridge University Press
- Lo, F. & Marcotullio, P. (2000), Globalization and urban transformations in the Asia-Pacific region; a review.
  Urban Studies, 37, No. 1, pp. 77-111
- Markusen, A. & Gwiasda, V. (1994), Multipolarity and the layering of functions in world cities: New York City's struggle to stay on top.
  International Journal of Urban and Regional Research, 18, pp. 167-193

- **Palomäki, M. (1991),** On the Possible Future West European Capital.
  Geo-Journal, 24, No. 3, pp. 257-267
- **Porter, M. (1997),** *The Competitive Advantages of Cities.*
  First Annual Rouse lecture
- **Porter, M. (1998),** *On Competition.*
  Boston (MA): HBS Press
- **Proulx, P-P. (1995),** Determinants of the growth and decline of cities in North America.
  In: Kresl, P. & Gappert, G. (eds.), *North American Cities and the Global Economy,* pp. 171-186
  Thousand Oaks: Sage Publications
- **Sanchez, J-E. (1997),** Competitive Political and Administrative systems.
  In: Jensen-Butler et al. (eds.), *European Cities in Competition,* pp. 446-467
  Aldershot: Ashgate
- **Shachar, A. (1995),** World Cities in the Making; the European context.
  In: Kresl, P. & Gappert, G. (eds.), *North American Cities and the Global Economy,* pp. 150-169
  Thousand Oaks: Sage Publications

F DETERMINANTS OF COMPETITION

F 1 DETERMINANT: CLUSTERS

- **Porter, M. (1998),** Clusters and Competition.
  In: Porter, M., *On Competition,* pp. 197-288
  Boston (MA): HBS Press
- **Steiner, M. (ed.) (1998),** *Clusters and Regional Specialisation.*
  London: Pion

F 1.1 CLUSTER: MULTINATIONALS

- **Cohen, R.B. (1981),** The new international division of labour, multinational corporations and urban hierarchy.
  In: Dear, M. & Scott, A. (eds.), *Urbanization and Urban Planning in Capitalist Society,* pp. 287-315
  New York: Methuen
- **Doremus, P.M. et al. (1998),** *The Myth of the Global Corporation.*
  New Jersey: Princeton University Press
- **Godfrey, B.J. & Zhou, Y. (1995),** Ranking World Cities: Multinational Corporations and the Global Hierarchy.
  Urban Geography, 20, No. 3, pp. 268-281
- **Kee, B-N. & Semple, R.K. (1995),** Concentration and dispersion of global control links and changes in the multinational quaternary place system.
  In: Green, M.B. & McNoughton, R.B. (eds.), *The Location of Foreign Direct Investment Investment,* pp. 223-246
  Aldershot: Avebury
- **Lyons, D. & Salmon, S. (1995),** World Cities, Multinational Corporations and Urban Hierarchy: the case of the United States.
  In: Knox, P.L. & Taylor, P.J. (eds.), *World Cities in a World System,* pp. 98-114
  Cambridge University Press

F 1.2 CLUSTER: FINANCE

- **Budd, L. & Whimster, S. (eds.) (1992),** *Global Finance and Urban Living.*
  London: Routledge
- **Edwards, B. (1998),** Financial Centres; Capitals of capital.
  The Economist, May 9th.
- **Gehrig, T. (1998),** *Cities and the Geography of Financial Centers.*
  London: Centre for Economic Policy Research
- **Meyer, D. (1998),** World Cities as Financial Centres.
  In: Lo, F. & Yeung, Y., *Globalization and the World of Large Cities,* pp. 410-433
  UN University Press
- **Reed, H.C. (1989),** Financial Centre Hegemony, interest rates and the global political hegemony.
  In: Park, Y.S. & Essayard, *N., International Banking and Financial Centers.*
  London and Boston: Kluwer Academic Press
- **Sassen, S. (1999),** Global Financial Centres.
  Foreign Affairs, 78, No. 1, pp. 75-87
- **Zuken, S. (1992),** The city as a landscape of power: London and New York as global financial capitals.
  In: Budd, L. & Whimster, S. (eds), *Global Financing and Urban Living,* pp. 195-223
  London: Routledge

F 1.3 CLUSTER: CORPORATE SERVICES

- **Beaverstock, J., Smith, R.G. & Taylor, P.J. (1999),** A Roster of World Cities.
  Cities, 16, No. 6, pp. 445-458
- **Beaverstock, J., Smith, R.G. & Taylor, P.J. (2000),** U.S. Law firms in World Cities.
  Urban Geography, 21, No. 2, pp. 95-120
- **Beaverstock, J., Smith, R.G. & Taylor, P.J. (2000),** World City network: a new Metageography?
  Annals of the AAG, 90, No. 1, pp. 123-134
- **Boyle, M., Findlay, A., Lelievre, E. & Paddison, R. (1996),** World Cities and the Limits to Global Control:
  a case study of executive search firms in Europe's leading cities.
  International Journal of Urban and Regional Research, 20, pp. 498-517
- **Bryson, J. & Daniels, P.W. (eds.) (1998),** *Service Industries in the Global Economy.*
  Cheltenham: Elgar
- **Coffey, W. (2000),** The Geographies of Producer Services.
  Urban Geography, 21, No. 2, pp. 170-183
- **Illeris, S. (1996),** *The Service Economy; a geographical approach.*
  New York: Wiley
- **Sassen, S. (1995),** On Concentration and Centrality in the Global City.
  In: Knox, P.L. & Taylor, P.J. (eds.), *World Cities in a World System,* pp. 63-78
  Cambridge University Press
- **Taylor, P.J. & Walker, D. (2001),** World Cities: a first multivariate analysis of their services complexes.
  Urban Studies, 38, No. 1, pp. 23-47

F 1.4 CLUSTER: INTERNATIONAL TRADE & TRANSPORT

• **Andersson, A.E. & Andersson, D.E. (eds.) (2000),** *Gateways to the Global Economy.*
  Cheltenham: Edward Elgar

• **Berg, L. van den & Pol, P. (1998),** *The European High-Speed Train and Urban Development:*
  Experiences in fourteen European Urban regions.
  Aldershot: Ashgate

• **Brotchie, J., Batty, M., Hall, P & Newton, P. (eds.) (1991),** *Cities of the 21st Century; New Technologies*
  and Spatial Systems,
  Longman Cheshire and Halsted Press

• **Bruinsma, F. (2000),** De strategische positie van Europese steden in het luchtvaartnetwerk.
  In: Boekema, F & Graaf de W. (eds.), *Nieuwe ideeën in Nederlands ruimtelijk onderzoek (RSE),* pp. 109-132.
  Assen: Van Gorcum

• **Bruinsma, F., Rietveld, P. & Brons, M. (2000),** Comparative study of hub airports in Europe.
  Royal Dutch Geographical Society, 91, No. 3, pp. 279-292

• **Cattan, N. (1995),** Attractivity and Internationalisation of Major European Cities: The example of air
  traffic.
  Urban Studies, 32, No. 2, pp. 303-312

• **Esparza, A. & Krmenec, A. (2000),** Large City Interaction in the US Urban System.
  Urban Studies, 37, No. 4, pp. 691-709

• **Graham, S. (1998),** Global Grids of Glass: On Global Cities, Telecommunications and Planetary Urban
  Networks.
  Urban Studies, 36, No. 5-6, pp. 929-949

• **Graham, S. & Marvin, S. (1996),** *Telecommunication and the City.*
  London: Routledge

• **Haughwout, A.F. (2000),** *The Paradox of Infrastructure Investment.*
  Brookings, Summer

• **Keeling, D. (1995),** Transport and the World City Paradigm.
  In: Knox, P.L. & Taylor, P.J. (eds.), *World Cities in a World System,* pp. 115-131
  Cambridge University Press

• **Meyer, H. (1999),** *City and Port.*
  Utrecht: International Books

• **Nunn, S., Klacik, D. & Schoedel, C. (1996),** Strategic planning behavior and interurban competition
  for airport development.
  APA Journal, Autumn, pp. 427-441

• **O'Connor, K. (1995),** Change in the Pattern of Airline Services and City Development.
  In: Brotchie, J. et al., *Cities in Competition,* pp. 88-104
  Melbourne: Longman

• **Rimmer, P. (1996),** International transport and communications interactions between Pacific Asia's
  emerging world cities.
  In: Lo, F. & Yeung, Y. (eds.), *Globalization and World City Formation in Pacific Asia,* pp. 48-100
  UN University Press

- **Smith, D. & Timberlake, M. (1995),** Conceptualising and Mapping the Structure of the World System's City System.
  Urban Studies, 32, No. 2, pp. 287-302
- **Stevens, H. (1999),** *The International Position of Seaports; an international comparison.*
  Dordrecht: Kluwer
- **Taniguchi, M., Nakagawa, D. & Toda, T. (1995),** The Changing Urban Hierarchy of Japan: The Impact of the High Speed Rail.
  In: Brotchie, J. et al., *Cities in Competition,* pp. 191-199
  Melbourne: Longman
- **Wheeler, J., Aoyama, Y. & Wharf, B. (eds.) (2000),** *Cities in the Telecommunication Age.*
  London, New York: Routledge

F 1.5 CLUSTER: REAL ESTATE & ARCHITECTURE

- **d'Arcy, E. & Keogh, G. (1999),** The Property Market and Urban Competitiveness.
  Urban Studies, 36, No. 5-6, pp. 917-928
- **Berry, J. & McGrea, S. (eds.) (1999),** *Cities in the Pacific Rim: Planning Systems and Property Markets.*
  London: E & FN Spon
- **DiPasquale, D. & Wheaton, W. (eds.) (1996),** *Urban Economics and Real Estate Markets.*
  Englewood Cliffs: Prentice Hall
- **Krabben, E. van der (1995),** *Urban Dynamics: a Real Estate Perspective.*
  Amsterdam: Thesis Publishers
- **Lambooy, J.G. (1996),** *The Urban Spatial Structure and Agglomeration Economies: Relations with Real Estate.*
  Tinbergen Institute Lecture
- **Oatley, N. (ed.) (1998),** *Cities, Economic Competition and Urban Policy.*
  London: Paul Chapman Publishing
- **Sudjik, D. (1992),** *The 100 Mile City.*
  London: A. Deutsch

F 1.6 CLUSTER: ACADEMIA

- **Bender, T. (ed.) (1988),** *The University and the City.*
  New York: Oxford University Press
- **Brouwer, E., Budil, H. & Kleinknecht, A. (1998),** Are Urban Agglomerations a better Breeding Place for Product Innovation?
  Regional Studies, 33, No. 6, pp. 541-549
- **Knight, R.V. (1998),** Building the "Knowledge-based City".
  Urban Affairs, 32, No. 2, pp. 225-260
- **Lambooy, J.G. (1996),** *Knowledge, Production, Organisation, and Agglomeration Economies.*
  AME-lectures
- **Lambooy, J.G. (1998),** *Agglomeratievoordelen en Ruimtelijke Ontwikkeling: Steden in het tijdperk van de Kenniseconomie.*
  Utrecht: Utrecht University Press

220

- Meer, E. van der (1996), *Knowledge on the move.*
  Amsterdam: AME
- Varga, A. (2000), Local Academic Knowledge Transfers and the Concentration of Economic Activity.
  Journal of Regional Science, 40, No. 2, pp. 289-309

F 1.7 CLUSTER: ARTS

- Chang, T.C. (2000), Singapore as a Global City for the Arts.
  International Journal of Urban and Regional Research, 24, No. 4, pp. 818-831
- Dziembowska, J. & Funck, R. (1999), Cultural Activities: Source of Competitiveness and Prosperity in Urban Regions.
  Urban Studies, 36, No. 8, pp. 1381-1398
- Garten, J. (2001), Cities: Investing in Culture is simply Good Business.
  Business Week, No.13
- Palmer, R. (2000), Cultural Capital in the City.
  In: Ooi Giok Ling (ed.), *Model Cities; Urban Best Practices.*
  Singapore: The Institute of Policy Studies
- Scott, A. (1997), The Cultural Economy of Cities.
  International Journal of Urban and Regional Research, 21, No. 4, pp. 323-339
- Scott, A. (1999), The Cultural Economy: Geography and the creative field.
  Media, Culture and Society, 21, pp. 807-817
- Scott, A. (2000), The Cultural Economy of Paris.
  International Journal of Urban and Regional Research, 24, No. 3, pp. 568-582

F 1.8 OTHER CLUSTERS

- Clava, l. P. (2000), The European System of Capital Cities.
  GeoJournal, 5, pp. 73-81
- Judd, D. & Fainstein, S. (eds.) (1999), *The Tourist City.*
  Yale University Press
- Rubalcaba-Bermejo, L. & Cuadrado-Roura, J.R. (1995), Urban Hierarchies and Territorial Competition in Europe: Exploring the Role of Fairs and Exhibitions.
  Urban Studies, 32, No. 2, pp. 379-400

F 2 DETERMINANT: INTERNATIONAL PERFORMANCE
F 2.1 GENERAL

- Ave, G. & Corsico, F. (eds.) (1994), *Urban Marketing in Europe.*
  Torino: Incontra+B30
- Avraham, E. (2000), Cities and their news media images.
  Cities, 17, No. 5, pp. 363-370
- Gold, J.R. & Ward, S. (eds.) (1994), *Place promotion: The Use of Publicity to sell Towns and Regions.*
  Chichester: Wiley
- Kim, K. & Barnett, G.A. (1996), The determinants of international news flows; a network analysis.
  Communications Research, 23, pp. 323-352

- **Young, C. & Lever, J. (1997),** Place promotion, Economic Location and the Consumption of City Image.
  Tijdschrift voor Economische en Sociale Geografie, 88, No. 4, pp. 332-341
- **Ward, S. (1998),** *Selling Places. The Marketing and Promotion of Towns and Cities 1850-2000.*
  London: E. & F.N. Spon
- **Wu, F. (2000),** Place Promotion on Shanghai.
  Cities, 17, No. 5, pp. 349-361

F 2.2 CITY CENTRE

- **Berg, L. van den et al. (1999),** *De binnenstadseconomie in de 21e eeuw.*
  Rotterdam: Euricur
- **Gratz, B.R. (1998),** *Cities back from the Edge: New Life from Downtown.*
  Chichester: Wiley
- **Porter, M. (1995),** The Competitive Advantage of the Inner City.
  Harvard Business Review, No .3, pp. 55-71

F. 2.3 MEGA EVENTS AND SPORTS LIFE

- **Danielson, M.N. (1997),** *Home team: Professional Sports and the American Metropolis.*
  New Jersey: Princeton University Press
- **Griffiths, R. (1998),** Making Sameness: Place Marketing and the New Urban Entrepreneurialism.
  In: Oatley, N. (ed.), *Cities, Economic Competition and Urban Policy,* pp. 41-57.
  London: Paul Chapman Publishing
- **Hiller, H.H. (2000),** Mega Events, Urban Boosterism and Growth Strategies.
  International Journal of Urban and Regional Research, 24, No. 2, pp. 439-458
- **Noll, R. & Zimbalist, A. (1997),** *The Economic Impact of Sports Teams and Stadiums.*
  Washington DC: Brookings Press
- **Rosentraub, M.S. (1997),** *Major League Losers: The Real Costs of Sports and who's paying for it?*
  New York: Basic Books
- **Thornley, A. (2000),** Dome Alone: London's Millennium Project and the Strategic Planning Deficit.
  International Journal of Urban and Regional Research, 24, No. 3, pp. 689-699
- **Whitelegg, D. (2000),** Going for Gold: Atlanta's Bid for Fame.
  International Journal of Urban and Regional Research, 24, No. 4, pp. 802-817

F 3 DETERMINANT: THE HUMAN FACTOR

- **Blakely, E.J. (2001),** Competitive Advantage for the 21st-Century City.
  APA Journal, 67, No. 2 (Spring), pp. 133-140
- **Elliot, J.R. (1999),** Putting Global Cities in their Place: Urban Hierarchy and Low-income Employment.
  Urban Geography, 20, No. 2, pp. 95-115
- **Green, Chr. (ed.) (1997),** *Globalization and survival in the black diaspora: the new urban challenge.*
  Albany: State University of New York Press.
- **Griffiths, R. (ed.) (1998),** *Social Exclusion in Cities: the Urban Policy Challenge.*
  Bristol: University Press
- **Hannerz, U. (1992),** *Culture, Cities and the World.*
  Amsterdam: Centrum voor Grootstedelijk Onderzoek

- **Hannerz, U. (1993),** The Culture Role of World Cities.
  In: Cohen, A. & Fukui, K. (eds.), *Humanizing the City.*
  Edinburgh: University Press
- **Hall, P. (1989),** The Rise and Fall of Great Cities: economic forces and population responses.
  In: Lawton, R., *The Rise and Fall of Great Cities: aspects of urbanization in the Western World.*
  London: Belhaven
- **Hofstede, G. (1994),** *Cultures and Organizations. London:*
  Harper Collins Publishers.
- **Kasarda, J. (1990),** The Jobs - Skills Mismatch.
  In: LeGates, R.T. & Stout, F. (eds.), *City Reader,* pp. 305-309
  London: Routledge
- **King, A. (ed.) (1995),** *Re-presenting the city: Ethnicity, Capital and Culture in the 21st Century Metropolis.*
  Basingstoke: MacMillan
- **King, A. (1995),** Re-presenting world cities: cultural theory / social practice.
  In: Knox, P.L. & Taylor, P.J. (eds.), *World Cities in a World System,* pp. 215-231
  Cambridge University Press
- **King, A.D. (ed.) (1997),** *Culture, Globalization and the World System: Contemporary Conditions for the Representation of Identity.*
  Minneapolis: University of Minnesota Press
- **Marcuse, P. & Kempen, R. van (eds.) (2000),** *Globalizing Cities: a new spatial order?*
  Oxford: Blac1kwell
- **Rusk, D. (1993),** *Cities without Suburbs.*
  The Woodrow Wilson Center Press
- **Sandercock, L. (1998),** *Towards Cosmopolis: Planning for Multicultural Cities.*
  New York: Wiley
- **Shaw-Taylor, Y. (1998),** Profile of social disadvantage in the l00 largest cities of the United States, 1980 to 1990/1993.
  Cities, 15, No. 5, pp. 317-326
- **Short, J.R. (1996),** *The Urban Order: an introduction to cities, culture and power.*
  Oxford: Blackwell

F 4 DETERMINANT: CITY GOVERNANCE

- **Altshuler, A. et al. (eds.) (1999),** *Governance and Opportunity in Metropolitan America.*
  Washington DC: National Academy Press
- **Berg, L. van den, Braun, E. & Meer, J. van der (1997),** *Metropolitan Organizing Capacity.*
  Aldershot: Ashgate
- **Body-Gendrot, S. (2000),** *The social control of cities? A comparative perspective.*
  Oxford: Blackwell
- **Fisher, P. & Peters, A. (1998),** *Industrial Incentives: Competition among American States and Cities.*
  Michigan: Kalamazoo
- **Garvin, A. (1996),** *The American City: what works, what doesn't.*
  New York: McGraw-Hill

■

- **Hall, T. & Hubbard, P. (eds.) (1998),** *The Entrepreneurial City.*
  New York: Wiley
- **Merrifield, A. (2000),** The Dialectics of Dystopia: Disorder and Zero Tolerance in the City.
  International Journal of Urban and Regional Research, 24, No. 2, pp. 473-489
- **Stewart, M. (1998),** Partnership, Leadership and Competition in Urban Policy.
  In: Oatley, N. (ed.), *Cities, Economic Competition and Urban Policy,* pp. 77-90.
  London: Paul Chapman Publishing
- **Newman, P. & Verpraet, G. (1999),** The Impact of Partnerships on Urban Governance: conclusions from recent European research.
  Regional Studies, 33, No. 5, pp. 487-491
- **Rothblatt, D. & Sancton, A. (eds.) (1998),** *Metropolitan Governance Revisited: American / Canadian Intergovernmental Perspectives.*
  Berkley: Governmental Studies Press
- **Sharpe, L.J. (1995),** *The Government of World Cities: the Future of the Metropolitan Model.*
  Chichester: Wiley
- **Sivaramakrishnan, K.C. (1996),** Urban Governance: Changing Realities.
  In: Cohen, M.A. et al. (eds.), *Preparing for the Urban Future: Global Pressures and Local Forces,* pp. 225-241
  Washington DC: Woodrow Wilson Center Press
- **Stone, C.N. (2001),** The Atlanta Experience Re-examined: The Link between Agenda and Regime Change.
  International Journal of Urban and Regional Research, 25, No. 1, pp. 20-34
- **Stubbs, J. & Clarke, G. (1996),** *Megacity Management in the Asian and Pacific Region.*
  Manila: ADB
- **Ward, P. (1995),** The successful Management and Administration of World Cities; Mission impossible?
  In: Knox, P.L. & Taylor, P.J. (eds.), *World Cities in a World System,* pp. 298-316
  Cambridge University Press

F 5 DETERMINANT: NATIONAL COMPETITIVENESS

- **IMD (2001),** *The World Competitiveness Yearbook.*
  Lausanne: IMD
- **World Economic Forum & CID Harvard University (2001),** *The Global Competitiveness Report .*
  Oxford University Press

F 6 OPTIONALS

- **Mercer, W.M. (2001),** *Worldwide Quality of Life Survey.*
  Croydon: William Mercer Ltd.
- **Rogerson, R.J. (1999),** Quality of Life and City Competitiveness.
  Urban Studies, 36, No. 5-6, pp. 969-985

GLOSSARY OF TERMS USED

Citymakers - *Companies and institutions that contribute to the international competitive profile of a city by their presence and level of activities.*

City Profile - *Illustrates the competitive position of a city based on (at least) the factors that are of overriding importance to international city competitiveness.*

Perception - *In the generally understood sense of the collection of factual knowledge and opinion stored in the brain. As this definition is close to that of 'image,' it can also be referred to as the 'individual image'.*

Functional perception - *The perception that 'citymakers' have of the quality of a particular city function, for example academia.*

Integral perception - *The perception that 'citymakers' have of the overall quality of all the relevant and interdependent functions of a city.*

Plausibility - *The likelihood that something is probable to the point of certainty, seems to be true.*

Plausibility check - *Method developed by the author to determine the degree of plausibility.*

PL index - *Plausibility index: The degree to which (in %) it is probable that the results of the research reflect the opinion of an entire cluster or of all clusters taken together.*

Shift method - *Method developed by the author, on the basis of budgeting techniques, in which the upgrading of a factor or city must be compensated by the downgrading of a different factor or city. The method aims to ensure that respondents are forced to choices and preferences, in this case for cities and competitive factors.*

FP index - *Free Publicity index: The frequency with which a city is 'in the news,' expressed in relation to the value for the city with the highest frequency.*

Cluster - *A small group of companies/institutions in a city and its surrounding area, involved in very similar or closely connected activities, who in most cases compete with one another but also cooperate. The nucleus of such a group is often one or more 'magnets,' around which the others group themselves. This definition is significantly narrower than Porter's (1998).*

Magnets - *The trend-setting companies and institutions within a cluster. Their functioning determines to a significant degree the functioning of all the others in the cluster.*

Hospitality - *A collective term for the cluster in which hospitality is central. This includes hotels, congress services and tourist agencies.*

QUESTION 1 (The Leading Cities in the World)

☞ **1-A In your view, which are the 25 most important, trendsetting, prominent cities in the world?**

To indicate your choice please mark the box ☑ of **five cities or more** which you <u>DOWNGRADE</u> from division I (the top-category!) to II and conversely, mark the box of **the same number of** cities which you <u>UPGRADE </u>from II to I.

☞ **1-B In your view, which cities are at the top for your professional field; that is, which are the major global centers of/for INTERNATIONAL TRADE & TRANSPORT.**

Please circle the names of **at least five cities** in the list below.

DIVISION I: Leading Cities		DIVISION II: Other important Cities	
Washington	❏	Zürich	❏
Tokyo	❏	Vienna	❏
Toronto	❏	Vancouver	❏
Sydney	❏	Tel Aviv	❏
Singapore	❏	Taipei	❏
Shanghai	❏	Stockholm	❏
Sao Paulo	❏	St. Petersburg	❏
Rio de Janeiro	❏	Seattle	❏
Paris	❏	Seoul	❏
New York	❏	San Francisco	❏
New Delhi	❏	Rome	❏
Milan	❏	Osaka	❏
Mexico City	❏	Mumbai (Bombay)	❏
Los Angeles	❏	Moscow	❏
London	❏	Manila	❏
Johannesburg	❏	Madrid	❏
Hong Kong	❏	Jakarta	❏
Frankfurt	❏	Istanbul	❏
Chicago	❏	Houston	❏
Buenos Aires	❏	Dallas	❏
Brussels	❏	Caracas	❏
Bangkok	❏	Caïro	❏
Beijing	❏	Boston	❏
Amsterdam	❏	Berlin	❏
Atlanta	❏	Barcelona	❏
		Any city that is missing?	
		. . . .❏	
		. . . .❏	

227

PLEASE DON'T MISS QUESTION 1-B (see above)

QUESTION 2 (The Competitive Advantages)

☞ **2-A In your view, which LOCAL factors make a city prominent, trend-setting, leading?**

To indicate your choice please mark the box ☑ of **five factors or more** which you <u>DOWNGRADE</u> from division I (the top-category!) to II and conversely, mark the box of **the same number of** factors which you <u>UPGRADE</u> from II to I.

☞ **2-B In your view, what should be on the Agenda for the Future of the city where your office is located?**

Please indicate your choice in the list by circling the asterisks (*) of the factors from the list below **(five at most)** which your city should give priority to in the coming years.

DIVISION I: Most important local factors	DIVISION II: Other important local factors

Population
| * Very large population ❏ | * Open to an international world ❏ |
| * Rich choice of highly skilled labor ❏ | * Multi-cultural community ❏ |

Center of economy and management
* Home for multinationals ❏	* Seat of international organizations ❏
* Major Stock Exchange ❏	* Presence of major production facilities ❏
* Home for international banks ❏	* Home for major media firms ❏

Government and politics
* Positive international performance ❏	* Good public safety ❏
* Political leadership ❏	* Commitment to invest in quality ❏
* Favourable LOCAL tax climate ❏	* Seat of the national government ❏

Physical infrastructure
| * Major intercontinental airport(s) ❏ | * Stop for high-speed trains ❏ |
| * International seaport ❏ | |

Knowledge
| * One or more leading universities ❏ | * Prominent business schools ❏ |
| * Renowned R&D institutes ❏ | * Large and richly varied network ❏ |

Other facilities
| * Modern congress & exhibition facilities ❏ | * Prestigious shopping facilities ❏ |
| * Numerous international-class hotels ❏ | * International professional services ❏ |

Cultural and social life
* Famous museums ❏	* Mega events ❏
* Performing arts of high internat. standard ❏	* Major international congresses & fairs ❏
* Attractive nightlife ❏	* Sportlife of high international standard ❏

General
| * It happens there! ❏ | * Impressive skyline ❏ |

Anything that you miss?
* . . . . ❏
* . . . . ❏

PLEASE DON'T MISS QUESTION 2-B (see above)

QUESTION 3 (Concepts)

☞ **Here are a number of concepts concerning (leading) cities. Do you agree or disagree with them?**

Concepts	agree	disagree
1. The label of 'leading city' provides prestige for a city and gives it a competitive advantage.	❏	❏
2. A leading city has so many advantages that you accept higher costs, congestion, and (some) criminality.	❏	❏
3. The largest threat to leading cities is the (growing) gap between privileged and unprivileged.	❏	❏
4. It's culture that makes cities different.	❏	❏
5. You should be entitled to elect the political authorities of the city where you **work**, even though you **live** in a neighbouring municipality.	❏	❏
6. The city center is the core influence in the (good or bad) image of a leading city.	❏	❏
7. The hotels show the importance of the city.	❏	❏
8. When cities have comparable qualities, the perception decision-makers have about a city is paramount.	❏	❏
9. • It's important for a city to be in the news.	❏	❏
• It's more important to be in the news than what is said.	❏	❏
10. The way "my city" performs internationally is very much in my (company's) interest.	❏	❏
11. The best way to promote a city internationally is to:		
• be the subject of a worldwide hit-song	❏	❏
• advertise in magazines, tv spots, etc.	❏	❏
• gain publicity in the media	❏	❏
• be known for low costs	❏	❏
• having a famous sports team bearing the city's name	❏	❏

☞ **Data about the respondent to this questionnaire**

Age	**Professional field**	**Position**	**Sex**
❏ below 40	❏ Aviation	❏ Senior management	❏ Male
❏ 40 - 60	❏ Shipping	❏ Other management	❏ Female
❏ above 60	❏ International Trade	❏ Non-management	
	❏ Other		

Do you live in the city in which your office is located?

❏ yes   ❏ no, in another municipality

Did you feel any constraint in your response because the research is being conducted from the Netherlands and/or the dissertation is for the University of Amsterdam?

❏ no   ❏ yes (please explain)

☞ ❏ Yes, I would like to have an abstract of this part of the research.

❏ Yes, I would like to participate in the prize drawing for an European roundtrip for two. Participants in the prize drawing are all respondents who return a completed questionnaire within three weeks from posting date. The winner will be drawn by the rector of the university at the end of the graduation ceremony.

If yes, please fill out the data below.

Name ....

Organization ....

Address ....

City/code ....

Country ....

☞ Please use this sticker to return the questionnaire by mail to:

World Cities Research
P.O. Box 5806
NL-1410 GA NAARDEN
The Netherlands

ITR/E/

ACKNOWLEDGEMENTS

When you leave a large organization like the municipality of Amsterdam, you also say goodbye to a huge national and international network, and to having masses of information and excellent assistants within easy reach. When I decided to start the worldwide research project that would ultimately form the basis of this doctoral thesis, I was very aware of this. You are on your own, but you also know that you will need the assistance of others. At first you can still fall back on the network that you had built up over the years, but this rapidly shrinks and in the beginning you do not know exactly what support you are going to require. So you just make a start, anticipating that it will be possible to get the help you need at the moment you need it. Looking back, that help was needed very often and was almost never refused, certainly not when people heard about the project on which I was working. At the close of this book I would like to take the opportunity to reflect on this.

Beforehand I knew that the research I had in mind would be a costly exercise, and with a pretty high risk of failure. When I was asked before I left what I would like as a leaving present from the city of Amsterdam, I suggested, after some thought: the financial means to make the research possible. The then alderman Peer thought this was, "for someone of my age, a productive thought from which Amsterdam itself might also benefit." It turned out to be a most generous gift, and I expressed my grateful thanks at the time. Six years later there is a certain feeling of satisfaction in delivering a work from which the city and its 'citymakers,' I believe, may indeed benefit.

From the beginning there was a great deal of communication necessary, mostly written, and in English. Larry Sewell, as editor, has been a constant pillar of support. With his handwritten corrections he transformed my first concoctions into what he called "appropriate nederlish." In addition he took a personal interest in the topic, regularly forwarding articles of potential relevance. Over countless cups of coffee in a café in the Jordaan area of Amsterdam, he was always prepared to function as the conscience of the world whenever I doubted how to approach something anywhere on the globe. This support continues to the final day, when he shall accompany me as my 'paranimf' (witness and supporter) when I defend my thesis in public.

Translations were regularly required in six other languages, in addition to English, and these were obtained partly through friendship, partly at a friendly price, and partly at the going rate. However, Heinz-Gerd Roes (German), Wouter Tieleman (French), Nicoline Meijer and Sandrien Banens (Italian), Mrs Saéz (Spanish), Mrs de Souza (Portuguese), Suiling Yan and Zheng Wu (Chinese) and Nabuko Karthaus (Japanese) were all unfailingly helpful, often having to work at high speed and showing much empathy for the subject matter.

The translation of the manuscript, however, was done by Belinda Stratton. In a short space of time she translated the original Dutch manuscript of this book into English, doing "a first-rate job" according to Larry Sewell. This is not so much a reflection of her knowledge of International English (she is British), but rather of the knowledge of Dutch that she has managed to acquire in a few years and her capacity to comprehend the material which she saw for the first time only recently.

A manuscript does not only have to be translated, but also transformed into a book with a decorative cover. That is a complex task, especially when a number of figures and tables have to be placed within the text. I have experienced this at close quarters, watching the precision and artistic talent of Anja Felder. Speaking of artistic talent, Walter van Broekhuizen was so kind as to allow me to use for the logo of the research an image of his sculpture 'The ideal city,' which can be admired in the headquarters of Fortis. A number of years ago, in a very pleasant restaurant, Jacob van der Kind wrote a poem on 'leading cities' that also fits extremely well in this book.

A worldwide study that is performed in a traditional way, by mail, requires a lot of paperwork: typing addresses, designing questionnaires and adjusting them, producing bulletins and photocopying. Fortunately I could rely on two trusted former assistants for this, Nel Bonneveld and Astrid Stol, while the copying firm TenSet in Bussum processed an awful lot of paper, almost always 'urgently.'

For multifaceted research you need multifaceted support, sometimes just once, sometimes for longer or more frequently. Usually it involved access to documentation or acquiring addresses. Whether I was knocking at the 'door' of the Chamber of Commerce, or the main office of the university, or the Port Authority or KLM or Schiphol airport, or the ING Bank or the Association of Publishers, the Concertgebouw or the Rijksmuseum, the congress center RAI or the Amsterdam Tourist Information Office, I was always welcomed.

In this book I mention several times the contact persons that, at the beginning, I had recruited to help me with the survey in about 50 of the 80 cities. In most cases they worked for the city or for the chamber of commerce. Their willingness to help was always contingent upon only being used if absolutely necessary. Perhaps I interpreted this too literally, with the result that when I really needed them for the first time during the final stages of the research, most of them had unfortunately moved on. The bulletin on the progress of the research that I had sent to them regularly did not prove to be sufficient to keep them involved and committed. Describing this less positive experience, however, does not do justice to the few faithfuls who ensured the completion of the final part of the research. These were the contact persons in Amsterdam (Paula Stelling), Brussels

(Lo Bremer), Frankfurt (Ulrich Lohrmann), Geneva (Hans Peter Graf), Glasgow (Steve Inch), Rotterdam (Jos Geerling), Sao Paulo (Hans van Hellemondt), and Vienna (Helmut Naumann).

But what would a survey be without the respondents? Almost 1400 made the effort to study the questionnaire and to return the form. Here I would like to express my thanks to them all; the majority (73%) I have also been able to thank personally when I sent them, at their request, a short summary of the results of the research.

"Undertaking research, even worldwide, and reporting the results is very different to writing a doctoral thesis," Professor Jan Lambooy, my supervisor, has emphasised repeatedly; "that is a challenge of a quite different order." It did indeed take some time before I fully realized this. That it has at last been completed is thanks not only to the free hand which he gave me, but also to the fact that he stepped in at critical moments to remind me of the requirements of academic research. For this project and for this doctoral candidate this was an ideal combination of characteristics!

When I retired in 1996, my wife, Trudi, and my four grown children knew what I was planning. Whatever they imagined it was going to mean, I am sure it has turned out differently: even at home you can still be absent or unapproachable. When the results of a survey have to be counted and grouped even during the holidays, the initial understanding could so easily have faded. They, and especially Trudi, coped with it all and I am very grateful to them for that. Now it is full speed ahead to the next challenge, but definitely one that allows more time for other things!

* * *